THE RED SLIPPERS MYSTERIES

A NOVEL

by

LLOYD C. GARDNER

FOR

MY GRANDFATHER, FRANK LINCOLN GROVE

and

With special thanks to Nancy for reading earlier versions with detailed suggestions, as well as to Tim, Marion, Warren and Ivan for their comments, and also Becky and Erin.

FORWARD

Like nearly everyone who read the shocking stories about the "Red Slippers" murder in the early fall of 1953, I had imagined that it was an obvious crime of passion. The victim was a pregnant young woman who had been summoned to the Ohio college town, West River, by her boyfriend and killed after an argument. Her killer, Robbie Stanson, confessed immediately after identifying the body as that of Wendy Peters at the funeral home where it had been taken for postmortem reconstruction. He told the authorities how they had planned to run away to Kentucky to be married. The secrecy was necessary, he said, because both sets of parents opposed their plan. Her death was supposedly "accidental" in the sense that Robbie had not set out to kill Wendy when he grabbed her by the throat during an argument over her teasing him about being seen.

Given the circumstances known then and the youth of the killer, the county prosecutor accepted a plea to Second-Degree murder, resulting in a sentence of twenty-five years to life. The case had been likened to the events in Theodore Dreiser's famous novel, *An American Tragedy*. It was very surprising, nevertheless, when Stanson was released on parole after serving little more than a decade in the Ohio State Penitentiary. At the time, there were serious questions raised about his behavior while driving a prison vehicle on official business. Nevertheless, the parole board confirmed its decision in a second 3-2 vote. He then finished his college degree and earned a master's in sociology and counseling. For a time after that, he remained near his parents' home in the Cleveland suburbs. He opened an office offering therapy for trauma and emotional problems. He never pretended to have done graduate work in clinical psychology. But he never attracted many clients. It was said that stories about his crime and prison record prevented him from succeeding, and then, in the summer of 1971, he announced he was going on vacation in Yosemite National Park in California.

From that point, it all becomes speculation about what happened. Stanson disappeared. No body was ever found. Nor was there any trace of what might have happened. Nothing. Park police and state investigators could discover no clues about what might have happened. His parents died soon after that, and he had no brothers or sisters. Thus it seemed there was little incentive to keep looking for any answers to the disappearance.

But then, two years later, a paper presented to a private Philadelphia seminar on unsolved cases by a professional therapist and amateur crime investigator somehow got noticed even though the participants had been pledged not to talk about the presentations they heard in a booklined study located in a renovated colonial-era house, where, it was said, Benjamin Franklin and friends might have once gathered to explore current issues, perhaps including similar crimes?

Suddenly, everything changed. The brother of the original victim, who had been tracking Stanson since his release from prison, heard about the seminar and the suggestion the case had not been solved. Eventually, the search Carl Peters launched came together over a few days in one place. What happened then remains the ultimate mystery. You may conclude what you wish after reading my reconstruction of the events that ensued.

Lloyd C. Gardner

PROLOGUE

THE REPORT

It had been raining all morning, but now there was just a drizzle where Miriam Stronge stood waiting inside the nook of a jewelry shop, where she could see reflections of passers-by in the windows. She always did that. Force of habit. She often felt she was being shadowed by someone. And sometimes, she *was* being watched. A tall woman, Stronge attracted attention in many situations. This fact was both an aid and a hindrance in her adopted profession as a Tracer of Lost Persons, incidentally the title of a popular radio show in the first postwar decade. But at this moment, she had spotted a nice watch on a tray near the back of the display. Maybe, she thought. She would see after she met with Mr.Peters and settled their next move - if there was to be one. She dallied a bit longer and then moved back onto the sidewalk and down a few doors to the Blue Ribbon Deli. At the entrance, she stood aside for two women to exit. Busy finishing their conversation they hardly noticed her waiting for them to pass.

But the woman in big glasses who sat on a stool at the cash register did observe the gesture and smiled at Miriam as she took off her hooded London Fog coat and shook out her black hair. People who saw Miriam for the first time always remembered her piercing blue eyes and were a little intimidated. After a momentary pause, she nodded to someone in the last booth and moved on to where a man sat, fidgeting with a menu. He gave the impression of someone always in a hurry, not just by the way he kept opening and closing the menu but especially the worry lines on his forehead.

As she reached the booth, he put down the menu and waited for her to slide into the seat across from him. As he did this, he looked over her head, staring at the door as if expecting to see someone else appear. He did this repeatedly even as they began talking. It was a bit off-putting at first, but Miriam refrained from saying anything. She also noticed his long white fingers that suggested someone who worked in a laboratory and wore gloves eight hours a day. He shrugged his shoulders often as well, another nervous gesture. She had noticed these things when they first met several weeks earlier in her office, and she had agreed to take on the assignment to find out what had happened to Robbie Stanson. Now, he looked even more intense than he had that afternoon.

"Lousy morning, Miriam," Carl Peters said. "Fit for discussing your report, I fear." He pressed his lips together as if ready to hear bad news. She looked across at him with raised eyebrows as she removed an envelope from the portfolio she always carried and set it on the table.

"Let's see it, then," he said, anticipating the worst. "No, just tell me what's in it. I'll read it later."

Stronge tilted her head in a gesture of sympathy with a sad smile and pushed the envelope across the table. On the front, it read simply, "For Carl Peters." It was thin, and he guessed two or three sheets at most.

She did as he asked. "Stanson's gone. Nobody knows what happened to him."

Peters shrugged and puckered his lower lip. "That's it?" he said, frowning and turning the envelope over and over.

She waited, nodding.

He repeated, "That's all there is?"

"Yes, I'm sorry, that's all I have found out."

"But you are still looking?"

"Yes, but I don't expect much more to show up - if anything."

"So." Carl shook his head slowly, keeping his eyes on Miriam's - a gesture of disbelief.

"So, he just walked into that national park, and - and that's it! No one knows anything."

"It seems so. We can't find anyone who knows anything. He was there a few days and then gone. Registered at the lodge. Never checked out. We found nothing in park records as best as we could, but he didn't sign into any of the small lodges and was not registered at any other of the hotels, at least not under his real name. And no one of his description, either. There might be two reasons for that. He could have altered his appearance with glasses, hair dye, and so on. Or he could have sneaked into one of the unrented cabins, obviously, and gone on from there the next day. I've discussed those possibilities with park staff, as you will see in my report. But anything might have happened on one of those high trails to the top of Vernal Falls or someplace else. It really is a good jumping-off place."

"Yes," Peters nodded in a dark grimace at the double meaning. He opened the envelope, scanned the sheets, sighed, and dropped them on the table. After a pause, Peters drew in a breath and posed a question. He had asked it once before when he hired Stronge. "What about that Walters guy, the one who was up for parole at the same time?"

Miriam folded her hands on the table, leaning forward, doing her best to look sympathetic - which she really was. "I talked with him. It could be he knows something, but we don't have anything on him or any way of pressing him no matter what he knows. He says he hasn't seen Robbie since prison. I think that's a dead end. All he can tell us is how Robbie maneuvered in prison."

Carl shook his head in disbelief. "Jesus, how can this be? How can he walk away from the world and nobody noticed?"

Miriam leaned back, straightening her arms in front of her and spreading them out. "Yosemite is a big place. If you want to disappear, it's a good place to do it. Plus, he might have gone out into some remote area where something happened. We don't know. You know, several people disappear from Yosemite every year." She paused and stared at Carl. Then went on: "And are never found."

Peters shook his head again in an unbelieving gesture, turning the envelope over and over. "And you checked: he never, ever communicated with an old friend - in prison, like Walters, but someone before that - or the girl he met driving around in the prison bus?"

"Not that we can find. Dina Stevens, you mean. Well, she got married and moved away from Columbus. We asked everybody he knew. And there aren't that many - he was a loner pretty much all his life. He left few traces anywhere; of course, maybe people aren't talking. The college has no records of Stanson in any activity - ditto the fraternity, not surprising that, of course. They have no desire to claim brother Stanson."

"What about that other college girl he wrote the day Wendy came down to meet him?"

"She won't talk to us but claims she wasn't ever interested in him, just wanted to find out where Wendy was - an old schoolmate of hers from high school."

"You believe her?"

"Not necessarily, but that doesn't matter now, does it? She's got a family herself now, and..."

"You offered her money?"

"Yes, but she just shooed me away. Made it clear she wanted nothing to do with the past - at least that past."

"All right, think it'll do any good to keep looking around there?"

"Just spend more of your money without much chance, but I'll do what you want."

"So, all we know is that he headed for Yosemite and -whoosh - he's gone."

Stronge nodded.

"No one at that clinic where he worked for a short time has any idea what happened?"

"No."

"None of his patients?"

"Nope, he only saw most of them once or twice - and folks who go there don't get much acquainted. And don't like to talk about things like therapy."

"There's got to be something."

"You'd think so. But he closed all his bank accounts a few days before he left for California."

Peters looked up at the ceiling, brought his eyes down to meet Miriam, took a thicker envelope out of his coat, turned it around once, and passed it over. Getting up out of the booth, he gave Stronge a small smile. He looked like someone in a funeral receiving line, his eyes hunting for someone not there.

She looked up at Peters and shook her head slowly, extending her hand. "Sorry. I know it must hurt - even now."

Carl reached down to take Miriam's hand. "Yes, well, I'll be in touch," he said. Then he looked back. "It never stopped and never will until I know. There may be something to go for I'm onto. - I'll let you know if - no, when, I need you."

She nodded. "I'm here when you need me."

Carl nodded back, sighed deeply, and walked out of the restaurant to his car. As she watched him go, she thought he had aged years in the few months since they had met and first discussed his sister's murder and the man who had killed her.

Stronge finished the breakfast she had ordered, left a big tip, exited the restaurant and walked the few steps back to the jewelry store. She emerged a few minutes later with a small package.

She felt very uneasy about all that had passed between them that morning, not just, indeed hardly at all, that he was obviously disappointed, but that he would do anything to find Robbie Stanson. And then what? His eyes had darkened since he last talked with her. At least, it seemed that way. Certainly, the intensity of the stare filled with determination. It now struck her full force, and she blamed herself for not thinking about where this might end and, most concerning of all, whether she might find herself having to "save" Peters from himself if he came near to committing some irrevocable act. She realized that she couldn't walk away from the search. She found herself hoping Robbie Stanson really was gone – forever.

§

Carl did not trust her findings all that much- just as he didn't trust anyone who had been involved in the original arrest and what followed. Miriam Stronge's report went unopened. He knew what was inside. But now he suspected there was much more to find about the disappearance of Robbie Stanson. There was the new Philadelphia angle he had learned about and would soon ask her to investigate. But he had kept the details to himself that morning, especially about his visit months ago from Stuart Freed, who said he was interested in revisiting the case. A psychologist or something, Freed had left him with the impression that there were new things to learn about "the case." Carl had offered him money to pursue his suspicions. Freed declined the offer but promised to keep him informed of what he learned. Apparently, his research involved a possible accomplice. He had explored his theory in a paper to a select group of unsolved crime buffs in Philadelphia. He did not say in his seminar presentation that perhaps the notion of an accomplice had something to do with Stanson's disappearance. Perhaps not. Perhaps he just wanted a fresh start as someone else, somewhere else. Something had set him out to disappear.

Jesus thought Carl as he left the deli, thinking about Stronge's failure. In the light of Freed's theory, Wendy's killer had successfully manipulated things, even going back to that "Honeymoon" sentence he got for killing his sister. Jesus, what an outrage!

Peters didn't really care if the killing was pre-meditated or done in a rage. That was for the lawyers to argue about. Anyone who saw what he had done to Wendy... He sat there in his car as the rain outside continued, harder now, thinking once more about that last time she visited him in Columbus before she went home to tell their parents she had "flunked out." She had given no hint that anything was wrong, terribly wrong, in her life beyond her grades - my God, her grades! What was that? Why hadn't he sensed anything? She had given up *everything because of that monster.* "Wendy, dear God, Wendy, I swear I will not fail you again."

He put his hands over his face and wept. When he looked up at himself in the mirror, he repeated that vow. A promise he had first made to himself at the trial's abrupt conclusion: "I will not fail you again."

CHAPTER ONE

THE RED SLIPPERS

Saturday, September 23, 1953

Daniel Brockman worked for the Ohio Department of Transportation. In September 1953, he was thirty-five years old, with degrees from Capital University and Ohio State. A supervising engineer, he lived with his wife and daughter in Worthington, just north of Columbus. On weekdays, he was either in his office in Columbus or out and around the state supervising road crews. Ever since high school, he'd kept his hair cut short. He was often kidded about his "flat-top." It was like a brush he rubbed often when trying to solve a problem. On this trip, he planned to stay overnight near Upper Scioto because someone at the county public works office had called in about a deteriorated stretch on a secondary road off Route 23, a main north-south artery passing through the center of the state. He had promised to check it out the next time he came up to supervise some work on a project nearby.

"Not a lot of people drive along that stretch of two-lane, actually, mostly woods there for a good piece," the hotel bartender told him on Friday night. "Used to go once in a while myself - hunting pheasants. No big deal."

"Ok, I'll take a look on my way home tomorrow."

As he finished eating a burger and fries, down at the end of the bar, an argument was brewing over details of the capture and killing of the notorious Pretty Boy Floyd near East Liverpool some forty miles away. A new feature story had just appeared in the local newspaper: *Pretty Boy Floyd's death: Justice or Judicial Murder*. "It happened twenty-years ago, right about this time," said Pete Hammil.

"He supposedly passed through here and spent time in this very room on that last escape route - but it didn't work. They caught up with 'im."

"Well, that's close, but it was only nineteen years ago, 1934."

"O.K., so I'm a year off. He tried to run and got shot near a corn crib. 'You got me twice,' Floyd cried out and died."

"Not quite." said Harry Gardener, "Floyd was lying there on the ground, and Melvin Purvis - the one who shot Dillinger in Chicago - told another FBI agent to shoot him with a Tommy gun."

"Really?" said Hammil. "I never heard that!"

"Yep, they laid him out in a barber shop window for a day."

"My, God." Hammil shook his head. "Why'd they do that crazy thing?"

"Well, think for a minute - if you had a nice clean funeral home back then, would you want all those Floyd-folks barging in to see his bloody corpse?"

"Well, I guess -"

"No guessing about it. You wouldn't want it, neither did the owner, for sure."

"Pretty Boy was damned popular. He had a reputation, whether it was so or not, for giving stuff to poor depression-struck people outta work."

"Yeah, I did hear that. Think it was really so?"

"I don't know. But lots of people trooped by that barber shop for a day or so. And then, at his funeral down in Oklahoma, there were over 10,000 present. That's always the legend stuff you hear, isn't it, the story they tell about all these guys - some Robin Hood stuff. I don't like it much."

"Well, folks differed about how he got killed - and whether it was justice catching up with a man who supposedly killed ten people."

The bartender smiled and said. "Yeah, his ghost has been seen around here a few times."

With that, the conversation ended, and the barroom emptied soon after.

§

At breakfast Saturday morning, someone else who had heard the conversation in the bar about the road problem said with a grin as Daniel walked by: "Watch out for copperheads."

"Thanks, I sure will."

"They like woodpiles, you know. I saw a whole bunch of them once in a pile of old dead branches. Smell like cucumbers, they do, so you keep an eye out."

"I'll be careful," Dan said as he went out the door, "but I don't expect to get too far off the road."

§

It was a clear, crisp morning in early fall. He drove with the window down, enjoying the air and the late summer flowers along the side of the road. When he got to the spot where the erosion was and put on his jacket, he remembered the warning and looked carefully as he stepped out of the car. "Aha," he said to himself. He saw the decaying berm and what was probably causing it. A rivulet one could barely make out was running into the road from the undergrowth. Dan decided to see where it might be coming from back in the woods. He kept an eye out for anything that moved or otherwise slithered out of dead branches. Probably, the guy had been teasing a stranger. Still, he was careful where he put his feet. But the only thing that got him as he pushed off into the brush was wild berry branches that snagged his pantlegs.

He was paying so much attention to the copperhead story he lost sight of the tiny stream of water. "Damn, gotta stop this nonsense." As he looked around, searching for it, he saw ahead through the leaves a glimpse of something red on the ground. Couldn't quite make out what. Then, a few steps on, he could see two red slippers. He pushed back a branch and could see it all. The slippers were on the feet of a woman, or what looked like a naked woman, flat on her back. But it couldn't be that could it? He ducked under another branch and could see the face - or what had been the face. "Oh, my God. Oh, God. What an awful mess." He stood stark still, not believing what he saw. His hand went to his head to rub the brush haircut and give himself a second more to think.

"Couldn't be real. It couldn't." But his breath had quickened. "Must be a life-size doll, that's it, or a store manikin someone had thrown away onto a trash pile because it was broken and useless. But what a strange thing to find a way out here."

Of course, that was it. Store dummy. He stood still for a few seconds more, not really looking at the figure, not daring to, wondering who would bother dragging it so far from town. Maybe there was something else. Did he poke in the weeds, looking for a broken-off piece - maybe something broken off another store display figure? An arm or something.

But he knew what he did not want to believe. He had walked into the aftermath of a brutal murder. And as reality grabbed him by the throat and spread down to his chest, he became afraid. Really afraid.

"That poor woman," he said to himself. "Oh, my God," he kept repeating. "Oh, my dear God, no." He felt his heart stop for a second, then start to pound and skip out of rhythm. The back of his neck tingled, and he saw spots. Then, it was the aloneness that took over, closing all around him. His aloneness - no, her aloneness, too. And he thought about the killer. He had left her here and gone away back to his life. He would be talking now to someone he knew or maybe crying about what he had done. He might even still be around. More likely far away. But who knew? Jesus, who knew?

Dan had seen pretty terrible things during the war. But they were somehow connected. This was different. There was no noise like it had been then. All there was around him out here in a quiet place was one death, one young woman. And he was here as the only witness to the loneliness, the terrible loneliness. No one else was there with them. No one could hear him if he called out. He looked back at where he had come from, where the car was, but there was no sound. The world he knew did not exist here. Only "she" was still here, of course. How long ago had someone dumped her here? He continued staring at the body, what he had first believed had never been alive, just a broken shop window piece of composite material - something ruined somehow and no longer useful because its face had been destroyed - no other word for it- had once had a real name. A real person who had once breathed and laughed - and cried. "Oh, yes, had cried, most certainly had cried."

But now there were no tears to see - just what looked like a smashed Halloween mask. An even worse thought crowded into his shattered consciousness: Was she alive when whoever it was struck his first blows? "Please tell me she wasn't," he asked the silent woods, looking for something to lessen the horror. Did even an owl, unblinking - staring down see what terrible thing had happened? Dan finally pulled himself away from the cursed, lonely place and the terrible images in his mind and found his way back to the road where he had parked. He was breathing hard like he had been running. Across that road he could barely make out a Ferris Wheel several fields away. He had not noticed it when he first stopped. He stared at it for seconds. It was too early for it to be running and for the tinny, grinding sounds and then the music when the lights were turned on, and it began to move. Was she somehow connected with that? He would never forget the Ferris Wheel, now a silent witness to his retreat from the woods and what he had seen as if it had joined with him in mourning for the dead woman, the two the only mourners.

For a time - how long? - Brockman sat stock still in his car, staring down the road. A farmer in a pick-up coming toward him slowed down to a crawl, then stopped and rolled down his window.

"Need help?"

Dan paused a second and rolled down his window, smiling. "No, thanks - just went to take a leak."

The driver of the other car gave him a funny look and stopped momentarily about fifty feet down the road. Then, as he drove away, he made a note of the license plate on the car.

§

A few minutes after 10:30 a.m. that Saturday morning, September 23, the phone rang in the Wyandot County sheriff's office.

Corporal Gerald Watts answered.

"I'm at the Sohio gas station," the caller said, "at the corner of Route 23 and County Road 8. I need to talk to someone who can come quickly. We'll meet here. Then I'll take you to a place you need to see right away."

"What's this about, sir?" Watts put his coffee cup down on the desk nearly spilling it out on the day sheet, and not a little irritated at what sounded like a nuisance call. Dead deer on the road, probably. Or maybe just a skunk. People get all agitated about nothing. Caller ought to calm down, he thought. He picked up a pencil and repeated his question. "I need to know something more," said Watts. "Tell me what you see."

"I can't tell you on the phone. Just someone come. The *Sohio* station. I'll be outside in a cream and blue Chevy Bel Air. Just come."

"Sir, we need to know if you need medical help - or something like that."

"No, dammit, I don't need any medical help - I need you to come - NOW!"

"I'll connect you with Sheriff Lewis. Just hang on."

Watts sighed and raised his voice: "Sheriff, you better pick up, some guy all rattled. Probably nothing, but you need to handle it."

When this call came in, Sheriff Russell Lewis was reading in *The Morning Express* about how Humphrey Bogart had decided to break with Warner Brothers after seventeen years to form his own film company. Often lost in thought when he read something that struck a memory gong, Russ was imagining himself in Rick's Cafe in *Casablanca*. He was a big movie fan having seen *Casablanca* so many times he almost knew Bogart's lines by heart. Folding the newspaper, he picked up the phone, not quite concentrating on the voice. It just happened he was in the office on a Saturday morning after a trip to the grocery store. "Sheriff Lewis here. Who am I speaking to?"

§

Awaiting the young county sheriff - youngest in Ohio - at that *Sohio* station was his first murder case. Drafted near the end of World War II, Pfc. Lewis had arrived in Germany just as the European war ended in May 1945. He thought at first he would be shipped out to the Pacific. But then came the dropping of the atomic bombs on Hiroshima and Nagasaki. Now, you could guess safely no one was going to be shipped to the Pacific, at least not to fight the Japs. The atomic bombs speeded up V-J Day, and the new president, still uneasy in the White House, had been dealt all the cards. Or so it seemed then to a nation that had suffered no mass bombings and stood alone on top of the postwar pyramid of broken nations.

Meanwhile, the young soldier, a lanky six-footer with a deceptively easy-going manner, a former hot-shooting forward on his high school basketball team, had done very well on standardized tests and had been assigned to OSI (Office of Special Investigations) in occupied Berlin, where he was soon engaged in helping track down missing shipments of high-priced items from the States. The burgeoning black market involved lots of bad apples. He discovered he liked investigative work and actually had a knack for interviews for spotting contradictions revealed even in the subtlest of eye movements, let alone the more obvious, like restless legs. Upon discharge at the end of the year, he knew another thing for sure. He definitely did not want to go back to the family hardware business. And yet he had no real desire to leave the area around his hometown - not right away, anyhow.

You could say he had a typical adjustment problem to civilian life. But it was more about feeling bored. If he heard some skeptics call him the "Accidental Sheriff," Russ might nod and say he agreed. He fell into it. Russ had been restless even before he was called up in the draft. Now, he could use the GI Bill to go to college and maybe play more basketball. But he had no "calling" to speak of when you think about careers like law or medicine. So, he put off deciding about college and decided almost as an excuse for not deciding on a future "career" to run for sheriff on his "war" record. Now, believe it or not, he was sheriff. His opponent had been as ill-suited as he was for the job in terms of political experience, and the county's voters apparently decided they owed a "veteran," no matter where or when he served.

What Russ was thinking about when he picked up the phone that morning was far from the reality ahead of him only a few miles and a few minutes away off a country road in a wood. So far his job had been about penny ante stuff. It would soon seem in the press, however, that he had been handed the big "story" of the decade, what would be called *The Red Slippers* mystery.

§

Russ nodded to Watts to stay by the phone in case this guy called again. "Keep him calmed down. I'll let you know if I need anything once I see him."

Dan was standing by his car smoking his third cigarette since he called the sheriff's office. "When the hell would he get here?" He pulled it out of his mouth when, at last he saw the car with the big star on the door and waved, throwing it down on the concrete as he waited for the sheriff to come over. Instead, Lewis stood by his car and studied the man's behavior to see if he was on something. He had his doubts.

They shook hands, and Lewis noticed he had trouble standing still, shifting from foot to foot. And he kept brushing his hair back and picking at his shirt collar. "Follow me down that way," Brockman gestured, pointing to the side road. "Hundred yards or so. I'll stop when I see the marker I left on a big stone, a golf cap. Then we'll go in the woods together."

Lewis was still not too sure what was going on - the stranger seemed excited and barely in control of himself. But there wasn't too much reason not to do what he asked, he guessed. He wondered why the man had parked a bit short of the marker but decided it didn't mean anything. "Lead the way," he said. "I'll be right behind you."

He saw the marker, and he saw the Bel Air pull over. Brockman got out and waited. Russ had put on his holster before leaving the office. He hadn't seen this man around town, but there didn't seem any reason to be concerned. Still!

"Over here," Brockman motioned. "I work for the state highway department. Right beside this stone, I started into the woods, looking for a tiny stream of water that might be eroding the road."

The man might not be any dangerous type, escaped from an asylum or something. But - he was starting to sound "funny."

"You go ahead. I'll be right with you."

"Yeah, look out for copperheads, I was told," Brockman said with an ironic grimace. "Look out for snakes. Sure."

Lewis thought the guy really was wired up. They had gone in about fifty feet when Brockman called out and pointed, "Over there, over there, see the red shoes? The red shoes, yes, that's what I saw first." He brushed his hair back again

Lewis caught up and understood - and didn't understand.

What he saw was just about the worst thing anyone can see. A naked girl with a missing face. Brockman pointed while turning his face away from the body. He just stood there, frozen in this place where nothing seemed alive. Russ broke the spell. "You stay here," he ordered. I'll go back to my patrol car and radio in for the right people to come and take her out of here."

Dan stared at him and nodded. Now that he no longer had any duty to perform but to stand there, he was still struggling to regain full control. Lewis put his hand on Brockman's shoulder. "Just don't smoke any cigarettes," the sheriff ordered. "Can't have this place contaminated."

"Yeah," Brockman responded, patting the cigarette pack through his shirt. "Can't have the place contaminated." Lewis nodded with a slight smile, not sure if the man was aware of the sardonic tone of his voice.

§

In a short while an ambulance and medical team arrived, along with other deputies. Soon, they were gone. The woods were as quiet as they were before Dan had entered. A few cars passed by slowing down, but there was no traffic jam. Warned by Lewis not to say anything until he was told it was o.k. Dan was allowed to leave the area until and when he was called back. He returned to the hotel to check out and go home. "See any copperheads?" yet another resident repeated this stupid warning. It had gotten crazy, these folks playing around with strangers, all with that same inane smile. He started to speak to tell this yokel what he had seen, put him where he belonged. He would have loved to see the look on his face then! But he only paused, shook his head and cleared his throat. He gave the wise guy a beaming smile. "No, no - no snakes," he managed to get out and hurried to his car, wishing he could see his face tonight or tomorrow when the news reached him and wiped away that smile.

§

By evening, the local press had indeed gotten the story of the body of a girl in "Red Slippers" found in a nearby woods, hardly more than fifty feet from the road. New details emerged the next day in Sunday's edition of the paper, *The Independent*. Alan Pierson, a farmer driving by, told a reporter he had seen a car parked near the spot where the body was later found: "I asked him if he needed help. He was taking in the scene, he said. Now, that sure enough wasn't true. Hope they bring him in."

The *Independent's* story of Pierson's mysterious encounter with a "suspicious out-of-towner" continued with Sheriff Russell Lewis's terse comments at the county jail. She had been "brutally beaten" by "many blows." "We don't know anything more as yet."

"Not even who she was?

"No, we don't."

"She wasn't local?"

"I said we don't know anything more yet."

The corpse had been evacuated from the scene to the local hospital. Scene of crime teams came and fenced off the area, as suddenly the road became a popular route for gawkers. But no evidence ever turned up. A post-mortem was held but not completed until Monday, when tests had been done and read. After examining the body again Monday, the coroner confirmed details of the beating and added that she had been defaced "with some sharp instrument." But then he declined to say whether the beating was the actual cause of death. As the case developed, these initial caveats played a big part in the calculations of both the prosecutor and defense attorney.

On the autopsy table, without reporters around, Doctor Samuel Borgen estimated the young woman as between 18 and 20 years of age, five feet four inches, and weighing 120 pounds. She was well-nourished with no indications of any disease. Her right arm had been broken probably ten years ago but had healed well. She had died, very probably, between midnight Friday and three this past Saturday morning - only a few hours before she was found! Had he been out early in the morning, it occurred to Lewis that Brockman might have encountered the killer as he left the scene of the crime. Not likely, of course. But Dan was never to know that. Her face had been nearly eradicated by someone wielding a crowbar or perhaps some wedge-shaped tool.

"Whoever did it hit her with all his force," Borgen told Russ and the worried county prosecutor, Tom Jackson, watching their reactions, "and then went on and on crushing in her jawbones, mashing her teeth, destroying her eyes - at least 20-30 blows, hard to say exactly how many times." Borgen looked from one to the other and grimaced with a deep breath, raising his eyebrows. "It appears he wanted to make her unrecognizable, it seems, to the living world. But the rage, my God, the rage behind those blows! Never seen anything like it. I can't even tell for certain if she was killed first and then de-faced because there are marks on her throat that indicate it might have been strangulation. I'll need more time. Maybe a second opinion."

"Somebody deranged," said Lewis.

"Perhaps," Borgen allowed, nodding slightly. He did not believe that. "But determined, that's for sure. And maybe not alone." He looked at both of them for a reaction. "That might account for confusion and the red slippers being left behind. Also," the coroner paused with a deep breath and looked at Lewis over his glasses, "she was pregnant, about two months, it looks like. Very hard to say for certain, but definitely pregnant."

"Sounds like we have our motive," the prosecutor said what they all thought.

§

"You're going to need a lot of help finding anyone to identify this woman," said Borgen as he took off his rubber gloves. "I've never seen anything like this. The first thing I'd do would be to call Hanrahan, the funeral director. He's done some great work on car crash victims. None may be as bad as this, but he might be able to reconstruct her face enough, and, of course, there are fingerprints to take if she's registered anywhere."

He waited, but there was no reaction. "Oh, I almost forgot," added the coroner as he put on his hat, "she had sex sometime in the last 24 hours."

He raised his chin to put an exclamation point on his ritual-like findings. And then Dr. Borgen exited the room as two solemn aides - who seemed to appear from nowhere - gently pulled the sheet back over the head of the dead young woman as if performing a final tender gesture to a dead princess.

The sex evidence might explain why she was found in nothing but slippers, but maybe not, thought Russ. It could be he panicked and stripped her, but it was dark, and he forgot the slippers. Still, what happened to turn her lovemaking into a final sacrifice? Or had it been something else? Did a third party - a jealous lover - interrupt the scene and carry out the murder, leaving another corpse someplace else? Even more heinous, was she a victim of a gangbang that ended in violence? But the coroner had found no evidence she had been drinking or had been drugged into semi-consciousness.

Worst of all, there was no indication of how she got there sprawled out, something like the way kids made angels in the snow. Lewis hated thinking of it that way, a dark vision of evil worse than he had ever seen. It was first speculated that she might have come from the people who ran the concessions and rides at the county fair across the road not more than a quarter mile away. But the possibility was quickly ruled out. No one there was missing, he would learn. And there were no suspicious characters among temporary workers and no missing women from town.

§

Now, it was up to the funeral director to do his best. A familiar figure around town, Chester Hanrahan, often came into the restaurant where local business leaders gathered around a table for a second coffee in the morning. Some who met him for the first time this way felt uneasy by the mortician's soft voice and perfectly groomed fingernails. Unlike the others, of course, he never talked "business" to his morning companions.

He had had some tough assignments, but none quite like this. Normally, this would be a closed casket case. But he would do his best. The autopsy over, the dead woman was met outside the hospital and transported in a hearse for the short trip to Hanrahan Funeral Home on Winter Street. The sheriff was left standing alone with the slippers in an evidence bag as he thought about another destination much farther away, the state crime laboratories in Columbus. He was determined to speak with them in person about the question of what had caused her death.

A day later, Hanrahan called the sheriff to come to view the results. Bracing himself for the renewed shock he knew he would feel, no matter how well the post-mortem "surgery" and make-up had gone to restore the young woman's face, he got out of the patrol car and took deep breaths as he walked to the double-door entrance with the lace-curtained windows. Once inside, an aura of fresh flowers surrounding a coffin overflowed out of the main room where two women dressed in black sat twisting handkerchiefs and into the doorway where Russ stood.

"Sheriff," Hanrahan broke the spell. "Over this way," shaking hands, he motioned Russ toward another door across and to the rear. "In here."

On the other side of that door something of a miracle had taken place. Now, the woman lying in state was no longer anonymous. Anyone who had come in contact with her in life would recognize her in death - if so tragically premature - so willfully unfair. Hanrahan had worked hard. He had piled makeup over the stitches, restoring something like her natural color. Even so, she would never appear just to be asleep. Now, it almost seemed she was ready to name her killer. To shout to the world when he was brought near: YOU! See what you have done.

§

The first reports from Columbus came on Wednesday morning. Like the county coroner, the state medical examiner hedged when he read the autopsy report. It might have been strangulation, not the blows to the head, that killed her. However vicious the attack had been. The report was not definitive down to no doubts. That raised the possibility of a crime in two locations! And then a contest over where the trial of the killer would be held. That was not what Lewis wanted to hear. But there was better news about what she had been wearing that last night. The red slippers had an identification number and the name of the manufacturer imprinted on the inside of the heel. Lazara Shoes, a firm in Columbus, had made the slippers. That model sold very well, unfortunately for the searchers, and could be found in stores in several states. But - here was the best thing - the serial numbers inside one heel were from a shipment made to White Plains, New York. In fact, to a specific department store that had taken delivery of the order in early June.

So now Russ knew that a woman in White Plains had purchased these shoes and had brought them with her to Ohio. Why? There were no obvious signs of a wedding or engagement ring, so presumably, she had traveled alone or with a friend. The first thing to try to find out was whether the White Plains police know of any missing woman who fit the description of the corpse found in the woods. Thanks to Hanrahan, he could send a picture. The answer came back no. There had been no reports of a missing person. How best to proceed? He decided to go to White Plains to the store to find out if the sale had been recorded and the customer's name appeared on the sales slip. He told himself that was the best way to proceed. Maybe the task could be handled by the local authorities - and he would ask for their help when he got there - but it was now his case, and he wanted to be there to meet her parents and anybody else who might know her.

§

He arrived in West Plains late Thursday afternoon. He learned that four pairs had been sold so far. The first two customers were easily confirmed as present in the city. The third pair had been sold to a young woman whose mother said on the telephone had taken the slippers with her when she left town in early July to go to Cleveland. Her name was Wendy Peters. "I just had a card from her last week," said Mrs. Peters when Lewis told her who he was and why he was calling. "She said she was doing well -not to worry about her. She had gotten a job in a large department store and rented a room. I know she planned to visit her brother in Columbus." She breathed deeply as if throwing up a shield around her fears. "Maybe she's with him right now."

"Would you check that, Ma-am, we need to know just as soon as possible."

"Well, I can call Carl, but he would have let me know if anything were wrong." Ellen Peters was stalling, desperately afraid of finding out something terrible had happened. The truth was, she did not know where Wendy was, physically or emotionally. Why had they let her go? Wendy had left White Plains telling her parents she would fly to Cleveland and find a job there. Her boyfriend lived there. Mrs. Peters had met him once when he visited White Plains in mid-June. His name was Robbie Stanson, a young man Wendy had met during her very first week at college.

She did not tell the sheriff about the terrible arguments before she left home for Cleveland. Wendy had declared her parents were being totally unreasonable for not letting her get married. Moreover, she had announced that she had no interest in going back to Bashford College, even if she was allowed in, despite her low grades from last semester. Ellen seemed apologetic about Wendy's record. "Her poor grades were no indication of her ability to do college-level work, sheriff. She was always a good student, as well as active in all aspects of high school life." But Wendy had not seemed eager to go back to school fall. Maybe that was the trouble, and maybe why she suddenly wanted to get married - a case of homesickness that wound up making her dependent on the young man. Strange as that might seem, it appeared to explain the desperateness of her attitude. But she didn't know for sure, frowning at her incomprehension.

Shaking her head, Ellen brightened a bit. Twisting the phone wire, she then told Lewis that her daughter said she had finally broken up with this young man. Then she frowned again and paused as her mind tried to deny what she was thinking:

No, she didn't really believe that was so. Why else, she admitted to herself, would she have gone to Cleveland near where he lived? She could have found a job here.

"I'm sorry, Ma'am," Russ broke into her thoughts, "please tell me who that is again?"

"The boy who came here to see her, Robbie Stanson." Her parents had not disliked Robbie, not at all. It wasn't that. When he visited early in the summer, her Dad thought he was a nice young man, likable in many ways, and seemingly eager to please her parents. "We thought they had had a falling out, or something like that, when we said they should wait. And I think it was because Wendy saw we were right. It was time to take a step or two back and think about the long-term future."

But she didn't really believe anything she was saying now as dark shadows crowded against such thoughts, pushing them aside. Already blaming herself, Ellen wondered if they had been right in pressing Wendy not to make such a hasty decision about marriage. She had never gone off the deep end before like she had this past summer. She had been popular in high school, never lacking friends or dates for the big events. Her brother had gone to Bashford and now had a very promising career as a chemical engineer in Columbus. Surely, she could understand her parents' reluctance to bless such a whirlwind courtship. Couldn't she?

Still on the phone, Lewis said he understood, but he would need to talk more. He had their address and would come out. Ellen was trembling as she hung up, not worried about Robbie. He had seemed to accept the situation, but had she met someone out in Ohio on the rebound and wasn't thinking straight. She hadn't tried to gain re-admission to college. But if they had broken up because she and her father objected to the idea of early marriage, maybe in her state of mind, she had fallen in with someone else, someone who had harmed their daughter!

Her next thought was to call her husband at the garage he owned. "You better come home," she said on the phone, "someone is coming here - a policeman- asking about Wendy. Hurry!"

§

It took Byron Peters fifteen minutes to get home change out of his work clothes, and put on an Arrow shirt he usually wore on Sundays. He was a sturdy-looking man who had a sense of the fitness of his home as a place where he had raised his children in safety and warmth. Wendy had sometimes seemed uncertain of her self-image, but not unlike many teenage girls. Byron thought about that as they waited to learn more, fearing he had missed some signal, something that they failed to do or understand. Byron took Ellen's hand and rubbed her knuckles as they waited in the living room. He knew she was on the verge of tears, and he really had little comfort to offer. They sat there looking at one another with false, grim smiles on their faces.

The sheriff arrived a few minutes later. Byron and Ellen sat across from Lewis on the brown couch, their hands entwined in a silent plea that would go unanswered. Ironically, she had returned from a late lunch with the mother of one of Wendy's friends not long before the call. She had been about to change clothes to do some garden work when the phone rang. When the sheriff arrived, he said only that he was in search of information about the purchase of some red slippers, "Yes," said Ellen. She remembered when Wendy brought them home. "Maybe they're upstairs in her room right now, pushed to the back of a closet," she said - and prayed. But she knew they weren't.

Still, they looked, Lewis following Ellen upstairs. After they checked her room, he sensed they knew as well as he did what had happened to Wendy, if not who had killed her.

"Maybe we can straighten this out pretty quickly," Lewis said, smiling a reassurance he did not feel. "You said you could call Carl. Can we do that right now? I'll ask him to come to Upper Scioto to look at the person we have at the funeral home."

He hated the way he had said this - but what other way could he have done? His stomach tightened as the silence went on. He could hear car horns on the street outside. Someone shouted - noises you wouldn't normally register. The couple looked at one another. Ellen began to cry. Byron got up and walked to the hall, where on a table below the stairs, the telephone could just be seen from the living room. Lewis watched him pick up the phone and heard the dial sound, all as if in a scene from a movie.

In the silence, waiting for their son to answer, Ellen looked steadily at her husband, twisting her wedding and engagement rings. Something she always did at tense moments - like when Carl had been in the hospital with pneumonia in his teenage years. Wendy had only had measles. She had been lucky, Ellen smiled to herself - in a last second of disbelief.

§

"Carl," Byron said, "I have someone here who wants to talk to you, son. Listen carefully to what he wants you to do. I'll talk to you when he's finished."

Lewis took the phone from him with both hands, nodding and bringing it to his ear gently. "Carl, this is Sheriff Russell Lewis from Wyandot County. I need to ask you to come up from Columbus and help us out in identifying a victim that we think might be your sister. The sooner you can manage this, the better it'll be for your parents."

He heard what he needed to hear.

"Thank you, Carl, much appreciate it. I'll tell you where to meet when I call tomorrow."

§

Russ turned back to the Peters, husband and wife, both now standing near, Byron with his arm around Ellen's shoulder as if staring through him to a black curtain that had fallen over their lives. He hated the final question he had to ask. "Mrs. Peters, do you have a recent photo of Wendy I could take back with me - just to make a comparison?"

"Yes, of course, let me get one of her senior pictures." She managed a smile. "They came out pretty well. She - she - was pleased," Ellen managed to get that out before she fell back down on the couch. Her husband was up and standing over her. But Ellen had recovered and pushed him away. "No, no, Byron, let me get the photos." She got up and went to the old secretary against the wall, opened one of the doors and took out a large brown envelope with the address of a local photographer's shop. She took out one of the photos and held it out to Lewis - but not looking at it herself. She was afraid she would faint.

Russ dared not to look at it until he was out of the house. "Do you have another envelope you could put it into?" he said to Mrs. Peters. He could not have managed to look at Wendy's picture while still with them. Ellen found one and gave it to Russ, turning away as she did.

Russ warned himself that he had to be a "real" sheriff, now, and not just the traffic cop he seemed to have been up until now, his first moment of truth on the job. "Thank you, folks. I'll be in touch as soon as I know anything more." He had lied, and they all knew it. He hadn't said anything about the girl in the woods.

CHAPTER TWO

IDENTIFICATIONS

SEPTEMBER 28 - October 4

Russ got in the car he had driven to New York, his car so as not to attract unwanted attention, dressed in "civies" for the same reason. And he still did not open the envelope. He knew what he would see. Ellen had given him a copy of Wendy's graduation picture. It was the usual studio shot that made all high school seniors look assured and in control, with no blemishes, no shadows as they faced the future. Russ remembered how he had hated his. He sensed Ellen watching him from the window with a plea in her eyes that they both knew would go unanswered as he started the car without looking at the house and drove away.

§

They had gone into Wendy's bedroom and turned on the lights when Russ looked for letters from Robbie or anyone else. A teddy bear watched them closely from Wendy's dresser. That bothered Russ. He thought about his five-year-old son's bear and blinked back a tear. They found nothing. Ellen pretended to believe that was a good sign there was no suicide pact - or something. *Maybe they had just run away? They had really wanted to get married. She and Byron had been wrong to try to stop them. It would be difficult, but with help from both sets of parents, they could make it work. Yes, they could make it work. Why hadn't she thought of that earlier when the sheriff first talked with them? He hadn't really said what he thought had happened to Wendy, had he?*

Then another thought had come to her: "Maybe Robbie has heard from her," she had said to Russ in an almost pleading tone. "He's surely back in school now.

Maybe if you ask him and find out something, Carl won't have to make that trip?" She looked at him, denying the meaning of his visit, not yet believing.

"Yes, Mrs. Peters, I do intend to find Robbie to ask him about Wendy - just as soon as possible." He did not say that he also intended to have their daughter's picture given to the press once Carl made a positive ID.

Russ had shaken hands with both parents, hoping to get outside the house and into his car without breaking into angry tears. He drove a few blocks and stopped outside a Woolworth's "dime" store like the one in Upper Scioto, where he had once bought his mother "Evening in Paris" perfume. He took out the picture. Wendy's slight smile hit him like a punch in the stomach. It was as if she were there, next to him in the car, encouraging him, guiding him on to his next step in finding out who had done this terrible thing to her. No matter what the undertaker had accomplished, she would never look like this picture again.

He gripped the steering wheel and started the long drive back to Ohio. He dared not stop for fear of losing all control before he got home.

§

Carl Peters arrived at the Hanrahan Funeral Home the next day. At first, he declined to make an identification, saying that the person on the table looked like Wendy, but he really could not be sure. Lewis had the impression - probably too much his thinking - that Peters was in denial because he had not been attentive to his younger sister. Probably thought she was a nuisance, Russ mused, and Carl was blaming her for what had happened - like she was a naughty girl. The more Russ thought about it, the angrier he got. She was still a teenager, he thought to himself. What was wrong with this family? Didn't they care?

He knew he was not being realistic. His kids were still -well-kids. Then he heard Peters ask if the "person" had had a broken arm. *God, what was wrong with him?* "Yes," Lewis managed to keep an even tone, "the coroner said about six years ago, and it healed well." Carl nodded with pursed lips. He kept looking at the face, and then, all at once, tears came into his eyes. "It's Wendy," he managed barely above a whisper. Then he turned as if fleeing and headed to the front door. He stood there with his hand on the knob. Then he turned back: "I should have helped her - but I had no idea of any trouble. Can we take her home now?" Lewis shook his head. "We have a lot of other people to talk to - including her last boyfriend. Robbie Stanson. Did she ever mention him?"

By now, he had realized Carl was in shock and apologized silently for his first impression. That had been terrible of him. He was learning all sorts of things about himself and his job from this terrible event.

Carl's voice brought him back. "Not to me," he began, but then stopped himself, "Oh, yes, she did say something once, maybe, but I thought it was over."

Russ was shocked yet again. Did he not know about Wendy's desire to get married to Robbie? Maybe not! He told Carl he would let him know when Wendy's body could be released, still wondering why she had seemingly been so completely on her own.

He heard Carl talking about funeral arrangements. His parents had asked him to do all the preliminaries.

"Well, we haven't officially released Wendy's body pending our preliminary investigation yet."

"This is about Robbie, isn't it?"

"I didn't say that." But it was indeed about an ID plan he had - to see the young man confronted by Wendy but not in a "comfortable" setting - a cushioned casket. Avoiding talking about his plan, he told Carl they needed to clear up some things before he could release Wendy to the funeral director. "We'll let you know just as soon as possible."

Peters nodded, looked at the floor, the ceiling, and finally back at Russ. He seemed unsure where he was. And then he walked toward the wrong door, stopped and turned back with an apologetic half-smile, no longer quite the same upward-bound postwar young scientist who had left his past life forever. After watching this scene play out and seeing Carl falter, Russ felt ashamed of his first thought that Wendy had been neglected by her big brother.

Carl hesitated as if he could not leave Wendy alone with these strangers. Finally, he turned and said, almost in a whisper, "You'll let me know - about everything?"

Russ felt ashamed again as he heard the sadness in Carl's voice.

"Certainly will," he said goodbye to Carl with a strong handclasp as their eyes met, now feeling sad for the living brother's burden of guilt.

In any event, Lewis was now ready to go down to Bashford College, two hours away. He had had several copies of the photo printed out. These he planned to give to college officials for identification and distribution. And he called the president's office to alert school officials that he planned to interview students who might have known Wendy Peters the previous year - particularly a former boyfriend named Rob or Robbie Stanson.

§

At the college the next day, Russ's first stop was at the Registrar's Office for a quick confirmation that Wendy had been a student at the school last year but had not tried to gain re-admittance this fall. This time, he had driven an official car and worn his uniform. He went to the Dean of Students' office, where he learned that the primary object of his visit to campus was supposed to be in ROTC class at this time.

He asked Dean Snyder if he could summon someone from there to his office. "I'd like to talk to Robbie Stanson in connection with the possible death of one of your former students, Wendy Peters, but I don't want to go barging into a class. He's not a suspect in anything at this point, only someone who knew her."

"We're not certain yet that it's even Wendy," he lied, pretending an identification had not been made already, "so if you could send someone just to ask him to come to your office after class, that would be the best way to handle this. We're just looking for help."

§

Robbie arrived at the dean's office dressed in his blue Air Force ROTC uniform. A fresh-faced young man - handsome with a ready smile was shown where Lewis awaited him alone. He had an appealing way of nodding to everyone and did not falter at Russ Lewis's serious demeanor. He looked straight at him with a serious nod. Lewis broke the silence, trying not to show his eagerness to rattle this young man. "We have to ask you about someone you know - or knew."

Stanson nodded again, frowned sympathetically with a worried look, and immediately asked as if eager to help the sheriff: "It's about Wendy Peters, isn't it?"

Lewis feigned surprise. "Yes, when did you last see her?"

"I guess it was in July. At her house - we broke up. I hadn't heard from her for a long time, so I was worried."

Robbie had jumped right in, behaving for all the world as if eager to help. Lewis saw that this fellow instinctively knew the best ways to project total cooperation as a defense mechanism. He seemed very concerned about Wendy, looking as if to say, "Hey, we're on the same team here." He pursed his lips and went on with his account of the end of their romantic relationship. Even though they had broken up, he said, and he hadn't seen her since summer, he still cared a lot. Then he explained that since one of her closest friends had not heard from her in weeks, he was naturally worried when summoned just now to the Dean's office.

Lewis told Robbie to sit down, fully aware he was dealing with a very self-possessed young man. But before he could ask his next question, Robbie jumped in ahead to continue his narrative and promised he would tell them all about her - and them. "She was needy, you know, that's the first thing." Lewis had given him no clue that they had her body and let Robbie go on telling his story.

Thus began a narrative of how he had met Wendy. They had first met at the Freshman Mixer the previous September: "We danced every dance together. I asked her for a date on the next Saturday. We went out a lot and quickly became 'steadies.' We were even there that day Ike's campaign train stopped in town," he smiled another disarming smile at the memory as if to confirm the beginning of a treasured love story.

He was so damned smooth, thought Russ. Maybe thinks we don't know she's dead, that I'm here because her parents asked me to find her. Something like that. Well, thought Russ, let him go on. I'll play along. And Robbie did go on. "Walked right up to the train where Ike was standing on the rear platform with Senator Bricker and Senator Taft and handed him my freshman dink and he put it on! You know that's the hat we all had to wear first semester." He looked around as if for signs of approval from someone else but had apparently forgotten they were alone. There weren't any, but Robbie added some self-congratulations, "That was pretty neat. Ike - soon to be President Eisenhower, of course, put it on!"

"But you haven't seen her this fall?" said Lewis, trying to suppress his dark thoughts about this clever young fencer.

"No sir, she finally wrote me in August, weeks after I had been there at her house, that we were all over. She must have found someone else to coach her, I guess. I did the best I could, you know, but she had a pretty tough time last semester. Failed one course. I tried to help her, but you know, she didn't really have the interest I did."

What gall! Thought Lewis.

Looking very serious now about his plans, he added, "I hope to go to Oberlin next year to get ready for theological school."

"Really," said Sheriff Lewis, with a half-smile. "Want to be a preacher, hunh?"

"Yes, sir, I do. Last Sunday made up my mind in church. Told the minister so."

"Really, that's interesting because her parents told me you two pleaded with them to get married?"

"We did talk about that, you know, once or twice maybe," he explained, looking very thoughtful, "but we both decided they were right. We were too young. And I was thinking about several more years before I could be able to support a family - financially or emotionally."

"Yes, I can see that. Really do." Lewis thought two could play this game. "You know, you could help us a lot by coming with me to positively identify this body we found Saturday morning."

A perfect look of astonishment spread over Robbie's face to go with the rising inflection of concern in his response. "You mean you think it's Wendy?"

Lewis had realized almost from the first that Robbie Stanson was a challenge. How long can he keep it up? "I didn't say Wendy. I said we found a body we think could be her."

He waited for Robbie's reaction. There wasn't any beyond a slight shake of his head. "Now, to repeat, I think it would be very helpful if you could ride up with me to Upper Scioto."

The well-mannered college student looked around as if determined to do his bit to help the sheriff and nodded yet again with a solemn look. "Sure."

§

Robbie appeared to enjoy the ride north. "I come this way when I go home to Mayfield Heights." Then he looked thoughtful, remembering something he had to do. "I have to get Dad's car back to him next week. He's been taking the bus to work." For all the world it could have been a ride to a football game or some other function. He and the sheriff exchanged stories about local high school football teams. Robbie had played baseball for his high school. "I got beaned once," he said with a laugh. "Knocked me out. I had headaches for about a month."

He looked over at Lewis for his reaction.

I'll play along, thought the sheriff. "That right? Any long-lasting effects?"

"Yeah, well, every once in a while, I still get a little dizzy. Nothing serious." But he caught Robbie looking for a reaction out of a corner of his eye. Lewis only nodded slightly and kept his eyes on the road.

Then he asked almost casually, "When again did you say you last saw Wendy?"

"Oh, it must have been sometime middle of last month, yeah, in August, I guess. That's when she wrote me."

He had finally slipped up. Lewis had asked when he last *saw* Wendy. But still, it was not a real slip. They drove in silence most of the time until the city limits.

"OK," Russ said, "we're about there. Now I want you to take a good look when we get to the place we're going and tell me for sure if it's Wendy or," he paused and stared hard at Robbie, "if you don't recognize this person. She's been beaten up pretty badly. Real bad."

Robbie flinched at that and put his hand on the door handle, tapping it with his fingers, a gesture that did draw a glance from the sheriff.

"You o.k.?"

"Yeah, sure."

§

They did not go to the funeral home. After a few turns, they were outside a one-story annex to the medical center, where Russ had had Wendy's body moved back from the funeral home for another "identification." This one by the person he believed had been the last one to see her alive. A lawn sprinkler caused a rainbow to dance across the grass along the walk to the revolving door with its notice to Keep Moving. Once inside, where the morgue was located, all the colors of the outside gave way to the gray and white of the walls and ceilings, black floors, and the nurses' starched uniforms. The smell of disinfectants filled the hall. They walked onto an elevator. Lewis pushed the floor button for LL. When it stopped, Lewis nudged

Stanson forward. For the first time since they had met, he seemed hesitant. After a pause Robbie stepped into a hallway where boxes took up most of the space.

"Kinda crowded just now down here," Lewis said. "Putting in new office furniture. Ahead, on your right, you'll see the door." Lewis wanted to draw out these last moments as long as he could to see Robbie's reaction.

"Stay here just a minute," said the sheriff, walking through an inner door and then stopping to call out. "George, I've got someone here to see our unknown victim. He might know who it is." The attendant offered Robbie his hand. This whole scene had been plotted out ahead of time.

"Sure hope you can help," said George with a friendly look, a key part of the ploy to confront Stanson with a supposed mystery. George thought to himself: Yes, Lewis was a young sheriff - youngest in Ohio, but he had police "smarts" for sure from all that experience in occupied Germany and with lots of new ideas about how "cops" laid mental traps to increase pressure on suspects.

The small room they entered seemed designed to induce claustrophobia, with its white walls and shelves crowded with brown glass bottles pressing in from two sides. A draped sheet covered the form on the medical table. There was hardly room to move around - all planned by Lewis. It was actually a storeroom, set up for shock effect at the sheriff's orders, never used for actual medical examinations of the living or the dead. Russ had actually been pleased quite a bit that no one had raised doubts about the suitability of his proposed plan to get a quick confession. He had told the County Prosecutor he was going to bring Stanson back with him to make an ID, not how he planned to accomplish a confession.

George uncovered Wendy's head. Her eyes were open, another part of his "project." As he had hoped, Stanson recoiled and seemed at last shaken - if only for seconds. That would be expected, of course, from anyone. He looked at the sheriff. "I can't be sure," he whispered. Lewis appeared to lose patience for the first time, "Oh, come on, man, you know it's Wendy. Let's get that settled right away, and then you can tell us what you know about what happened to her."

"OK, yes, it's Wendy. It's just... I haven't seen her for weeks, and I was so hoping this was not going to be her. You surely understand that."

"Yes," Lewis nodded, staring hard at Robbie, "I think probably someone hoped we wouldn't recognize her after a terrible beating almost destroyed her face." He paused for several seconds, waiting for a reaction. There was none he could see, wondering what in hell was going on inside Stanson's head. So he continued. "I also think we need to check your story about the breakup with some other folks down back at Bashford. See where you... where she was the last couple of weeks because her parents thought she was living in Cleveland. Let's take another ride down to the college and ask around if anyone has seen Wendy this fall? You don't mind that, do you? Who knows, maybe she stayed in Cleveland. Her parents have her address in Cleveland. I'll ask around. But be sure we'll find it all out. You still have a place to stay down there?"

Robbie nodded and asked to tell his parents about what was going on.

"Of course, you can use the phone back in my office."

It was the first sign Robbie had given that he was worried. He put in a call but managed a calm front and did not say anything about getting a lawyer. *"He'll break. I know he will,"* Russ thought to himself.

§

They drove down again the next day after putting Robbie up overnight in the local hotel. Russ dropped him off at the Dean of Students office, explaining that the college had arranged for the sheriff to meet with some students in the MUB, the student union building. He asked if there was somewhere "safe" where Robbie could wait and was led to a small office where paper supplies were kept. It was perfect, Russ thought. Let him stew a bit. Russ had thought about putting him in the county sheriff's office but decided to hold back on that for a while until he had better indications Wendy had actually been in West River recently.

West River was a small college town, about 8,000 and with 1,800 students, so there was a good chance Wendy would have been seen and recognized if she had been there. At the arranged meeting, about two dozen students showed up. Several said they might have information. He planned to meet with them as a group first and then with some individually.

"Had anyone seen anything of Wendy Peters recently?" Lewis asked to open the meeting. "Seen her on the streets or in a restaurant? Maybe right here in the building?" A sophomore girl named Lorrie had not seen Wendy this fall, but she had lived on the same corridor freshman year and was very explicit about what she had seen several times in her dorm. "Wendy used to come in from dates with him with marks on her face, and one time even a black eye." Pausing for dramatic effect, Lorrie went on: "She just laughed about it."

"Who was him?"

"Robbie Stanson."

"You know," Lorrie continued, "he was there nearly every morning at the dorm waiting to walk her to campus, and he always walked her back, I guess, every afternoon. We all knew about it, but Wendy didn't seem to care."

Lorrie looked around the room, seeking confirmation. Another student towards the back of the room nodded and said, "He was a sicko! And she ought to have listened to us."

"Why didn't someone say something about it to a dorm counselor or the dean of women?" Lewis asked.

The second girl shrugged, now sensing she might be blamed for not caring, and looked down at her lap, "I don't know - should've, I guess."

"But you haven't seen her this fall?"

"No, I don't think she came back to school."

As it turned out, no one had seen Wendy since school began, let alone with Robbie anywhere. Nor had anyone seen her old boyfriend that particular night, September 21, the time frame police seemed the most concerned about. A fraternity brother had seen Stanson the previous night, however, in a local restaurant. "He was with a girl when I saw him about ten p.m., but it wasn't Wendy. I didn't know her." Another student saw him the next morning in a required phys ed bowling class. "I don't know, he seemed kinda agitated," the student told Lewis. "Got really mad a couple of times when he didn't make a strike. Practically threw the second ball down the alley!"

"Big temper, then," said the sheriff. "Anyone ever see him go off on someone else?"

No one had, but then it emerged that Robbie Stanson was not someone who hung out around the student union or other gathering places.

"He had a few friends, I guess," said one student, "but never saw him in a group of guys."

§

This was disappointing. It appeared no one had seen Wendy in town or on campus. Then came the break Lewis had hoped for. A student who had been quiet through all this as if waiting to hear something decided he might, in fact, have information and spoke up. What he then related seemed to mark the first turning point in the case: Around nine o'clock on the night of September 21 or 22, 1953, his story began, two couples had sat necking in a car on Herndon Street south of the football stadium. It was a favorite spot because few people drove out of town that way. Almost directly across the street from their car was a practice field with an old unpainted shed, not more than fifteen feet square, with one small window, not quite abandoned but hardly used in recent years. None of the four had heard or seen anyone actually go in or out of the shed. "No, we didn't see anything, really, just some shadows and maybe a flashlight once," said a student named Ted. "It was pretty dark, and... you know." But no one else offered anything more.

Russ decided to visit that shed before he went back for Robbie, who was sitting in the dean of students' outer office. What he found astonished him, and not all to the good. It raised uncomfortable questions from the get-go but made some sense - in a vaguely disturbing way. Surrounded by tall weeds these days, the dilapidated old storehouse was almost always left alone. Once it had housed mowers and bags of limestone for maintaining the grass in the stadium and marking yard lines, now it was empty except for rusted cans in one corner and a set of fence poles bound tightly with twine leaning against the rear wall. *Could they have met there? Not really a romantic spot, but there was nothing romantic about the way this story was developing.*

§

Lewis went back to the Dean of Students Office. "Well, Robbie, what I understand from your friends here at Bashford and girls who lived close to Wendy is that you treated her pretty roughly..."

For the first time, he seemed alarmed. "No, that's not so, that's not so," he said, shaking his head. "We wrestled sometimes, that's all."

Lewis pushed harder. "Not what I gathered. Seems like you dominated just about everything in her life, going to class, coming from class..."

"She counted on me, you mean," he shot back. "I already told you that the last time. She pleaded with me to be there when she needed help..."

"Really, you actually mean she pleaded to be hit and..." Lewis paused. "Now I want you to take us to a place where some students saw something that last Friday night before her body was found, ok?"

"Ok"

With Robbie once more beside him in the front seat, Lewis asked Stanson to show the way to the football stadium as if he had never been there.

"Cut down this street and turn right. You'll see it."

"Thanks."

After they passed the stadium, Lewis pointed to the old shed on a practice field. "Let's get out here and walk over there - towards that shack or whatever it is. Someone said a little while ago this morning, they saw a flashlight near it that night."

There were no obvious signs anyone had come near this grey outpost in recent weeks, let alone a couple in search of a place to make love. Russ felt its forbidding solitude as they got close. Here, he thought again. Hard to believe a bright young woman would agree to go here? And no one had seemed interested even in tearing down the eyesore.

"Ever been here?" Lewis asked, not sure *he* believed anything happened in this abominable place.

"No, Sir."

"Let's take a look." The sheriff led the way across the field with Robbie keeping pace, for all the world as equally concerned in finding out about Wendy. At the shed, Lewis asked Robbie to push open the door while he got out some gloves. Robbie walked in, looking around without any hesitation as if there were no dark memories to overcome. "See anything over there," Lewis asked, sweeping his hand around in a questioning gesture.

Robbie looked hard all around. "No, sheriff, what are you looking for?

Oh, well, maybe it wasn't here, mused Lewis to himself. But somewhere.

Still, he was a little bit disappointed his little play-action scenario hadn't turned out the way he had hoped it would. He would force the issue another way.

They returned to the patrol car, and Russ told his passenger he wanted him to return with him to where they had found Wendy's body. "Any objections?"

"No sir, if I can help, I will do all I can."

Man... thought Lewis again, he is a cool one, yes, a damned cool one.

§

Reaching Upper Scioto, Lewis put Robbie in an unlocked holding cell detained, he told him, for some further questioning to clear up "a few points." He was not quite going by the book, but Robbie still had not requested a lawyer, even when the sheriff notified his parents in Mayfield, a suburb of Cleveland, about his being "detained." They were mystified and unbelieving that all this was happening. He decided to make a quick trip to their house. Almost as soon as he got there and explained why he had to see them, still not using the term - arrested - Robbie's mother Ann started repeating what would become her mantra, "It's all my fault, it's all my fault. They wanted to get married, and I wouldn't let them. I wouldn't let them." She went on to talk about how conscientious Robbie was. Whenever he was out late, he would always tell them when he got home. He didn't drink or hang out with any of the boys who did. Robbie's father picked up on that theme, talking about how he had taught his son to catch deep-hit fly balls in the field nearby. "How could this be? He was never cruel to anyone, never in a fight."

"Mr. Stanson, Robbie told us he had been hurt one year. I got hit on the head in a baseball game. Do you remember that at all?"

"Yes, I do. His junior year."

"Did he see a doctor? He also told us that he has had headaches ever since. Anything you can add to that?

David Stanson picked up on that theme. "Yes, I remember that incident. Robbie did complain about headaches. But we never thought it was serious enough to take him to the doctor. Maybe - probably - we made a mistake there. Do you think that had anything to do with what happened?"

With what happened! What was that, an admission and a line of defense? Robbie's father had seized on a possible opening and had moved ahead to the outcome of the investigation. Russ backed off quickly. He had just offered a medical alibi of sorts - on his own! *Bad mistake, he said to himself. Watch that sort of thing.* If some defense lawyer asked... Not a good move, not at all. He should have just kept quiet about what Robbie had said in the car. "I'm taking him down to West River again to clear up some things. I expect to bring him back as soon as we do that, and possibly formal charges will be placed. I hope you will take my advice and secure legal assistance in the meantime."

"Can we see him first?"

Russ avoided a direct answer. "Oh, we'll arrange that when we get back from another trip. Shouldn't be there long." He realized he was treading on dangerous ground here, but the shock of the "arrest" still hadn't completely sunk in with Robbie's parents. In part because Russ still called it a "detainment." This slip-up caused some trouble later.

§

The next day, it was back in the car for another trip down to West River. Again, Robbie was silent on the drive down. He had given the sheriff an eight-page "statement" about how they had met and gone steady, his visit to her in Westport, their plans for getting married, their parents' disapproval and their break-up. Robbie showed no signs of panic - or remorse. Seeking to find a weak spot and produce a quick confession, he took Robbie back to the shed. "Nothing happened here, then? Those wrestling matches you talk about, where did they take place? If I bring in a forensic crew, they're not going to find anything?"

"I already said we wrestled some."

"Yes, you said that, and I don't believe you for a minute. But are you now saying you were here? Let's get clear, at least on that point. And you are going to tell me again - this time the full story - about your relationship from the beginning and when and how you said it ended."

"It did end. I couldn't help her anymore and..."

"Well, her parents thought you two had broken up..."

"That's right. That's right, I wrote to one of her friends about it. Check with her. She's at Wittenberg, and her name's Jane Stafford. Call her up; interview her. She'll tell you."

"Oh, we will, we will."

But Lewis had been taken aback a bit by Robbie's confident assurance that Miss Stafford would at least confirm that he had written such a letter. Was he wrong to think this was coming to a rapid ending? Was he wrong about who had killed her? He felt outflanked at almost every turn. Still he was convinced it had been Robbie, maybe not here but someplace.

§

Dropping Robbie off at the county jail, Russ called Wittenberg and located Jane Stafford. "Yes," she said, "Robbie had written me." She had been concerned because she and Wendy were good friends, and she had not heard from her since mid-August, so she asked him what he knew about her. He then wrote saying they had broken up and he did not know where she was.

"What else did he say."

"Well, he implied that he was available now. I didn't exactly respond to those hints because I wanted to talk to Wendy."

"Did you try to contact her parents?"

"No, I wasn't certain about that."

"The police?"

"Why should I talk to them? I just thought Wendy might be shutting herself off from someone who knew them both. I decided to wait."

Lewis decided he would not tell Robbie about the phone conversation for a while. Meanwhile, he would concentrate on Robbie's story on the break-up and the circumstances around it.

§

He also made a call to Detective Robert Carpere in Cleveland, who had been assigned to check Wendy's landlady in Cleveland to see what she had left there when she went missing. So far, he hadn't heard anything. The landlady was visiting her sister in Pittsburgh. Russ hung up the phone and went back to the West River cell. Stanson still had not asked to see a lawyer and was calmly chatting with deputies in the county sheriff's office. Lewis had still not told him he was under arrest. How long could this go on?

"Tell me again. When you saw Wendy at her house in July that was the last time?"

"Yes, that's right. The last time. I had a job in Cleveland driving a delivery truck for the May Company. I lived at home with my folks."

"Did you date anyone else this summer?"

"No, I didn't really have the time to meet someone - and, frankly, after Wendy, I didn't want to get involved for a while."

"Well, Jane Stafford tells me that you sounded like you wanted to date her."

"No, that's not so, not at all."

"So she misinterpreted what you wrote? I expect to get hold of that letter to see how you put it. Did you try to break it off with Wendy because you didn't want her to get pregnant?"

"No, nothing like that. As I said before I just couldn't handle her neediness any longer." He raised his voice. "And I didn't know she was pregnant."

"Really, well, she was. She must have found someone pretty quickly."

"Yeah, I guess so - must have."

"Come on, Robbie, you don't really expect me to believe that. She was carrying your baby."

Robbie shook his head, but Russ could see sweat on his upper lip. "Her parents told me she was going to Cleveland. I think she was coming down to see you that week. And you met her. There was no break-up."

Robbie stared at Russ. After a minute, he smiled and nodded in a way that said he knew he had been lying but that now he was going to tell the truth. "Yes, o.k., we wanted to get married. Her parents and mine were against it, so we decided that the only way for us was for her to get pregnant. Then they couldn't stop us. We worked it out that she would come to Cleveland and get a job. Then, early this fall, we'd go down to Cincinnati, go on over to Kentucky and get married. But it was her idea to come down here last week."

"But you didn't want to get married," the sheriff paused, "you killed her," Robbie said nothing, so Russ went on. "How do I know? One of her classmates saw her outside that shack on the athletic field." He was lying. No one had actually seen Wendy. But it seemed to hit home.

The only sound for a minute was the clock ticking on the wall. Then, as if mystified about how it could have happened, Robbie broke down: "I don't know what happened. It all happened in a fog - these headaches I told you about... I loved Wendy."

CHAPTER THREE

TO TELL THE TRUTH?

"You're going to tell me everything from the time she arrived in West River until you left her beside the road that Friday night." This moment would prove to be one of the most contested issues in the "Red Slippers" case. As things played out, Russ's failure to warn Robbie about his rights, pretending he was not really "under arrest," only "detained," became a real issue. And he would regret it all mightily later when the case came to court, and even later. But not at the time. Nothing like this had happened to him in the army, but then, in the army, he had never faced a Robbie Stanson, who seemed (as he later realized) to be one step ahead all the time.

"I can't remember everything." Robbie had said, shaking his head in response to Lewis's "order."

"Do your best." Russ managed to keep his voice calm and measured. He had never confronted a murderer. "Maybe it'll come back to you. Start from the beginning."

But the uncertain Robbie, who had appeared bewildered a few moments ago, was already gone from the room. He even seemed pleased with himself at the way things were now playing out. He had regained his footing - and seemed thankful to the sheriff for giving him the opportunity to get it all off his chest. Then, they would be square. The danger would be over.

"Damn him," Russ said to himself as he watched this rapid transformation. He knew he had messed up, just not how badly. He had overplayed his hand. Robbie could claim he was tricked into a confession, that he said he had killed Wendy only because of the sheriff's badgering about a witness that Lewis feared did not exist. Was he that clever? And the "detainment" ploy Russ had used instead of a formal

arrest at the start that would have encouraged the suspect to get a lawyer on the phone pronto.

All in all, the sheriff had good reason to worry about his handling of the case so far. And added to this, something was nagging at the back of his mind, something that had not taken shape yet, but it concerned how he had managed all this without any real witnesses. That shed was out in the open.

But that thought had to wait. Robbie's narrative now picked up with Wendy's supposed initiation of a plan for them to get married, packing up all her stuff at the apartment where she lived and coming to West River earlier than he had expected, on a Thursday. He had not instructed her to come down just yet. That was why, he said, she had had to stay in that shack on the old practice field. He hadn't had time to find a place before she showed up on a bus from Cleveland on Thursday night. He had worried that if he didn't agree to her plan, she might do something "dangerous," like committing suicide. He left her there that first night, he said, and came back to his room. He barely slept that night, afraid for her, he said and returned as early in the morning as he could with coffee and rolls in between phys ed and botany classes and tried to talk her into going back to Cleveland. He told her they weren't ready to get married. She still hadn't told him she was pregnant. But she said she was going to stay until Robbie was ready to go to Cincinnati and then on to Kentucky. "That was not such a good idea," he had told her, "all our plans could be spoiled."

"OK," said Russ. "I'll get you some paper, and you can write it all down so we have something in writing to go on." Robbie still hadn't asked for a lawyer and picked up the narrative again, now in writing where he had left off - not quite what the sheriff had asked him to do. But the sheriff knew that Robbie felt he was in charge of the narrative, even so, no matter what he said or wrote. "I got a little upset and warned her to stay out of sight until we figured all this out." He left and did not come back again until the early evening. Right away, there was trouble about a man she said she had seen walking across the field toward the river. But then she undressed and put on a blue nightgown. She said she wanted him more than anything. So they had sex. "Then she sprung the rest on me." She had not only seen this man she had talked to him for a few minutes.

"For God's sake, Wendy, why'd you do that?" She slapped him. "And I lost control. I hit her, and she fell back and banged her head on that table in the shack. I didn't know what to do." He stopped there, tears welling up in his eyes.

Russ looked at what he had written. "Was she conscious?" Lewis asked after reading that assertion. The question seemed to stump Robbie. "She moaned a little, I think," he then said. Lewis continued reading the confession: "Then I took her out to my car and drove around. I wasn't really thinking very clearly at that point, just hoping she would revive and I could tell her how sorry I was about how all this turned out." At this point, Robbie stopped short, looked like he had a new idea and added that he planned now to write her parents about how sorry he was she had died. *Yeah, just as if she had been sick. Robbie was playing the real victim now.* And he had a sense of losing control of the situation with his sarcasm. It hit him then that he couldn't really go on this way another minute. Whatever he admitted here might be ruled out. Russ hoped the way he had conducted this interview did not foreshadow trouble in getting justice for Wendy.

Taking a deep breath to calm himself, he said, "You better get a lawyer - now."

§

After placing Robbie under arrest in the county jail located near the courthouse in West River, Lewis spent the night in a hotel. Despite Robbie's "confession," there remained the question of a murder weapon and what had happened to it. Without that, the case might still be difficult to prove, especially in terms of where the murder had actually taken place. That question was crucial. Stanson's narrative left open the time of death, as had the autopsy. There were no obvious signs of violence in the shed - at least to the naked eye - and worse, no signs Wendy had even been there! And Lewis was anxious to know more of the back story about the time Wendy spent in Cleveland. Robbie had "confessed" in his way, but the sheriff needed a lot more.

Russ had pretty well figured out where Robbie was trying to go now: to some temporary insanity plea, better put, temporary incapacity. It seemed like he was making it up on the run, but it was pretty clever. "You know she was defaced, don't you," he began the questioning again the next morning. "You were conscious of that, right? You were still in a fog?"

Robbie still did not give a straight answer. And despite Russ's warning, he still had not asked to talk to a lawyer. He apparently thought his statements would elicit more sympathy if made totally voluntarily. Also problematic for everyone was the slip-up of leaving the red slippers with Wendy's body. Or was it a slip-up? Did he mean to argue that he was so far off in an extended trance that he failed to notice what he had left behind?

The first thing, however, was to get Robbie to tell him exactly what he had done with the "thing" (he could think of no other word for it) he had used to deface Wendy and the suitcase he said she brought with her. A search of his father's car that he had used to transport Wendy to the spot where he had wielded the weapon had not turned up anything like such a bludgeon - nor anything else either, including no bloodstains, and that was really remarkable. In a fog one minute, detail man the next. It didn't fit - not at all.

Robbie said without emotion, barely above a whisper: "It was just handy. At the fraternity house. I threw it in the river." But he refused to look Lewis in the eye.

§

By this time, most students at Bashford and indeed the whole town knew that a student had been "detained" in connection with the disappearance and death of a "Pretty Young Co-Ed" found in the woods outside Upper Scioto but little more. Newspapers ran pictures of Wendy from the copy of her high school graduation portrait, and, alongside, much to the discomfort of the ROTC Department, pictures that had had been snapped of Robbie leaving the Dean of Students' office, his uniform jacket unbuttoned, his tie loose, accompanied by Lewis, who had a firm grip on his arm. Someone who worked in the Dean's office had tipped off the local press even as Robbie was being interviewed. There were also pictures of the sheriff's car. So now there was a vigil around the county courthouse and jail, and when Robbie and Lewis exited the early twentieth-century red brick building and walked down the back stairs to the car, deputies were present to keep a small crowd back. As they walked to the car, Robbie did not duck and look at the ground. Instead he smiled a little at the crowd that had gathered outside the jail and pushed back a lock of hair from his forehead. He was not in handcuffs.

It was as if, Lewis thought to himself, he believed he had called them there to watch. Why? For Chris-sakes! He wants to feel in charge! That must be it - he's delusional. Robbie gave directions, and the sheriff drove to one end of the bridge over the river on the east side of town, close to the railroad station and near where Eisenhower's campaign train had stopped a year ago. Robbie finished his account of the crime by explaining that when he got back to town after leaving Wendy's body in the woods, he had thrown the "thing" into the water. Car traffic was blocked, and no one was allowed on the bridge itself. But by now, both students and townspeople had heard stories of a terrible murder and appeared in growing numbers crowded along the riverbank as if a traveling circus had come to town. This added to Lewis' discomfort - a great deal. The main attraction was Robbie, standing there in the middle of the bridge between two local deputies.

§

It was a sunny morning, and the crowd could see Robbie gesturing to the sheriff when Lewis waded out into the shallow water. The river at this time of year in early fall was not deep under the bridge, and Russ stood in hip boots and undershirt dipping his hands, feeling for whatever the "thing" was Robbie said he had flung into the river that connected him to Wendy's death.

Lewis could see the blue sky and clouds reflected in the clear water, along with glints of sunshine popping on and off on the surface. The swelling crowd of people (where did they all come from!) waved and shouted and pointed from the street and were now on both riverbanks.

How much longer would this awful search take, Lewis thought? He waded back and forth, trying to see something among the rocks besides broken beer bottles, afraid there was no weapon here. Had Robbie planned out a scheme that would make it appear as if he had lost all memory of his crime? It wouldn't surprise him.

Then he saw it: An iron bar about four feet long with an eye at one end, used, he was later told, by railroad workers to switch a train from one track to another. Nearby, as well, he now glimpsed a suitcase, half open with a piece of a blue blouse trailing out of it. Russ picked up the metal bar and waded back to the shore, retraced his way to the suitcase, freed it from where it had caught between rocks, and pushed the blouse back in and shut it. Nothing else was left of Wendy's clothes. He wondered about there being only one suitcase. Perhaps Robbie had dumped some of her belongings in another spot? One more thing that bothered him about Robbie's "confession."

But there was no time to think about that possibility at the moment. He would have to ask about that later. He had the murder weapon – well, not exactly, of course, because of the continuing doubts about the time of death. A swarm of reporters awaited his arrival back at the county jail. Once Robbie was placed back in a cell, he met them in the front office.

"Show us how he did it, Sheriff!" Russ refused. It was beyond disgusting. He could hardly bear to hold the metal bar in his hands, as if even touching it made him feel complicit in some strange way in exploiting what terrible thing had been done to Wendy, her face destroyed, her life ended so brutally in such a horrifying scene alone in the woods.

But press photographers insisted he at least pose with it pointing at the eye on the end. He shuddered as flashbulbs recorded the scene. He could not wait until he got out of their sight, and he had his prisoner in his jail cell up north.

§

If Russ was unhappy about the crowd that watched the gruesome scene play out at the river and the worse aftermath at the county jail, college administrators were horrified at what had ruined the fall semester. Besieged by reporters who clogged the halls around the main administration offices shouting questions at deans and secretaries, normal business was almost impossible. Worst of all, beyond the dozens of alumni reactions – especially from those who made large gifts - were the dozens of parents writing - and calling - demanding to know what was going on: "Where were the dorm counselors? Did no one notice what was happening all last year?" The president talked with the college's lawyers about how to keep a trial out of West River, but none of them had ever experienced anything like this. Panty raids and pranks that had turned into sprains and broken bones, yes, but nothing like this. Reporters stopped students passing to or from class, descended on the student union to interview coffee drinkers. Urgent orders went out to maintenance crews several mornings in a row with buckets and brushes to wipe away the graffiti that had appeared overnight on the walks throughout the main campus. Students circled around them gawking at the obscene comments scrawled in chalk on the sidewalks ("Bashford Murderers" was the mildest) along with crude drawings depicting a supposed murder scene, and the sex before it. The sidewalks did not stay erased. Every morning for close to two weeks the scene was repeated. Normal life at Bashford College had disappeared into maelstrom. How long would that last?

§

Meanwhile, the discovery of the "weapon" had convinced Robbie he needed to make a full "explanation" of how his "black out" had led to Wendy's tragic death. Sherriff Lewis brought him a yellow tablet and three newly sharpened pencils. Robbie did not call it a confession, and instead said it replaced everything he had admitted to earlier:

Robbie's Story

When Wendy arrived at the Cleveland airport, I was so happy to see her. We hoped that our parents would relent in their opposition to our marriage. But if they didn't, we planned for what we would do after we told them she was pregnant, and we loved one another. I was working as a delivery man for the May company, driving trucks around the city and suburbs. She applied for a job in the lingerie department and got it. Oh, yes, but first we found an apartment for her only a few blocks from my house. But we did not go there together, because we had agreed that we would say we had broken up - this was because we didn't want to have to explain everything, we just wanted to go ahead through the summer both making some money so that we could manage for a few months. Then I would get a job, and we would figure out how to get enough support from my parents to allow me to continue my education.

That was the plan, anyway. When I went back to school, Wendy stayed behind to continue working until I came up with details for our marriage. But she got lonely, and just a day or two before she came down, she wrote me and said she was coming. I told her this was not a good idea. But she really wanted to see me. So I said, o.k., take the bus down and I will meet you. I tried to think of some place, a motel where she could stay for a day or two. Then I thought what if she is seen by some of our friends and they told everyone? Our plans would be blown up. So I told her to make sure she brought all her things, and all her money, and I would meet her a block away from the bus station. It was scheduled to arrive at 1:10 a.m.

When she came around the corner, we kissed and got in the car. I told her the new plan, and she was happy to stay in the shed because we only supposed it would be for a day or two - at most. I got her settled there then went back to my room at the fraternity. Next day I saw her several times. It was her idea to have sex right there. Afterwards she teased about this man who had seen her, and she did it in a way that made me mad. She gave my nose a little tug, and I lost it. I just got mad and shoved or hit her. She fell back and hit her head on that table in the shack. Then she slipped off onto the ground. I tried to revive her but she just moaned a little. I guess I thought she was playacting. "Wendy, I said, cut it out, cut it out" I was starting to cry at this point, and I guess I had her by the throat and was squeezing. "Wendy," I remember shouting, "cut it out. Wake up." Then everything started swimming, and my head hurt - really bad. I slipped down on the ground beside her and she wasn't moving.

I thought I had to take her to the car, and somehow I dragged her along. Then went back and got her things and suitcase. Some stuff wouldn't fit in. I drove around West River in circles. I thought I heard her moan once or twice. But then it was pretty clear that was not the case. I didn't know what to do. I thought, "What would Wendy want me to do?" "Go to the Police?" "Take her to the hospital?" "What would she want?" And I decided that she wanted to help me more than anything else - we were a team. I would just have to work it out for us even though I was now alone.

So I decided on a plan. I drove up to the fraternity because I remembered there was something I could use to help me - help us - survive this tragedy. Then I drove north out of town and kept going until I was pretty far away and turned off the road near the woods. I carefully lifted Wendy out of the back seat and into the trees. Then I tried to make sure no one would recognize her dead - she wouldn't want that, she was always so happy when we were together.

I went back to the car - my Dad's car that he was letting me use - and drove back to West River. On the side of town where Ike stopped on his campaign trail the year before there was a river. I stopped on the bridge and dumped her suitcase over the rail. Then I tossed what I had used to make Wendy unrecognizable into the water a few feet further along. Nobody came by while I was there.

I didn't sleep that night. It was a pretty bad weekend. But on Sunday I went to church - the big Methodist Church on Central Street. I prayed about what I could do now for the both of us. The more I thought about what had taken place, the more it seemed to fit in to God's plan for me. And I decided that the only way our commitments would mean anything was if I dedicated my life to God's service. I was to forsake any personal goals I might have had before Wendy's death. I felt better right away and knew that was what Wendy wanted me to do. Maybe it had all been His plan - from that very first date to the "fight" in the shed. And I felt better at once. And as things developed, I came to realize as well that I had left those red slippers with Wendy because it was all part of the plan God had for me - so that everyone would know her role in my making the right decisions. Without her none of this would have happened. The minister at the church (I didn't tell him about Wendy's role) thought it was a fine thing that I had decided right at the beginning of my sophomore year. There was time to do it right!

And if the sheriff hadn't come down last week, I was going to go to the police myself.

§

Russ read this incredible conclusion and decided he had one more thing he could do to try to shake Stanson's belief in his "explanation." There was no one to write Wendy's story unless he did it. Yes, he would write "Wendy's Story," not only from what he learned from her parents, but from information he could get from the people who rented her a room in Cleveland. It also turned out that one of Wendy's classmates had seen her working at the department store and tried to strike up a conversation. So he had made his first trip to Cleveland to interview Wendy's landlords, and consulted with Cleveland detectives who had found letters from Robbie.

Mr. and Mrs. Hallett had rented Wendy a room and they had developed a strong relationship with the young woman in a short time. She confided in them almost like she was their daughter, and when she felt bad about her situation, they invited a local minister over for coffee on a Saturday morning. And there was a letter Robbie had written her a week before she took that last bus trip to West River. It turned up caught in a drawer when Mrs. Hallett cleaned out Wendy's room the afternoon she left for West River. "I didn't know where to forward it," she then said to Sheriff Lewis, looking at him almost in tears.

§

Later, with Robbie in a cell down the hall, Russ Lewis went to his desk, took off the cover of his typewriter and began:

Wendy's Story

I met Robbie Stanson at the Freshman Mixer in September 1952. We seemed to hit it off right away and I was very pleased when he asked me out for a real date on the next Saturday. Very soon we were "steadies," and I got used to the idea of him stopping by the dorm in the mornings to walk me down to class. I had never had a boyfriend in high school like Robbie and I guess I did like to show him off a little bit to some of the other girls on my floor. He was handsome and seemed to know his way around college life pretty well already. I never thought he was intruding or keeping me away from other people. A couple of my friends told me I ought to watch my step, but I just thought they were jealous. Robbie needed me also to help him with his studies. It made me feel happy to do that, but, yes, sometimes it kept me from finishing up my own work in good time. He told me not to worry, I would be fine. My first semester grades were not great, but he said everyone went through that. If I helped him, then he would do the same when I needed help.

But the second semester made me worry about what my parents were going to think. My brother, Carl had done well at Bashford and was now a chemical engineer in Columbus. He didn't seem all that concerned about me. We had hardly seen one another since I came to school. And I had the strong feeling that he didn't want his little sister messing up his life. Anyway, I had Robbie.

Of course, it was getting pretty hard to keep from "going all the way." Late in the spring he had his Dad's car and we did "do it." I was feeling less concern about my grades all the time and wondering if Robbie was thinking about getting married, because I was - very much. You weren't supposed to go all the way with someone just casually, were you? We did talk about it and Robbie seemed to agree - or so I thought. After the semester ended, I was ready to talk to my parents - alone at first to see how they felt. They said we were too young. Robbie told me his parents had said the same thing. I wondered if he really did talk to them and they really had said that? So what were we going to do?

When Robbie came to visit in July we were still trying to figure it out. We went "all the way" a couple of times in his car on that visit. Maybe we intended I should get pregnant. Maybe it was an "accident." But after he left for Cleveland, I decided that I would go out and be with him sort of like we were married, seeing each other every day. The truth was at this point that I did not tell Robbie I thought I was pregnant. I felt strange about things. And when one of the girls from my floor came up to me in the store, I pretended not to recognize her. I don't know if she believed me, but she went away with a funny look on her face.

September came pretty fast. And Robbie told me he was going back to school and he would think about what we had to do. That made me a little uneasy - but I really, really loved him and I was now sure that I was pregnant. All I told Robbie was that I "thought" I was pregnant. He got very mad at that point, which I understood - a little bit - and hit me. This time I did get a black eye. When I told Mrs. Hallett, she was really upset about it and I told her I was worried about Robbie's reaction, because he hadn't said we were going to get married soon. She suggested I talk to her minister, Rev. Sherry Bell. I didn't know what to expect, but I did decide I would tell him. He was nice as he could be. He said the first thing I had to do was talk it out with Robbie. I thought he was right so I wrote him about it.

Wow. Robbie called me up and said he hadn't really planned on this so soon. He needed to think about it - almost as if having a child was something one could change your mind about and it would go away. Then I was really, really upset two days later when I got his letter. Instead of anything nice, he wrote that "Under the law, when the mother is older than the father, he cannot be compelled to take any responsibility for the child." That's when I broke down and went to Mrs. Hallett again. She was really kind and got me to talk to Rev. Bell. He thought I had to be very strong, and if Robbie loved me the way he had said he did all these months, then with God's help it would all work out. But he also said that I had to be prepared to talk about this with my parents. Most important, I should not try to face this alone. That's when people make bad decisions.

I went to my room and thought about it - and cried a lot. The next day, however, Robbie called. He wanted me to take the bus and come down! He was working on fixing out a plan for us. "Bring everything. All your clothes and money. And don't tell anyone. We can't let anyone stop us." I was really happy. I told Mrs. Hallett about the call and she was very happy for me, too. But she cried a little and told me to be careful. The bus would get in late, Robbie had said, and that was good. He would meet me on Spring Street, a couple of blocks from the place where the bus stopped. And take me to a motel for a day or two while he got his stuff ready. It was all going to work out, he promised.

When I got there and walked to Spring Street I saw his car flash its headlights and I crossed the street to get in. I put my suitcase on the back seat. Then I got in the front street. "Hi, Wendy, it's great to see you. You didn't tell anybody, like I said not to?" I lied, because I thought he was just being silly. "No, course not." We drove off and he said that he hadn't been able to get a motel, and the downtown hotel would have too many people passing by who knew us and might spoil everything. We had to carry through our plan and get married before anyone could stop us. I felt that way, too. Robbie was being careful, and I nodded when he said there was one place that would be safe.

We drove down to the old practice field south of the football stadium and he pointed out an old shed. I wasn't too happy about this. But Robbie had some blankets in the trunk and I would only be there for a day or so, just until he got his money out of the bank, and made our final plan! I fell asleep some time - I don't know when, because I didn't wake up until Robbie came to the shed and knocked on the door. I got up and got dressed. He had brought some coffee and donuts and we ate breakfast.

He left then, and I did not see him until late in the afternoon. This time he brought a bag of hamburgers and French Fries. After we ate, I told him to go outside for a couple of minutes. Then I put on a new nightgown and told him to come in. He really liked the nightgown and we had a wonderful time - maybe the best ever. He was so gentle and I wanted him so much - now for the three of us.

Afterwards I told him a man had seen me during the day. He didn't stop or anything, but I couldn't just stay shut up in that shed all day, could I? So I waved to him and smiled. I guess I really hoped that would help persuade Robbie we needed to start our journey to a new life. But he got all serious. "You sure it was someone you never met?" he said. "Course not," I said and pinched his nose. He got very mad, and hit me - hard, harder than he ever had. I fell. He picked me up and started shaking me. All I could do was moan some words out like, "I hurt, don't hit me." Everything was all blurry. Then he grabbed me by the throat...

§

Finished typing, the sheriff took "Wendy's Story" down to the cell where Robbie was sitting on the bed attached to the wall. He was scribbling away on a tablet with a pencil he had asked for that morning. "Read this Robbie, and then tell me how things really happened. Remember I now have the letter Wendy left behind and I've talked with the Halletts." He looked up at me with a somewhat puzzled look on his face.

"I will when I finish this."

"What is it you're writing?"

"A letter to Mr. and Mrs. Peters. I want to explain what happened and how sorry I am, and that I am dedicating my life to serving God as a minister - after I am punished, of course. And how important Wendy's role was in making this all clear to me about what I had to do."

Lewis was dumbfounded. "Come on, Robbie, do you really think they want to read anything like that from you? Come on. Take this and tell me when you want to talk seriously about what you did."

"When can I see my parents?"

§

Lewis had never encountered anyone like Stanson. He still hadn't asked for a lawyer. What did he think was going on? Was this all part of a scheme he had worked out? "I want you to look at 'Wendy's Story,' Robbie - to see how we can reconcile it with your "confession." (Russ was caught off guard, he later realized, because he had entitled what Robbie had written as his "story," and then referred to it as his "statement," not as his "confession.") "Maybe I don't have it all down right," he said. "Remember I don't have a memory of what actually happened. I need you to help me out here."

Lewis frowned, "Come on, Robbie."

"Well, o.k., I'll read it again, but I don't want to say much more until I see my parents."

"Understood." Russ waited as Robbie went through the typescript. He passed it over shaking his head. "That's not it, you've written things so it makes it look bad for me. If she were here she wouldn't sign anything like that." His face had reddened and his eyes were shining.

"Ok, Robbie, let's go over some of these things and you can help me figure out how to reconcile these two statements."

Robbie shook his head. "You are putting words in her mouth. I don't really want to talk any more now. I gave you an account of what happened. And remember sitting here now is nothing like it was. You can't claim to know better what was said, what happened."

"Well, no, I was not an eyewitness. But let's think together for a little bit. Wendy arrives - and you meet her at a lonely spot."

"We were both thinking that we did not want any interference with our plan."

"Yes, the supposed plan to go to Kentucky. Do you have anything - or better put - did you show her anything so she would have an idea what to prepare for?"

"No, but I knew we could find someone down there. You don't have to go through the same bunch of stuff to get married as in Ohio."

"Oh, yes. That's a good point. But how long did you think it would take you to do it all? Coupla days? A week maybe?

"We could have done it. Lots of people elope."

"Yes, that's so. Lots do." He paused and looked straight at Robbie's eyes. "And some change their minds about even getting married."

"What's that supposed to mean?"

"Nothing, just happens. Well let's go on to another point. You've said Wendy agreed to stay in that shed, no bed, no toilet, no running water. Do you think people will really believe that?"

"It was bad. I know that. But a hotel was out of the question."

"Oh, I think I agree with that. I just don't think someone, even someone all excited at the prospect of a 'romantic' elopement would agree to spend a night there - alone. Does it make sense to you? Can you help me out here."

"I've told you - it was just going to be for a short time. I was back early the next morning.'" Robbie ran his hand through his hair and started to say something more, then stopped.

"Yes, what is it? And you know that brings me to another point." Russ paused and looked hard at Robbie for a few seconds. "How do you figure that in all the time there she was seen by only one person walking across the field? The encounter that she told you about that set off your final fight - or maybe I should say, explosion?"

Robbie didn't reply. Russ went on with a thought that had been flitting around in the back of his head. "Sure, she just saw the one person? I'm wondering if maybe she saw you with someone else." It was Russ's way of suggesting another witness or - *an accomplice*! That would blow Robbie's story up like a needle in a balloon.

§

They stared at one another without moving. Finally, a small smile began creeping across Robbie's face. "I wouldn't know why she saw only one person and nobody she knew from college." Pleased with himself for handling Russ's ploy so smoothly, he added with a sad smile: "I can only tell you what she told me." He paused again, looked down at the table and then back at Russ. "I asked to see my parents. I guess I should have asked to see a lawyer - *a long time ago*, but then you played a little game, sheriff. Detainment, you said, not arrest."

Russ shrugged. He knew he had played it wrong, and inside, he was churning up regret for being so dumb - but he wasn't going to give Robbie any satisfaction by betraying his self-reproach. "O.K," he nodded as he got up. "Do you have someone in mind, or -" he couldn't resist a jibe even though he knew he should – "or do you want a phonebook?"

Robbie smiled broadly in a sort of triumph. "I assume you've told my parents about my being questioned, so I'm sure you have their phone number pretty handy."

Russ's face reddened. "O.K., I'll bring you a phone in here."

"Thanks, sheriff."

CHAPTER FOUR

PRE - TRIALS

After Robbie made his phone call to his parents, he went back to his "penitential" task of writing to Wendy's parents. It turned out his parents had already been given the name of a lawyer recommended by an official at Bashford College.

Robbie thought about that. Imagine that, he mused, Bashford College is interested in my defense! In a way, he couldn't have asked for anything better. They were scared. He was not quite sure what the issue was for the college. He could think of a couple of reasons - but it was not because they were afraid he would be set free. It had to be something about keeping the trial as short as possible and as far away as possible. The man was to come over to the jail the first thing in the morning. And his Dad told him he couldn't remember the name, it was all happening so fast, but the lawyer had said on the phone that Robbie was not to say anything more.

Meanwhile, Russ spent an uneasy night thinking about what he had done - or rather what he had not done. Nothing to do now but let things play out. He had forgotten for a while that he was no longer in Germany - where the "rules" were not quite so clear. He sat at his desk for several minutes, and slowly picked up the phone in this wary mood that had come over him and called the county prosecutor, Tom Jackson.

"Morning, sir, thought I would give you the latest. There's no issue here about proof. We have the weapon, and Robbie has confessed. I think he's trying out various temporary insanity pleas. He's pretty clever in his own way. I don't think he'll get away with it, but you never know."

"Thanks, Russ. The president of Bashford College has already been on the phone. He's really anxious about where the killing took place. I think that's going to be the big question for all of us. Have you told the young man about his need to get a lawyer? We don't want any mis-steps here, right?"

Russ groaned to himself, hoping he was showing no outward signs of what had actually happened. Robbie had simply broken down and seemed anxious to confess. There was never any "formal" interrogation -first - and Robbie hadn't made any comments when Russ challenged parts of his statement. So, there was no "interrogation" to speak about - he told himself, without really believing what he was saying. *But Robbie's smile grew in his mind like the Cheshire Cat's in Alice in Wonderland as more of a smirk than he had remembered it. But nothing to do except tough it out.* "Absolutely, he called his parents and they already knew about a lawyer," he paused, to stress what he was about to say, "and the lawyer was recommended by someone at Bashford College."

He let that sink in waiting. The wait lasted more than a few seconds. "Is that so, Russ?

"Yes, but Robbie is also playing his own game before he's talked with a lawyer. It's as if all this were happening to someone else and he's just watching the whole story play out - a slightly interested witness. May be planning some sort of psychological impairment defense. He's gonna say he doesn't remember hitting Wendy at all - something like that. Yet he told us where to find the weapon. I think we've just started on this chess game. It's our move. You agree?"

At the other end of the conversation, there was a bit of an uneasy feeling creeping down the back of his neck at the sheriff's breezy demeanor. "Yes, just be sure to keep me in the picture."

And that made Russ wonder a bit about what was happening. Then Jackson continued, "We have to look out, he's still a minor - if not under the law - then in some popular notions. In a sense, the very viciousness of this crime suggests mental issues are going to come up. And there's something else."

"Yes." Russ waited for more questions about the procedure. But that was not where Jackson went. "Do we know for sure when and where death occurred, can we pinpoint it?"

It was the way Jackson paused as he talked about the "case," unlike all the other matters they had discussed since Russ had become sheriff that made him feel not quite sure they were together. "Well, that's where Robbie is trying to fudge things, I think. He says he heard her moaning for a time after he choked her and drove around. Then nothing as he drove north. Trying to make it seem halfway at least accidental, from hitting her head - but besides what he heard that night from the back seat we have all that other stuff. The letters and his instructions to her not to leave anything behind in Cleveland. Pretty clear what he was planning."

"Hmm. Maybe, to us - but I'd feel a lot better if we had forensics lined up. We'll have to wait a few days on that?"

"Problem there is that the preliminary time frame our coroner signed off on extends back to when he hit her in the shed. And if she died before he started defacing her maybe Second Degree. But I think it's still clear-cut - Murder One. All that other evidence of planning, don't ya think?"

This time there was a pause. Russ could almost see Jackson purse his lips. "*Well*," that's where we are right now, but it's not gonna be that easy - bet on it. We may not even get to trial here. Those folks down in West River have yet to weigh in."

"Yeah, well, Stanson talked to David Wells, the lawyer, this morning. I looked up Wells." It was Russ's turn to pause. He ran a finger across his chin. "He graduated from Bashford. Maybe something going on there. I feel sorry for his parents. His mom keeps saying it's all her fault. She should have let them get married."

"Not surprising. Their only child."

"Well, long and short of it, we still have a ways to go," said Jackson.

"Yep."

Russ hung up. He had not told Jackson yet about his shadowy feeling there might have been an accomplice. There would be a better time, he thought, to pursue that idea.

§

A University of Michigan Law School graduate, Tom Jackson had already built an enviable record in his first term as prosecutor. He had lost only a couple of cases in two years, one when the county's best witness admitted not being where she had said she was on the night of a break-in. Tom still thought the guy was guilty but had realized a conviction was unlikely. So the case was dropped. On the personal side, he was friendly with everyone, but not too friendly as to give the impression of a soft touch. Perhaps most impressive was his courtroom "stare." Witnesses who had been "tough guys" in jail, or when questioned in his office, wilted when Tom bent forward with a sheaf of papers he wielded like a weapon and put his questions like a series of left jabs. That he was tall and thin with dark straight hair and horned-rim glasses made him appear even more formidable in action.

Already there was talk in local (and even state) Republican circles of Tom Jackson in the state legislature. Perhaps, some even said, he'd be a good candidate for Congress. Others were not sure: Maybe in a couple of years? Tom was aware of these background conversations, and thought "I'll be ready, hell, I'm ready now!" He very much desired a political career starting up a couple of notches, and was careful where he ate, what he drank, and who he talked to. He and his wife Maureen

71

-'Mo' to their friends - were quick to serve on a variety of public service committees, whether it involved selling tickets to a fund-raising event for girl scouts or the local library. They stayed away from anything that looked the slightest doubtful, such as – say for argument's sake – the firing of war hero General Douglass McArthur by Harry Truman, the haberdasher president from Missouri, also known as "President Accidental." A little young for Rotarians as yet, he was a perfect attendee at weekly Kiwanis luncheons. He even asked to be on the program committee to meet as many "up and comers" as he could, and to fill his address book.

The "Red Slippers" case was a big opportunity to cap that record with a smash performance of his office (meaning himself, of course) and he didn't want to jeopardize it. What Russ told him about how Stanson's parents got their lawyer, and the contacts Bashford had made with him so far increased his wariness about what games were being played with a murder case, and how he saw his role playing out to his best advantage.

§

Dave Wells, Jackson's would-be adversary, was a forty-two-year-old lawyer who dressed the part every day. He always wore three-piece suits, with a watch chain and fob, displaying prominently his Phi Beta Kappa key. Sometimes he rubbed the key like a good luck charm. Always, also, gold cufflinks. And that was only the start of it. He would take out an expensive fountain pen to write notes on a legal pad, recapping it with a great flourish to signal the end of an interview with a client. He was also tall, six foot-two, with sandy hair and a mustache much like that favored by politicians in bygone days. All that was missing was a pince-nez. Instead, he wore rimless glasses. He wanted to look the part of a learned jurist - whose word was as good as the best law professor at Harvard or Yale. It was very old-fashioned, but often very effective. He had made quite a reputation in the field of criminal law.

He was also a graduate of Bashford College -Class of 1931. (He graduated in three years, as he always managed to get into press interviews.)

The Bashford connection was critical. Robbie's parents were not in the usual income bracket of Wells' clientele. Almost as soon as charges had been filed, Andrew Hennings, the college president had consulted his closest allies on the Board of Trustees. Hennings had begun his career as an economics professor, climbed rapidly to department chair, and shown flair as a Dean who could raise money. He had been selected to lead the college only two years earlier. And now this! To a person, the Board wanted to minimize Stanson's links to the school. Fortunately, as it were, he was not a BMOC, Big Man on Campus. He was not engaged in any activities like a star freshman on the football or basketball team. He had not stood out in any of his classes, etc. Curiously enough, the best way to protect the college appeared to send Wells to serve as his lawyer in the hope of keeping any trial away from West River. Wells could be counted on to pursue the task of plea bargaining so no trial would take place near the college.

And Hennings was not the only one pressing for as much separation as possible. Stanson had appeared in the Dean's office that first time with the sheriff in his blue Air Force ROTC uniform. The senior colonel commanding the unit had been sitting at his desk enjoying a second cup of coffee when a warning phone call interrupted his plans for the day. "Colonel," the dean's secretary whispered into her phone, "I think you need to send someone over here on the double. Robbie Stanson is being questioned by police about a woman who was found dead in the woods outside Upper Scioto. He's still in uniform." Blast, thought Colonel Richards. "Captain Ferguson," he shouted down the hall," get over to the Dean's office and get that bastard out of that uniform. NOW."

Alas, that proved impossible, and besides reporters already had pictures. Richards could only think about the flail this would cause up the slippery ladder at the Pentagon, and perhaps determine his next assignment when he got the hell out of this ROTC trap – as he now saw it. The sticky problem for Hennings and Richards was that Robbie's evolving line of defense would appear to be that Wendy had died as a result of the blows, and or choking, that went on in that "Damned shed," sitting there all these years like a decrepit shanty occupied by half-starved, hairless rats as Hennings put it. "Why in God's name hadn't it been torn down years ago! What an image for the college - even besides the murder. It looks like the college is located somewhere off *Tobacco Road*."

The phones were ringing constantly - even worse than when the previous fall a GI Bill of Rights student who worked part-time in the reptile house of the Columbus Zoo had brought one of the Boa Constrictors up in a car and dumped it out inside a sorority house on steps leading to the basement. That had been bad, but nothing like what this latest mess would do to applications and plans to raise tuition. "Good, God," Hennings railed at the cluster of deans and secretaries huddling in his offices. "Just as soon as the police and all the rest connected with the case are finished, I want that shed torn down." Most of all, yes, most of all he did not want a murder trial in West River. And that was what alumnus Wells could do now for his college, much more than any cash donation. "Wells," he said over the phone, "is there any way to make sure the trial is up there?"

"He was apprehended up here, Andrew, but it seems the crime took place down in West River, so it's not a sure bet unless we can count on the prosecutor up here to want an easy conviction for his record. Murder One always presents serious challenges. Everyone has ambitions for the next step up the ladder. There might be a couple of ways to do this. Let me think about how to proceed - don't worry, the main thing these guys are worried about is how not to blow it. Let me have a good talk with Robbie, and then we'll see how to proceed. No guarantees, but we'll try to figure it out."

"The *main* thing is to get it out of here. Is there some way to do that?"

"I don't know Andrew, I just don't."

Hennings had been at Bashford for just a short time as college presidencies went. He had recently worked in Washington at the head of a foundation that depended on volunteers and big donors and knew what scared off potential big money. He was a big man, over six-foot-three, with a booming voice that carried to the back of large rooms without need of amplification. His grip conveyed strength and purpose. "He always looked you in the eye, often with a grin and a wink." But not today. He was hunched over his desk looking at a newspaper with a picture of that damned "shack" – there was nothing else to call it – on the front. He looked at the wall across the room, lined with portraits of his predecessors. He picked up the phone but put it down to think more about what to do.

§

Hennings' biggest worry was a trial spectacle. Otherwise, he would not have cared for one minute what happened to Robbie Stanson. He knew David Wells felt the same way. Their problem was how to use his confession to best advantage. He picked up the phone and called his secretary. "Doris, get me Horvath on the private line. He's usually in his Columbus office and if he's not there I have his home number." Horvath was an old Bashfordian, a three-letter athlete who had become a contractor and financial advisor, whose absolute loyalty had been re-affirmed financially many, many times over the years since his graduation. He had just finished a term as chair of the Board of Trustees. He had business contacts – as well as political contacts of great value – all over the state, and beyond.

This time Hennings wanted something different than a check. He sat there brooding at his desk when his secretary came on the private line. "Mr. Hennings, I have Mr. Horvath."

"Thank you, Doris." He waited a few seconds until he was sure Doris had hung up. "Don, Andrew here, how are you these days, staying in shape?"

"Great, thanks. As a matter of fact, I just came in from the handball court. And you, Andrew? I imagine, from what I read, that things are pretty stirred up right now from where you sit."

"That's an understatement, Don. Couldn't be at a worse time. Well, no time is a best time for something like this. But this is a big year for us. We need money for the library with more space for faculty offices. The science labs are so far behind they look like something from a Frankenstein movie. Well, not really, but you've seen the reports from outside consultants."

"I have, indeed, Andrew, I was chair of the Board when we asked for these reports."

"Well, you see my – the college's – problem then. We need to make sure that applications from good students – in fact better than just good – hold up. We're going to be making some big decisions about seeking private funds. It all comes together – and now this crazy kid kills his girlfriend and we're all over the national press with reports about that damned shack down on the athletic field. Have you seen the pictures?"

"Yep, I've seen 'em. Makes us look like some school on *Tobacco Road*."

"My thoughts exactly. Now, you know what can make this worse – a whole lot worse?"

"Well, I have some idea."

"Let me fill in that picture. What if it turns out he had help? How does that sound? "

"Terrible, obviously."

"Terrible isn't enough. Try catastrophic."

"Well, that's an overstatement, Andrew."

"Maybe. I'll grant I'm here at the center of the public relations storm. But let's agree it could have very serious consequences."

"Yes."

"Yes, and we have another complication with the prosecutor, a man named Jackson. He apparently wants to go with murder one, I hear, which is not a sure thing, and second, means a long trial, more publicity, and more press snooping around. The lawyer we got for the Stanson family – we're paying the freight, of course - is trying to keep things in line. But the prosecutor has his own ideas – I should say career – to think about."

Don Horvath still had the lean, long-legged body that had been "The galloping-gazelle" on the gridiron, and one of the pioneers of the one-handed shot on the basketball court. He still had most of his light brown hair that he was ruffling with one hand as he talked to Hennings with his feet propped up on his desk. "Andrew," he said, "I'll get in touch with Mr. Jackson. Don't worry about that. I know some people in that neck of the woods that he probably would like to have on his side come election day, or to guide him into a good firm. And I'll coordinate with David. I have known him for quite a while. He's as loyal to dear old Bashford as they come."

"Great, I'll wait to hear what you learn." His voice sounded less sure of himself than it ever had, and he knew it.

"Andrew, don't talk that way. This isn't a big deal – what we're asking. Come to that it's best for this young man. After all, his life may depend on it, keeping out unwanted 'helpers' whatever they did or didn't do."

He paused, thinking what to say next while fiddling with his pencil and drawing circles on a yellow pad. Then he asked, "What do you think really happened?"

He could almost see Hennings' reaction. "I don't know, and I don't want to know!"

"O.K., right, I'll be in touch."

§

Once Robbie's parents were persuaded that there would be funds to pay for the lawyer from some sympathetic parents who wished to remain anonymous, David Wells was an obvious choice. They were told it would be best for all not to talk about lawyers' fees and other expenses, especially not where they were coming from. Wells saw to it that the press was around the next time Robbie met with his parents, and that he had talked with Robbie beforehand. He encouraged Robbie's parents to talk to the press - especially about that head injury he had suffered. He hinted publicly that the defense would suggest psychiatric evaluation at one of the state hospitals, leading perhaps to a diagnosis of temporary insanity - not a mental condition. There might not even have to be a trial if he could reach an agreement there.

But first, he needed to get things straight with his client. He met Robbie in a conference room. The sun came in the window and splashed a streak of light between them. They sat across from one another Robbie's hands clasped – almost casually – with the slightest hint of a smile. "Now, young man," Wells began, holding him with a steady gaze, after polishing his glasses, "here is what we are going to do."

"Yes, sir, I've been thinking a lot about what happened - and why." Wells raised his eyebrows. This was not a typical client sitting here he thought as Robbie went on. "Did you read what I told Sheriff Lewis in my second confession, er statement? Confession's not the right word for it."

Wells smiled - a skeptical smile. "I did, but do you think we can really go with the divine intervention you toy with there - really?"

Robbie looked hurt. "What happened has made me understand that I need to be punished, but that God has a plan for me. He is testing me."

Wells was impressed with the boy's sense of his own brilliance but determined to show this young man he was the boss. "That's pretty good." Wells nodded at his client in a tone that did not hide his sarcasm. This young man needed to be put in his place. "Pleading guilty and seeking forgiveness. Maybe we could call Dr. Norman Vincent Peale to the stand. He would surely give you a bona fide stamp of approval for employing the power of positive thinking. But it won't work. We need to stir up the prosecutor's plans, give him some options that would get him a sure path to a favorable outcome - for his professional advancement."

Robbie smiled, nodded, and waited for instructions - now like a good boy. *But Wells believed the would-be conjuror still felt in control. It even made him a bit uneasy.*

§

Leaving Robbie to think about things, hopefully, to understand his culpability as a lot more than the repentant sinner whose temper got the best of him, and a truly guilt-ridden defendant, the defense attorney asked the authorities for a small favor. He wanted representatives of the press to see Robbie in his cell, meeting his parents. Out of deference to Tom Jackson's cautious signals - the sheriff allowed Robbie's parents to go into his cell, while reporters stood around right outside.

The session went well. Robbie told his parents, wrote one reporter, "That they should be strong. He was all right and everything was going to be all right. He did not know how this all happened. He had pretty much blacked out." He wanted to see a local minister, he said, to ask him whether he thought it was a good idea to write

Wendy's parents telling them how sorry he was that this had happened. That wish was granted, and Rev. Thomas Nelson duly appeared in Robbie's cell.

"I know it's all kinda strange," Robbie told the churchman. "But I think I really owe it to them." Nelson was flummoxed. He fidgeted with his thumbs on the Bible he had brought with him and hesitated to look at Robbie for a few seconds. He thought back over the last twenty-four hours. He had already marked several passages in the "Good Book" that he felt Stanson ought to read and meditate upon. He hadn't exactly expected a call to the jail, but he had thought about the crime. So when the phone rang at the parsonage, he had a premonition. "I don't know how I knew," he told his wife Diane, "but I did." Now, however, Robbie had faced him with an unhappy choice. He could say yes, go ahead, it is the right thing to do. But he really did not believe that for a second. Tom Nelson was not one of those preachers who consulted the Bible for everyday decisions, but this was beyond anything he had been exposed to in seminary, or in his fifteen years at the First Methodist Church.

"Very well, Robbie," he finally said, "let's pray on that. You've told some people, I understand, that your goal is to become a minister. Jesus asked for forgiveness for those torn souls who were up there on crosses beside him that Good Friday. So your impulse is a good one, yes" - Nelson looked past Robbie thinking about what to say next - "but how will you know what to say in such a letter?"

Robbie just looked concerned with pursed lips. So the minister went on. "I don't think something that comes in the mail alongside advertisements" - Nelson continued, drawing out his thinking but not really believing he was going to convince Robbie not to send such a letter - "would be a very good idea. And you wouldn't be reaching out in person. Perhaps it would be better at the trial. You could face them and demonstrate far better the remorse you want to express. I will leave it to you, of course, but my sincerest advice would be to wait and speak from your heart."

Robbie nodded solemnly and took Rev. Nelson's arm in both of his hands in a fashion as if *he* were the one giving comfort to one in need of spiritual guidance. It also left Nelson with a strange sense that he had been put in a box alongside other crayons Robbie could use to draw the pictures he now imagined would resolve this dark moment in his life.

§

Despite his lawyer and the minister, the letter went out that afternoon. Newspapers were also told about the letter. As everyone had expected, Wendy's parents were infuriated by Robbie's sorrowful admission that he had been responsible for their daughter's death - but that he had loved her and didn't understand how it could have happened. And to send it to the papers! "What kind of deranged, sick personality comes up with a plea for forgiveness, and dares to put it in such a letter?" That quote appeared in several press stories.

Wells then said to reporters that he had told Robbie he should not be surprised at such a reaction, shaking his head in a way that left the impression he, the defense attorney, also wondered about his client's mental health - and that everyone should, too! Having advised against the letter, Wells had re-thought the issue and decided Robbie had actually made a clever decision – the question he couldn't determine was how he could be sure it would work. It cast him as a confused young man, not a killer. How could Wells use that image?

CHAPTER FIVE

MANEUVERS

Dave Wells now had a plan - thanks in part to Robbie's letter - that he outlined over the phone to Andrew Hennings. "I think we'll start now by asking for a medical, psychiatric exam, with the notion in the back of our minds that Robbie be sent to the State Hospital in Lima to see that this is done right. If we try to introduce that at a trial for Murder One you're just going to get dueling head doctors."

"O.K.," said Hennings, "then what?"

"But we aren't going to go down that path very far. Just enough to make the prosecutor think he'll have a tough time. He doesn't want a tough time, obviously. He'd like a quick conviction."

"Yes."

"One without complications."

"Yes."

"We start with the Lima option. Then after we get Mr. Jackson thinking about that we offer a guilty plea to Second Degree - with a likely life sentence. And no big trial with student witnesses to talk about Robbie's behavior from the time he returned to school this fall until that supposed scene that no one witnessed in the shed."

"Yes, we surely do not want that shed brought up again and again. The pictures are all over the papers not only in Ohio, but someone sent me one, for heaven's sake, from *The Brooklyn Daily Eagle*. Can you imagine, *The Brooklyn Daily Eagle!*"

"To be expected, I fear."

"But not only that, then there might be courtroom testimony from a bunch of Robbie's friends about how while Wendy was tucked away in that shed for his enjoyment he and a pal were running around West River in a car with a girl in the backseat. I saw that gem mentioned in a local newspaper yesterday. What else is going to turn up? This Sheriff Lewis and the prosecutor are going for Murder One, aren't they? We really do not want that spectacle down here or up there, either."

Wells tried to calm Hennings down and reassure him he had a plan, but he was not so sure himself that it would work. For one thing, Robbie could not be counted on to go for a Second Degree - he might just think he had outsmarted them all, Rev. Nelson, Lewis, and Wells himself.

§

When the attorney checked in with the county prosecutor a day earlier he could see that his original strategy of suggesting a psychiatric exam was not going to the place where he hoped it would, a Second-Degree plea rather than force the issue of a murder trial. Jackson had shown him new statements not in press stories that Lewis had gotten down in West River from Robbie's friend who drove him around that Thursday night before Wendy arrived on the bus. And the damned letters Stanson had written about not being responsible for their unborn child, as well as yet another one to the girl in Wittenberg suggesting he was ready for a new relationship. No mental blackouts there!

Jackson had handed these over with a brief comment. "You might want to take a look at these, David (he had decided now to drop the Mr. Wells stuff), they're pretty indicative of Robbie's belief he could put anything over." Actually, David Wells needed no instruction about Robbie Stanson's self-confidence by now! Jackson handed over the letters in a studiously casual way, to emphasize the strength of his hand in this legal duel: "What do you think he really intended in asking her down? It looks like he had a plan already. He was gonna claim that they had broken up and he never did see her again. That's what these letters mean. What kind of person would keep a girlfriend shut away from everybody, excuse me, hidden away, if he had a plan to get married?"

Wells said nothing as looked at the typed sheets, and read the friend's statement taken down by Russ Lewis: "Robbie met me at 7 p.m. in the L&W restaurant, and he said there was a town girl he knew that we could pick up if I would drive around for a couple of hours. We could both make out with her. So we did. And then we left her out on Spring Street around ten or so."

"What do you expect me to say, Tom" - returning the first name gambit. "This just shows Robbie didn't know what to do, that he was not thinking right - that he was moving from one fantasy to another."

"Yes, sure, you're right. Fantasies. I'll be sure to ask him about his- mental lapses - at the trial, and what brings them on. Sounds like they come and go pretty much on order. You can have these. I already have enough copies." This last sounded like a warning of press releases in the near future. Jackson had said all this without allowing anything like a smirk to show on his face. But Wells realized he may have underestimated his potential courtroom opponent. Maybe he had underestimated *both* Robbie and Tom Jackson. With an inner smile, he thought of a film noir title for his position, *Double Jeopardy*!

§

Wells decided he had to be a tough guy again when he entered Robbie's cell with a copy of the Bashford student's statement about the hours before Wendy arrived in town, when they were driving around "making out" with a local girl. Pulling it out of his briefcase he pushed it at Stanson's midsection almost like a punch. "Here, I wonder what you make of this? Is Larry lying in order to get noticed? I thought he was a close friend - or maybe that's the problem. You tell me. And perhaps you better tell me everything you left out in those two confessions - so I won't be surprised in court."

Robbie read the typescript quickly and passed it back, actually smiling as if to sympathize with someone who had tried to help, but just couldn't see the real picture. Shaking his head sadly, Robbie looked at Wells as if they were both seeking truth out of a misguided witness: "No, that's not the way it was at all. The whole thing was Larry's idea. My notion was I just had to meet Wendy at the bus stop and..."

"Whoa, you didn't plan to meet her there - but someplace else. That's what you said, in order to make sure no one intervened - and - stopped you from your plan to take her to Cincinnati and Kentucky, right?"

"Yes, that's right, just not right at the bus stop, but close enough."

"Oh, good, let's nail that down shall we?"

"Well, we can talk about that later. The important thing is that idea of picking up the girl - I don't even know what her name was - that was Larry. He wanted to make out and I thought I could keep him in the dark, like everybody else."

"Yeah, keep him in the dark, like everybody else. Holy Jesus - are you serious? I'm the one in the dark it seems, and you're going to show me the light switch - *now*."

"It's the truth. Larry is lying."

"Why would he do that – do ya suppose? He's a friend, isn't he?"

"I thought he was, but maybe he wants to get clear of me. I might say the truth and that would embarrass him?"

"It doesn't really matter if he is lying or not, either way, it sounds bad. We're not talking about smart-ass boasting at a fraternity house bull session here. You're planning to say that you had a blackout because of an old head injury. That's not going to wash, Robbie – you planned too well."

"Not a black-out, exactly, but maybe in a trance - brought on by a past trauma."

"Where the Hell did you get these ideas?" Wells slapped his forehead, recapped his pen, put it in a shirt pocket, and stood up. "Deputy, we're done here." He said that staring at Robbie and shaking his head.

§

Wells left the county jail thinking about what was next. At the arraignment before Judge Kerwick the next day Jackson previewed the evidence for a solid First-Degree case and asked that Robbie Stanson be confined without bail. Wells had not been surprised at that when it happened, but he was a little surprised at the judge's demeanor as he nodded vigorously his agreement with the prosecutor. It was as if a verdict had already been rendered. Combined with the testimony of Robbie's classmate that Lewis had brought back, getting the charge rolled back to Second Degree with his client's guilty plea was not going to be easy now. But the real problem he faced, as he saw it, was how to make another change from Robbie's planned "Not, guilty, Your Honor," to "Guilty of Second Degree."

The problem centered in all the evidence of design. Right down to knowing where to get a "weapon" that would be hard to trace. Robbie's explanation of finding it at the last minute was not the planning of a professional killer, of course, and in some ways, it still really was last minute – as if Robbie had been weighing in his mind a final decision. But perhaps that was worse? You could use elements of Robbie's "confessions," but hanging over it all was the picture of this young man swinging that weapon at Wendy's head and face – over and over. Wells was pretty inured to crimes of passion, greed, what have you - but the violence done here? There was his youth, of course, and no record of violence - at least not beyond the bruises observed by Wendy's corridor-mates in the dorm. But he imagined himself standing before the jury. How could anyone sitting there believe this young man had ever loved a young woman and done this to her?

All that was left, it seemed, was the forensics. If she had died in the shed – at the very moment when Robbie was supposedly blinded by the whole situation – then, maybe he could pull this off. But the time frame for all that happened was hours not minutes. Who was going to believe that Robbie was in a "trance," as he put it to Wells, during all that time on the drive north to the lonely side road near a woods? They might find some shrink with a beard who would say that on the stand, but Wells did not want to be caught between guys with accents throwing Freud's complexes at one another. That was not the only time factor to worry about. A plea bargain had to be settled before a jury had been impaneled, before testimony was presented, before Robbie appeared in open court.

§

"What do you think, Russ?" Jackson asked the sheriff. "Are we missing anything?"

"Well, our medical folks are working with the people down in West River. Problem is if she was dead when he drove her up here, then the case might seem to belong down there, if she was still alive when he took her out of the car up here – no question. But it's not that simple. No one at Bashford College wants a trial down there, very bad for the recruitment of a freshman class, and very bad for alumni donations. Or so they are saying."

With a grimace, Jackson seemed to settle whatever doubts he harbored about the outcome: "I'm going with Murder One. The judge is with us all the way. I think I'm ready for whatever Wells thinks he has."

§

David Wells had in fact a plan in mind. If Jackson wanted to go for Murder One, Wells would counter with a promise to introduce testimony of what was usually called temporary insanity. His client had laid the groundwork already. It wouldn't work, but it would certainly introduce a factor that could muddy things up, and get reporters side-tracked on new stories that he would throw out like birdseed. It would take attention away from the central issue of brutal violence.

So he had to play on Jackson's determination not to lose. With that, he decided to call up the prosecutor again to see where matters stood.

"Tom, David Wells here. I think we ought to have a talk about how this is going. I've got some psychiatrists lined up who are experts in the after effects of head injuries like Robbie's. They are ready to see him here, or we can send him to Lima."

"Well, there's no evidence, is there that he showed any signs of memory loss or blackouts before, that I know of at least."

"Remember, his dad told Russ he'd experienced headaches."

"Yes, I don't know if that will convince anybody."

"Yeah you're right, but it's one of the things that make for uncertainty, isn't it? I remember a similar case a few years back, a man came home one night and killed his wife and baby child. He got sent to the state hospital and was out in five years."

Actually, he knew of no such case, and counted on Jackson's lack of experience with earlier capital cases.

"Un-hunh." Tom knew he was playing, but he might use the argument if need be with people like Lewis - or Robbie's parents if things started to go bad.

"Now if you'd agree to Second Degree, we both know that this judge will go for the long term. No get-out-of-jail card – for any reason. Then there's this." Wells paused. "President Hennings has some good friends in this county including the member of Congress from this district. I'm pretty sure he'd like to see the County Prosecutor win a conviction up here as a favor to Bashford College. If the trial takes place down there because of a disagreement about time of death, that would be bad in some ways – especially for the college. I might like it, because then the plea of temporary insanity makes more sense. But it is not certain for either side. And (another pause) I think I can get Stanson to see a plea to Second is also best for him – because we really don't know, do we, how all this will play out."

"I'll think about it."

§

Tom Jackson was a pragmatist, or so he told himself. There was in fact a chance that a Murder One trial would end in a hung jury. That would be bad. Even worse, Wells might convince jurors during the trial that a Murder Two charge would have been more appropriate, given all the imponderables, and Stanson's age. That what had happened was really, when you looked at it carefully, a lovers' quarrel that got out of hand. The only testimony about what happened in the shed was Stanson's to give, and he was sure Wells would have his client well primed. And for that matter, it appeared that Robbie had his own sense of how to deal with any questions Jackson might raise. Against that, there was the disputed statement of his classmate on the pickup date, or whatever you wanted to call it. But still, there were the two letters Robbie had written, the first declaring his relationship with Wendy was over, and the second stating that as the younger party, he was not responsible for the child. And, finally, his summons to Wendy to come down to West River and leave nothing behind to say where she was going.

Moreover, Jackson could call the couple who owned the house, the Halletts, to testify to Wendy's destination when she left Cleveland, and the joyful feeling she had that Robbie was now ready to do the right thing. All of that was fine. But there was still the possibility that Robbie would recall some other part of his story he would introduce under Wells's guidance, referring to the lasting effects of the head injury. For all he knew, moreover, there might be other classmates who recalled one or more of Robbie's "blackouts." That would be bad, possibly very bad. He simply did not know.

Lewis would not be happy, for sure, and Wendy's parents - well, that was the worst part of the whole thing now, wasn't it? He would have to convince them it was best to go for the sure bet. Of course, he did not need their permission or blessing in making his decision, but he had to try to get them on board – if only to forestall some bad press. This had become a national case: THE RED SLIPPERS MURDER. People were writing him from all over, some enclosing newspaper clippings. There were articles that discussed the forensic issues, and how difficult it would be to determine the exact moment of death.

He dreaded appearing to take the "easy way out" if he now stood up before Judge Kerwick, and said, "The prosecution accepts Mr. Stanson's plea of guilty of Second Degree Murder."

All these thoughts were racing through his mind when his secretary buzzed him on the intercom. "Mr. Jackson, I have a Mr. Donald Horvath on the phone from Columbus. He says he has some important information about the Red Slippers case. Do you want me to put him through?"

Who was this he wondered? Then his secretary added, "He says he knows President Hennings is anxious to help you with the case."

"O.K., I'll pick up."

"Mr. Jackson, Don Horvath. I think we have some mutual friends who are interested in helping you out. I understand you're trying to plot out the best course for the case so as to be sure you come away with a win for justice and a reasonably quick end to a very messy case..."

CHAPTER SIX

PREMEDITATIONS

When Tom Jackson thought about the mixture of inducements and implied threats David Wells had laid out in their meeting, and then the "helpful" phone call he had received from Horvath, he grew even more unhappy about taking a plea bargain. His father had once been sheriff of Wyandot County. He knew he would have disapproved just as Russ Lewis would if he went down that path.

"Tom," Russ began when the prosecutor hinted that he might accept a plea of guilty to Second Degree, "you know there's premeditation on every footprint in this case from the shed in West River to that woods where he dragged that girl out of his car and beat her."

"Well..."

"Besides that," Lewis went on, "you must have read what the homicide detective in Cleveland told the newspapers about Stanson's love letter to this other girl – not the one at Wittenberg –but someone named Carol."

"I did and I don't know how that got out – maybe you do?" Jackson's steady look made it seem that he was starting, somehow, to blame Lewis for having to accept a plea. He went on a few more paces down that path: " Do we even know if it's real?"

"I don't know, Tom, but it doesn't make any difference, does it. He wrote that unfinished letter just before he told Wendy to come down."

Jackson sighed deeply. "You know that they both feared their parents would try to annul a marriage if they found out?"

"But that was before she got pregnant, for heavens' sake!" Russ let that sink in. "He had her under his thumb from day one – or night one, when they met at that freshman dance."

"I can't try a case under our suppositions about their behavior. "

"You don't have to, right here on my desk is the Ohio State Medical Examiner's report: 'Death occurred in Wyandot County.' That means he drove her up here while she was still alive."

"Yeah, but that report also fudges cause of death. It says strangulation, Robbie admits to that in the shed. It doesn't say the blows with that awful thing. Wells can play on that. And besides, you remember our coroner was not so definitive about the timing."

"I don't think that will work. The state's got the best scientific lab."

Jackson shook his head as if he were a juror. "Doesn't have to work, does it, just create a doubt in the mind of one or two jurors."

Lewis sighed.

Jackson said, "Let's go see Robbie in his cell – I'd like to hear him spell it all out one more time."

"Besides all that, Tom," Lewis countered, "I'm pretty sure he had help. I just don't believe she stayed in that shed. We didn't find a damned trace anyone had been there."

"C'mon Russ," said the prosecutor, shaking his head. "You and I know you can't prove that. You went down there and talked to a lot of people."

"Yes, sure, but this has been so rushed, I just feel..."

"I have feelings, too, about a gap between reach and grasp."

With that, they headed to Robbie's cell. Jackson knew that Bashford College's interest was twofold: First and foremost, no trial in West River, but also no lengthy murder trial anywhere that might involve yet unnamed witnesses from the school.

§

When Jackson and Lewis arrived at the cell David Wells was there. But Robbie did not need any coaching. "I just don't remember. Everything is like it's behind a curtain I can't see through." That's all Robbie would say. Except this: "Mr. Jackson, did you know the sheriff didn't tell me for a long time that I had been arrested - just detained, as he put it." He looked at Lewis with a smile. "That's true, isn't it, sir?" he said looking his innocent best. Tom Jackson didn't show a sign of the concern that welled up inside him. As soon as Jackson and Lewis left, the defense attorney invited in three reporters. Robbie did not re-tell his story about all that happened, but he gave it out in his response to the questioning. "I didn't plan it ahead of time, and I'm not going to say I did." He then went on adding details to his written "statement" he had given the sheriff *without being warned*, or even arrested, all corrections that he thought were useful to his claims of being in a sort of trance the whole time since the events in the shed. He now said that he had left Wendy in the shed and driven around town for ten or fifteen minutes. When he came back he parked near the athletic field and tooted his car horn. Getting no response he then went on foot to the shed. He couldn't wake Wendy, but he thought he heard her moan. He shook her and got no response and somehow got her into the car.

"I was still scared," he said in a choked voice. " I hadn't meant to hurt her. But I told myself there was nothing more I could do for her now. The only thing I could think of was to make her unrecognizable." Stunned by this incredible assertion, reporters noted that tears were now streaming down his face. The moment passed. Seemingly regaining control, he continued as if he were simply talking about managing an unpleasant occurrence. "I stopped at a dump near the football field and looked for something to hit her with but I couldn't find anything. I finally found the iron bar behind my fraternity house. " When the fraternity house mother read this incredibly horrible statement in newspapers she retreated to her apartment to write out a letter of resignation - which she later tore up after thinking better of the impression that would make. President Hennings would call the fraternity president to ask if that were possible. "Did Stanson carry out this - this - murder weapon through the front door? How could that happen?" he shouted into the phone. "Did any of you see this - this - this - thing?"

"No, sir," replied John Lawson, the president of the fraternity. "No idea where it came from."

"I can't believe this. There are no more surprises - are there?"

And there was yet more from Robbie's cell. "I don't remember how I got to that place, or how I got back to West River, but I do remember I hit her with pointed end of the bar. The papers say that I stabbed her twice with it but that's not true. The blood on the handle was from the cut on my hand." The cut had occurred, he said, when they were "wrestling" in the shed. As if this somehow lessened the guilt!

David Wells tried to "clear up" what Robbie had now set out as the latest version of the tragic death of Wendy Peters in a lover's quarrel that ended badly. He praised Robbie for being so straightforward. There is not an iota of premeditation in this explanation of what happened, he claimed. Wells added that the letter that Robbie wrote to the Wittenberg co-ed about his relationship with Wendy being "all washed up," was part of the ruse the couple had devised to maintain the secrecy. As for the new letter from "Carol" that emerged in the press that seemed to establish an ongoing relationship with a high school junior, a letter signed, "Love," there was nothing to it. Robbie had already said, "She used to call me up when she had problems with her boyfriends. And if I didn't have anything to do I would take her out. She probably signed lots of letters that way."

He had added that he probably signed lots of letters that way. "There's no use asking me why I did it. Something snapped. What, or why, I don't know. Maybe if a psychiatrist heard the whole story, he could tell me." It now appeared that his defense would employ a plea to Second Degree, while at the same time relying on temporary insanity. Wells bolstered that by telling reporters about how disappointed Robbie was that Wendy's parents would not read the letter he sent trying to explain what had happened and asking forgiveness. Yes, he had decided to send the letter after he was told by a clergyman not to send it. Wells thought he could bolster a case for psychiatric examination by talking about the letter. It certainly did not seem rational. Robbie went on and on to reporters, talking about going to church back in West River. "I believe I would have turned myself in if they hadn't caught me. I went to church the Sunday after and that made a big difference. My parents took it kind of hard."

§

There was another reader of these stories who knew more of what happened than Sheriff Lewis, or either of the attorneys. He had wrestled with himself over whether to contact a reporter secretly - or go to the police. He decided to do neither. He had nothing to do with Wendy's death, whether Robbie's story was true or not about how it all happened. He was the one in danger now - and nothing his fault. But who would believe him? And Robbie could try to pin it on me. How can this be?

§

Sheriff Lewis was furious about the press coverage Robbie was getting because of Wells's maneuvers, and the smooth way he presented himself as a subject to some inner confusion instead of a desperate schemer who had planned it all along.

Russ pleaded with the prosecutor, "Listen to him: he is now saying it all happened because of their parents saying they couldn't get married. My God, listen to him! If no one will buy the temporary insanity, he's saying, then I'll blame her parents. I might even say she tricked me into getting her pregnant. Oh, yeah, that's when the tension started building up inside him all right, absolutely. I buy *that*, no question."

They looked at one another. "Tom," he pleaded with the prosecutor, "let's release everything we have."

Jackson frowned. "No, I'm not going to try this case in the newspapers."

Lewis got up from his chair, scraping it on the floor for emphasis, and walked to the door. "Sounds like we aren't going to try it at all. The only thing he's said in the last few days that's true is that the tension was building up inside him."

§

It had been a hard conversation. Things did not get better. When Tom Jackson returned to his office from the jail he found two phone messages. "Please call State Representative Tony Mauro," read one. "Please call Dr. Hennings at Bashford College," read the other. After those calls, Jackson asked his secretary to call the Peters. "Mr. Peters, this is Tom Jackson. We talked the other day and I want to bring you up to date about where we are from the viewpoint of a successful prosecution, which we both want in order to see that justice is done. I know nothing is ever sure, and especially not in a Murder One trial. We need to think hard about the best path to a conviction."

Peters said nothing. Perhaps he was thinking of a statement that the prosecutor had given out to the press in the early days. "It is not the kind of bar you find in the woods the instant you need one. Nor is it a bar you just happen to have in your car." There was the case for Murder One in a nutshell. But now he seemed to be coaxing the Peters along a different path. "I would not want you to lose this opportunity to see Stanson convicted."

Wendy's father still said nothing for another minute. Finally, he asked, "You've changed your mind, then?"

"Not really," said Jackson, "just facing reality."

Byron Peters hung up - he knew where things were going.

§

The final coroner's conclusion, that Wendy died of strangulation, not primarily from the blows to the head, posed a conundrum of sorts. If she died of strangulation, then presumably the case should be tried in West River as one of Murder Two. But there was something else - Robbie's statement that he heard her moan on what the press called the *"Death Route to the Woods,"* left open the issue of a proper charge. But the coroner had said she might have died in Jackson's county. It did not mean that he was bound not to accept a guilty plea to Second Degree murder. The case seemed full of double negatives, and for all the indications of advanced planning on Robbie's part, Wells had succeeded to some degree in portraying him as (the press said) a "handsome, sandy-haired boy, with blue eyes" - and a spotless record before this "tragedy of a lovers' quarrel." Even so, all public indications had been that the prosecutor was going to go for Murder One. And, finally, all indications were Robbie's lawyer wanted to introduce the possibility of temporary insanity, not a guilty plea to Murder Two. That was the playing field, so to speak, that confronted Jackson. Of course, he did not mention all the calls he had received. What had started out as a seemingly easy win had been put in doubt.

One problem was the issue of intent. As Wells pointed out despite all the questions about the place of death, felony murder was a state issue, not a county or city issue. Though he was trying to make sure the trial did not occur in West River, Wells could still delay things by asking for a change of venue. And Jackson wanted the conviction on his record. It was not clear at all despite the horror, and the letters discovered by the Cleveland detectives instructing Wendy to come to West River with all her belongings, that a jury could be convinced that Robbie had intended to kill Wendy when he grabbed her by the throat. There was nothing in his past that would indicate such an intention.

§

As the days after the indictment and arraignment wore on, still with no indication of any change in the original presumption that the prosecution would seek a Murder One conviction with the death penalty, two odd, and unsettling developments appeared in news stories without attracting a lot of attention. The first was the discovery of yet another suitcase belonging to Wendy. It was found in some bushes just outside the football stadium - not inside the shed, or near it. Authorities did not say much about the discovery. But one student said that there had been no suitcase there when he passed by a day earlier. Who was to say? But Robbie had not mentioned another suitcase, and it seemed odd that if Wendy was planning to be married the only suitcase found had just a few changes of clothing. How likely was that? Hennings read the story and was back on the phone to Wells. "Can't you settle this thing with a plea to Second Degree murder? Get it over with before something else turns up - this time inside the stadium dorm area?"

Hennings would now have nightmares about more than the shed. To house an influx of World War II veterans coming to school with the GI Bill of Rights, the college had put temporary dorm rooms in the stadium. Now, this second suitcase suggested that the shed might not even have been the place of the murder! Or at least raised doubts - and also doubts about everything else, including the possibility that Stanson had aid, or even - *God forbid!* - that Wendy had spent a night in one of those rooms.

It was essential to head off such an inquiry. Probably Robbie had tossed the suitcase there and avoided talking about it - but maybe not. Maybe an accomplice had kept the suitcase and then risked leaving it in those bushes? Back at the jail, Wells went to Robbie and told him about the finding. He took it in and said nothing. Yet another discovery also darkened the picture. A fisherman found a bracelet between the shed and the stadium. Could it have belonged to Wendy? The two discoveries seemed to point in opposite directions. What else was about to turn up?

§

But there was no follow-up on either discovery. Everyone wanted to close this thing up before it turned into an even bigger mess. Even, it seemed, the press. Two weeks later David Wells stood up before Judge Kerwick: "We would like to enter a plea of guilty to Second-Degree murder."

Judge "Stony Kerwick" looked over at Tom Jackson, fully expecting him to reject the offer so that they could move quickly onto the jury empaneling phase of a Murder One Trial. A list of potential jurors had been submitted to both sides, and newspaper reports had given the solid impression that the trial would not be a long one, the outcome almost predetermined from the words of Robbie himself and what Wendy had told the Halletts about her pregnancy and Robbie's summons.

"Your honor, we have decided after much deliberation to accept the defendant's plea of Guilty to Second Degree Murder in this case."

"You have?" Kerwick's raised eyebrows could be seen from the last row of benches in the courtroom. "I was under the impression you were ready to proceed with a Murder One case."

"Yes, your honor, but this step, we believe, is the surest way to obtain justice for Wendy Peters and her family."

Kerwick appeared stunned. "Was that your original position?"

"I don't want to get into the business of speculating about how we reached this conclusion."

"But the evidence...?"

Jackson risked cutting him off: "Yes, we have evaluated all the evidence and decided this was the surest path to a conviction."

Kerwick turned to Wells. "Your client accepts this surprising offer and is ready to plead guilty?"

"He is, your honor."

"I see. Well, then, I see no reason to postpone the sentence."

The judge looked down at some papers on the dais, stacking and restacking them, giving himself more time to think. He had not expected anything like what had just happened. He shook himself to an erect position. "Mr. Stanson, please come forward and stand before this court. Now, before I say anything else, I would like to say that this was a shocking crime, one that leaves us all feeling touched by its violence. Mr. Stanson do you have anything to say now before sentencing?"

"Your honor, all I can say is that I did a terrible thing to a woman I loved. I will never understand how it happened. I loved Wendy."

"So you say," said the judge looking at Jackson, and then back at Stanson. "I feel sorry for Wendy, for her parents, and for you - that it has come to this. (He did not explain the ambiguity) Mr. Robert Stanson, it is the judgment of this court that, having pled guilty to this terrible crime, the sentence of this court is that you be imprisoned for twenty-five years to life at the Ohio State Penitentiary in Columbus."

The courtroom had not expected this sudden end, and people in every row looked at one another with questions on their lips. Everything seemed to shift into high gear. As Robbie was escorted out past the judge's bench, he looked around to the small gathering at the back of the courtroom. One man stood up and walked to the center aisle where Robbie would have to pass. Their eyes met for a long few seconds and the man who had killed Wendy Peters felt a tingling at the back of his neck.

As he stood there, so close he could almost touch Stanson, Carl Peters thought again how he had failed Wendy. There was no way he could make it up – not yet. But he felt sure this would not be the end. He would wait and never stop hating.

He shouted after Robbie. "I will always be there, Stanson, I will always be there. There will come a day..."

§

At the back of the courtroom, Russell Lewis stood watching Kerwick deliver this sentence and rap once with his gavel. He could also see Tom Jackson exhale a deep breath and turn back to the prosecution table to pack papers into his briefcase as reporters swarmed in from two sides. As the newsmen gathered around Tom, Carl stood stock still at the end of the aisle. He nodded to Russ, who now, somehow, also felt guilt feelings, not knowing quite why. The two had not met since that day in the funeral home. They exchanged glances as if in agreement that something was missing and yet to be discovered just as one of the reporters began:

"Mr. Jackson, how did you reach this conclusion? What did you say to Wendy's parents?"

"Our office came to this conclusion after seeing the forensic reports. The exact time of death was unclear, as was the cause. We discussed this situation with several well-known attorneys, and they counseled that we follow this path." He did not mention his conferences with David Wells.

"But sir..."

"I've said all I can about our deliberations. They were careful and conclusive."

"About Wendy's parents?"

"We were in daily contact with them from the very beginning. They have suffered a great loss, and this was the surest path to secure for Wendy's family the justice they deserve."

"Did you discuss this specifically with them?"

"That's private, as I'm sure you understand." Jackson snapped shut his briefcase and started to wedge his way out of the courtroom. The parents would, in fact, tell reporters that they were satisfied with the outcome.

The reporters opened a path for him as over to one side Carl Peters stood motionless with no expression on his face. Jackson looked at him and nodded as their eyes met for a second. Peters continued standing there not sure what he wanted to say to reporters. Finally, he said out loud, "Stanson has to spend as many years in prison as Wendy would have lived." What did that mean? Life, apparently.

"Mr. Peters," a reporter turned to Carl. "Mr. Peters, can you tell us how your family feels about what happened this morning?"

"There's nothing more to say right now. Let's leave it at that."

§

Sheriff Lewis followed Wendy's brother out the door without speaking to him again, feeling sad there was nothing to say, and then walked over to the prosecutor's office. Jackson was waiting for him. "Well, Russ, no one's really satisfied, but it's the way it is."

"Yes, sir, the way it is." Jackson nodded in return, fully grasping Russ's meaning, and decided to add some additional thoughts. "Russ, do you really think that Robbie would try for a temporary insanity or blackout defense if we pushed Murder One?"

"I imagine he would, but the evidence..."

"O.K., the evidence - as you see it - but would a jury see it all the same way? And the matter of his age..."

"But there was someone else there, I'm sure of it."

"Really?" Jackson raised his eyebrows. "You didn't turn up anybody."

"Dammit, I didn't have the chance."

"What, I'm supposed to send you and a bunch of deputies down there..."

"Not a bunch of deputies, O.K., but we could have done more."

"*Really*," he said again with even more emphasis. "Perhaps you'd have taken the risk of losing a conviction - and, and, there's his age, don't forget that. Leave it. He's going to be put away for a long time, a long time. Maybe there's no place in your mind for redemption - no matter - just a simple eye for eye."

"Sure, I believe in redemption. It's just I feel like we've been conned, and not only by Robbie Stanson."

"Enough, Russ, enough." With that, Jackson started putting papers into his file cabinet and the sheriff exited - he thought to himself - as in a Shakespearean play he'd read a long time ago in high school. He thought about those exits - they were never final.

§

One newspaper Russ read in his office the next day headlined the story out of Kerwick's courtroom, *"Girl's Parents OK Slayer's Life Term."* Below the headline, the story continued: "An act of mercy by the slain girl's parents today allowed the killer to escape a possible death sentence in the 'red slippers murder case.'" It was not clear what act of mercy by the parents saved Stanson. The decision had been made by Tom Jackson.

CHAPTER SEVEN

THE SENTENCE BEGINS

Returned to his cell Robbie Stanson was allowed one more press conference before the trip to the penitentiary. "My prayers have been answered. I deserve to be punished, but I am a young man and I still have the opportunity to make something of myself." Two days later Robbie sat behind the wire screen in Sheriff Lewis' cruiser for the first time for the long drive to Columbus. Asked by reporters what they talked about, Lewis shrugged. "A little bit about the weather, but he was quiet most of the way." Warden Henry Allen had been asked what would happen to Robbie inside. He would get the usual orientation, including a medical - and then, depending upon his behavior and the prison's needs, he might be given a job.

His arrival at the prison, like everything else about the case was treated as an "event," followed avidly by local reporters and attracting even some national attention'. Bashford College President Hennings had made sure he had all the stories put on his desk first thing every morning. He hoped they would end soon. Other readers seemed sorry to say good-bye to: "The former divinity student as he entered the bleak penitentiary on the river's edge to serve a life sentence." When he entered prison, Robbie was dressed exactly the same way he had been during sentencing, in a well-fitting tan sport coat and grey slacks. He was pictured smiling with several heavy psychology textbooks in his arms. Lewis watched this scene drag on, greatly impressed yet again and despite all his other feelings, with Robbie's ability to stage-manage even this event - asking the reporters if they got what they wanted. "Is this o.k?" he said turning the books so the titles showed. Lewis's shoulders twitched but he said nothing. Robbie had made it seem like the beginning of redemption – a pictorial history.

In the newspaper pictures, he looked exactly like a student going off to a new year in an expensive private college! He smiled at the reporters and opened one of the books as if he were eager to get back to school, announcing: "Now I'll have a lot of time to study." There was no more talk about feeling a need to be punished. And the idea of going to divinity school he talked about after his arrest seemed to have been thrown out the car window during the ride down from Upper Scioto. Lewis marveled at the inventions he made for every occasion. "Maybe, I'll study psychology," he said, nodding a last time to reporters as he entered the open door. He offered his hand to Russ before reporters could put away their cameras. The sheriff took it and felt Robbie's strong grip. He'd been sandbagged.

§

"Christ," Russ said to himself, "he behaves like a celebrity! Wonder how long that will last?" Lewis guided him inside with his fingers tight around Robbie's arm and turned him over to the prison "greeting committee." There were a few preliminary forms for him to fill out, and then he was taken away by his new wardens out of sight to Russ. The sheriff's life went on as before, yet he believed he was not finished with the Red Slippers murder case. But how so he was not to discover for a long time.

As Stanson entered the prison, a news story filled adjacent columns about a stumbling drunk in Chicago, who was picked up on the street and was sent to a House of Corrections and fined $25. He was a former handy-man and chauffeur for crooner and movie star Dean Martin. The newspaper that ran the story paid the fine, and Martin's ex-wife took up the task of raising funds for Ira Hayes to get a new start in life. "I have every confidence this plan of mine - to help Ira find himself again - will work out to the advantage of us all." Ira was a Pima Indian from Arizona, and one of the heroes shown in a photo raising the American flag on Mt. Suribachi in

Iwo Jima. The photo of that scene - arguably the most famous of the Pacific in World War II - won a Pulitzer Prize, and was then memorialized on a postage stamp.

§

Once the preliminaries were over and Robbie was assigned to a cell, a guard came to take him to the Warden's office.

"Son, let me tell you how we do things around here," began Warden Allen. " I never assume anyone has nothing left in him to warrant some degree of usefulness to society, either in here - or, if it ever happens, you are sent back into society. In your case, it is a long road. You are a traveler on that road. It is not an easy hike, as you will find out, not a lazy walk on a Sunday afternoon. We do not tolerate stragglers or stone-throwers. Do you get my drift?"

Robbie nodded slowly, befitting, he thought to himself, the ritualistic nature of this scene, almost as he had imagined it would be when he arrived at the penitentiary. "Yes, sir, I understand what you are saying."

"Good. Now from your answers on our initial interview forms, it appears you are interested in helping some of the men in here to improve their reading and writing skills. We actually have a large 'school' here with what we call grade one through eight. Right now enrollment is around 200 with a waiting time for admission. But how do I know that you are a teacher?"

"Well, sir, I was a scout leader, captain of the baseball team. The guys depended on me for help with other stuff, too."

"I wonder, Robbie, I wonder. Now I have to ask: Do you still have these black-out spells you talked about after you were arrested or was that part of the rigmarole that defense lawyer threw up around you for the trial - the trial that never was?"

"I'm not sure they've gone away - but probably there won't be that kind of situation arise again!"

"Oh, that's for certain, but, if we do give you a go at it, it will be on a trial basis." Allen laughed a kind of ironic laugh and looked for Robbie's reaction to his clever remark.

Robbie responded with the sort of smile that said, very good Warden, very good - thinking that Mr. Warden Allen was not going to be too difficult to manage - at some point down that road he was picturing for the rookie prisoner.

§

Within a few weeks, the newcomer to the penitentiary had indeed established himself as one of the teachers in the prison school. He taught reading courses and simple check-book mathematics. He came across as sincerely interested in helping men out. There was a program where the prisoners with "jobs" on the inside could arrange to send small sums of money to family members out in the world. He would work with them on letters to their lawyers. He even started advising some on the right strategy to use in filing for parole hearings. He became known as the "prof." And, in the first summer, after he arrived at the prison, he began coaching the softball team. With all that was going on, perhaps it was not surprising that word got out about the convicted killer who had become a favorite teacher.

Not only that he was becoming something of a celebrity in the outside world as well. The prison allowed a reporter and a photographer to come inside and interview "Prof." Stanson at his "desk" while he advised one of his pupils. The photo of this session showed a serious Robbie, head inclined slightly toward the "pupil" as he jotted down something on a piece of paper. Stanson was also taking courses by mail, he informed the reporter. Soon he would have forty credits, not near enough to finish his degree, but it was a good start.

What could he do with his college degree if he earned one while in prison? the reporter asked. "Well, I had thought about becoming a minister or a teacher. But I guess with my prison record that's probably out. I would be barred from these fields. Perhaps journalism. What do you think about that?" The reporter had no opinion about Robbie's chances in journalism, so he went on enthusiastically describing the school inside the prison where he was a highly valued teacher. Besides courses in person, there were even "correspondence" courses - his idea - and cell study tutorials - another of his favorites. The reporter expressed some skepticism about Robbie's plans. It was doubtful if he could meet all the requirements while in prison, he wrote in his story, but Robbie assured him he would figure it out. "He had plenty of time."

It almost seemed as if he was becoming a perfect example of a justice system's ability to do more than punish the guilty for the benefit of society.

§

Eventually, the outside interest died down. "Robbie," the warden said to him one day, "how'd you like to come into my office and help out with the paperwork and do some filing."

"Of course, sir, whatever you want. When should I report to your office?"

"Tomorrow, when you finish your morning class."

The warden had been pleased with his Robbie "project." He related well to the students without seeming to talk down to them. And he had been awarded some privileges and trusty status. So began the second phase of Robbie Stanson's prison term, for that was now how he talked to himself about his situation: A preparatory set of experiences for when he was paroled. At the end of ten years? Yes, perhaps even that soon. Working in the warden's office would help. And the new assignment also helped him with the other inmates, who now sought out his inside information about what was likely to happen, or, even, what might be in their files in the outer offices, where Mary Ruth Austin held the reins.

Through this opening also, Robbie became acquainted with another one of the warden's favorites, Dave Wilkins, who was also favored by Mary Jane. In fact, they soon formed a tripartite inner circle - or so they thought of themselves. Mary Jane also had keys. And as the warden's trust grew, there were times when they were alone in the office. Dave was serving a term for armed robbery; in fact three robberies, but he only tripped up once and that was because - he had convinced himself - he had not prepared well. He did not have college experience like Robbie, but you could never have told that from listening to him talk. He had a radio baritone and sounded like one of the newscasters at six p.m. Mary Jane, who had gone to secretarial school, thought he reminded her of one of her high school teachers - one she especially liked.

He teased her, and her response indicated that she was open to a more "intimate" relationship. Robbie watched this develop into something that might be useful for him down this long road the warden had described in their first interview.

§

In Robbie's eighth year behind prison walls, as the saying goes, the warden recommended that he be made a special trusty, with new duties that took him outside and into the city, always under watchful eyes, of course. That was understood, if in different ways, however. His experience as a truck driver in Cleveland in the summer before Wendy's "accident" as he now explained her death to himself commended him to the wife of one of the senior guards. The prison had made arrangements with several funeral homes in Columbus to collect flowers left behind after the hearse pulled away for the somber trip to the cemetery. The police van would then take them to the prison hospital, where they served a second, life bringing cheer to those who suffered without friends or family.

And so, one day, Sally Kosmon asked Robbie if he would like to drive the prison truck and accompany her on her twice-weekly rounds. The warden had recommended him for this new job/privilege. "Sure, Mrs. Kosmon, I would like that very much." So now he had three jobs, teaching, office assistant, and flower fetcher - as he liked to joke about the situation. Mrs. Kosmon also had a part-time job at one of the funeral homes, so her experience was highly useful - much more so than one might imagine.

§

Like so many others had since his imprisonment, Sally Kosmon took to Robbie at once. If anything, he was more handsome now as he entered his late-twenties. But it was his contacts with other prisoners that she valued most. Soon Sally was inviting Robbie to have coffee and donuts during their bi-weekly collections. She never asked about what happened back at Bashford, though she had been briefed by her husband, Tommy, a ranking senior guard who had pointed her in Robbie's direction. "He's got the warden's eye - a friendly eye - and he can be useful."

Both Kosmons were always on watch for those who might be inclined to carry out simple "requests" for the prison inmates. For example, Robbie could perhaps deliver notes from some of his pupils to friends on the outside, and vice-versa. It was a connecting link worth thinking about. Those on the outside sometimes needed information about how their friends were being treated. And there was, to take an example close to Robbie, information "Dave" had about certain items "in storage" that could be converted to liquid assets to supply funds to needy souls outside or saved for when Wilkins got out. His release was an uncertain date, which made it all the more important to sell when the market was right. The Kosmons' fees for these services were quite reasonable - when you thought about it - five dollars a message.

The funeral home where Sally worked had an upstairs apartment. The Kosmons leased it. They had furnished it with an eye for a single young lady whose job brought her into contact with a wide range of the citizenry, perhaps a cashier at a restaurant on High Street? It did not take long for a good candidate to appear. Dina Stevens had graduated high school and was uncertain about her next steps, but she needed to get away from home and be on her own, yet not too far away. She was an attractive young woman, able to size up people without appearing to be nosy or in any way intrusive. The Kosmons interviewed her after she answered an ad in the *Dispatch* announcing the apartment and its location, "On a quiet street, not far from shops and restaurants, furnished with utilities paid."

At the end of the interview, Dina asked what the rent would be, and would she be expected to sign a long-term lease. Tommy and Sally looked at one another and nodded. "Well, Dina," (now their candidate for bigger things), "I think we can be reasonable on that score."

"Let's say we think our apartment is probably worth $100 a week...." He paused.

"Oh, I don't think I can pay that much!"

"I didn't finish. I said we think it is worth that much, but we might be able to take less - depending."

"Depending? I'm not at all sure about where this is heading. If you mean -" she said looking into the bedroom.

"No, no, heavens, nothing like that," said Sally with a concerned look to reassure Dina they were thinking of no such thing.

Still not sure where this was heading, her face a frown, Dina asked, "Like what, then?"

"Well, Dina," began Sally, "Thomas can explain more details later, but the long and short of it is we need a reliable person to handle some 'mail' for those without any ready access to the post office."

"I'm not sure I follow."

"I'm sorry, let me be more specific. Thomas is a guard at the prison. He sometimes gets requests from the inmates about how to handle private communications, such as family matters, so that the nosey folks in the main offices don't get involved. Nothing really shady. Not at all. But you must realize that these poor men have no means of a secure communication with family - or, perhaps, someone who can help them with post-prison positions. That sort of stuff."

"And where would I fit in?"

"There's a cashier's job open at the Capitol Diner not too far from here. Daytime hours. Decent pay - which we might be able to supplement from time to time, depending on traffic. And then there is the rent discount we talked about. So does this sound interesting?"

"I guess it might - but you're sure I won't get in trouble anyway?"

"Of course."

Dina was not gullible - at least she thought she was not - and felt she could back out if necessary. As it happened one of her uncles had served time in prison and could have used such a service. If anyone was naive, it was the Kosmons, for thinking such a service could remain secret for very long. But she was game.

§

The arrangements were really very simple. Mrs. Kosmon would bring notes to the apartment above the Arnold Funeral Home when she came for flowers -and pick up any return mail that Dina had received at the diner. That's all there was to it. Sometimes, she added, Dina's contact person at the funeral home would be a young man, Robbie Stanson. He was a trusty and had special privileges. Dina really wanted to be able to live in the apartment. And Mrs. Kosmon seemed like a very decent person who only wanted to help some men retain a small connection to the outside world. So she said yes. She would do it as long as she had no other plans for her immediate future. But it was only temporary, she warned the Kosmons, not something permanent.

Yes, the Kosmons understood that perfectly. The first messages did not arrive for transport to the diner for two weeks. Then there might be one each time. Never more than two. The only tricky part was how to handle the exchange. That was resolved by "break times," when Dina could step outside for a breath of fresh air. Why, then, didn't Mrs. Kosmon simply arrange to meet the recipients on the street, then? Because she would be in the prison van, along with Robbie, or in her car. The funeral home arrangement was perfect. Sally or Robbie would simply walk upstairs, spend a couple of minutes, and come back down with the mail. Or, they later worked out, there was a laundromat nearby that could also serve as a meeting point.

When Robbie started driving Mrs.Kosmon he and Dina also hit it off at once. This was something Sally and Tommy had counted on, and it gave an extra incentive to Dina to continue the meetings. Soon they were conversing over a cup of coffee, and then continuing conversations at the nearby laundromat.

§

And one day -"Robbie," said the warden, "Mrs. Kosmon's not feeling well this morning. I think it's alright for you to go alone." Here was a real opportunity to "branch out" a bit on the mail service. With inside access to prison records, the three, Robbie, Dave and Mary Jane could start charging for addition and subtraction, providing amended "vital statistics" about disciplinary matters in papers headed for the parole board. The fees for this service were a lot stiffer than for letters, even those that contained coded messages about buried treasure, or information about "rats."

The "system" worked this way. Robbie would talk to one of his students who needed a little help with his "records" before he appeared before the parole board, say, and Mary Jane could insert or delete an "item" from the personnel file of the person. The warden depended on his secretary and seldom checked the files before they went over to the board. It was risky, sure, a scheme within a scheme.

While Mrs. Kosmon's health did not worsen, more and more Robbie was going out alone in "civvies" and checking back in with the flowers from the funeral homes and other "donations." Dina had adjustable hours, and soon, perhaps once a week, she would ride with him as he made his rounds. They went to a city park and sat on a bench watching the pigeons scrabbling over bread crusts - just like any other young couple. Then the car became their "make out" place. Robbie now had money to spend and he trusted Dina to keep it safe. One day in late September she said she was sorry she hadn't worn a sweater. "Let's get you one," he said.

"Sure you want to do that?"

"Oh, absolutely," he replied, pulling her towards him for a long kiss. Unlike his dates with Wendy, furthermore, there were no swollen lips or bruises.

§

A few weeks after Robbie and Dina visited the big department store on High Street where he purchased a nice yellow sweater, things began to go wrong - just a bit. Robbie had been sent on a late afternoon trip to pick up some items in Columbus for the warden at a hardware store. He hadn't seen Dina for nearly a week, and so he stopped by the funeral home for a bit. The bit became an hour on her bed. And he was late getting back. At the car entrance to the prison, a guard checked him in - but made a notation on his schedule. The next day the guard who came on in the morning saw the note and decided he would pay special attention to the timeline for the van's trips when Robbie was driving.

For several days the morning day guard at the check-in post looked carefully at the previous day's hour-by-hour record. Nothing dramatic showed up, but he finally decided he would follow Robbie and see what might develop. He waited outside on one of the days Robbie carried out his "mission." When the prison van with OHIO DEPARTMENT OF CORRECTIONS pulled out and headed downtown, John Weiser followed in his Chevy Bel Air. The van stopped briefly at the first two funeral parlors, and Robbie had help carrying out the flowers. At the next stop a girl emerged when Robbie finished packing the van and got in on the passenger side. With her he drove to a park and stopped. A half hour later, they left the park and the van stopped outside a diner and the girl exited. Weiser blew a brief whistle through his teeth and drove back to the prison, walked to the guards' lunchroom and composed a note addressed to "Warden Allen: Confidential."

He dropped it off at the warden's office. He did not hear anything for three days. During that interval, Mary Jane had alerted Watkins. "Dave," she said, "what'll we do about this?" Watkins heard her out, puzzled for a minute, then replied, "Send it in under the day's mail. See if you can't manage to get it stuck a little in one of those manila folders. Then we'll tell Robbie to get a story ready, depending on what happens."

§

Nothing happened for a few days, then Weiser showed up in person at the office and asked the secretary: "Did you give my message to the Warden?"

"Certainly did Mr. Weiser." Still nothing for a week. Finally, Weiser asked for an appointment with the Warden.

Mary Jane showed him into Mr. Allen's office. "Officer Weiser to see you, sir."

"Yes, John, how are you."

That was the beginning of trouble for all three. Mary Jane was fired. She got the worst deal for keeping information from the Warden. Her successor found a box of condoms in her desk, and it was clear that his office had become a trysting place. Allen was, for good or bad, not informed about the "hanky-panky" that had gone on. The new secretary kept the secret for herself in case it might come in handy later. But neither she nor, obviously, Allen were aware of all the small changes that had been made to certain prisoners' records in his files. Allen was nearing retirement at this point, and his attention to all the little details had slipped a bit - quite a bit. One thing was clear: He had to remove Robbie from the flower runs. The Kosmons had planned well. Robbie got blamed for the "dates" with Dina Stevens, but the "mail service" continued with Mrs. Kosmon handling all the deliveries.

When Robbie's parents came to visit, he filled them in about all that had happened.

"You should leave that girl alone, son, until you get out," his father said.

"Of course, Dad, I don't really have any choice, do I?"

§

After a few days of solitary and weeks of extra-kp duty plus the loss of some of his privileges, Robbie seemed back in good grace. Warden Allen was not reprimanded by higher-ups because the story of Stanson's "courtship" had not gotten out - not yet, at least. Weiser felt some disappointment about what was not done, but he had no desire to rock the boat- until it could do him some real good. As a state employee, there were few benefits to whistleblowing at his level. Allen had taken care of his office staff problem, and life went on pretty much the same inside the "Big House."

The next year in October 1963, began Robbie's tenth since his confession. The parole board, a five-person panel of practically unknown Ohio citizens - at least to the public - met frequently and issued its decrees: either a thumbs up or thumbs down decision. Few people took much notice unless it was a big-time case. Robbie's had drawn much attention at the time, but seemingly over the years it had faded away; but that was not to be the case for long. Robbie's application was in a stack of manila folders on the table that month and passed back and forth by board members with a few murmurs, pencil jottings, and brief comments before a decision. No one had alerted the press that Stanson's parole was on the table one day in October, 1963.

The chairwoman, Mrs. Florina Seneca, the wife of a municipal judge, did notice that this was the first time for Stanson. As one might suspect, she was often the deciding vote on the panel. She had been in welfare positions in Franklin County before joining the board and then named chairwoman. She ran tight meetings and was known for quick judgments.

She rapped the meeting to order. "Henry," she looked to the guard at the door, "please ask Mr. Stanson to come in."

Robbie entered with an open smile on his face and waited until he was asked to sit down.

"Mr. Stanson, I think we will begin by asking you if you believe you are ready for parole at this time. You were sentenced to life ten years ago. It's only been ten years. Many people might say that's hardly sufficient time given the brutal nature of your crime. Why do you believe that we should recommend you be paroled?"

Robbie looked his studious best, concentrating on Mrs. Seneca. Then he began his statement, "I know that most people who did not know the whole story would feel that way. What I did will always be with me, the rest of my life. I know that I loved Wendy, and now I think that what I do with the rest of my life - if I can get back to school - will be some way to prove that love by helping others. I had intended to go to theological school after college. Now that might not be an option. But I am thinking about finding some sort of role in counseling. I'm not sure quite what, but there seem to be some good options."

"If we approve this parole," said Mrs. Seneca, " we would probably require that you return home for a period and live with your parents for a specified time. How would that impact your plans?"

"Not at all, I could take courses to finish my degree - I already have credits from correspondence courses." He nodded in a way to indicate he fully understood the terms and shifted in his chair to show he was ready for their decision.

Looking around the table, Florina raised her eyebrows in a questioning way. Turning to her colleagues, "Well, gentlemen do you want to ask Robbie anything?"

Ronald Carlson raised his hand, with a pencil pointing at Robbie. "Your prison record looks exemplary - but I wonder about some things. For example, your claim you blacked out. How is it that you then decided to dispose of Wendy - not knowing if she was dead, already? The county medical examiner said she was killed there - after you arrived at the woods. "

"Sir, I was in a state of shock. I've learned in my reading about unusual behavior in such circumstances that it is a little like being in a trance."

Carlson raised his eyes at that and looked at each of the board members."Un-hunh. So you were in a shock induced trance when you struck that young woman more than twenty times?"

"I can't explain it any other way."

"Might it be that you had another problem? Might it be that Wendy's pregnancy was not planned but an 'accident,' and that you saw your life - as you had planned it - going down the drain?"

"The only thing I can say, sir, is that, yes, the world turned upside down. But it happened because of a quarrel at the moment - it was not planned."

"I don't buy that for a second. But I will say you have spent most of ten years helping others. Perhaps you could continue that work inside."

"Yes sir, if that is the decision of this board."

"Anything else," Florina asked. The other two members passed. "No, then you may go, Mr. Stanson. You will be informed of our decision." After he left, she looked around the table, "Well, gentlemen, what do you think we should do?"

Carlson was clearly upset, "Florina, he has actually served the bare minimum, ten years by a few days later this month. I remember that case. He defaced that young woman. I've been on the board for more years than he's served. I'm not happy that we are even considering this right now."

So, indeed, was Alexander Martin, the only Black Person on the board. "Madame Chairperson, do you think we would even be considering this if Stanson was black or brown? I don't buy the youth argument. Everything in the record of this case shows careful planning, not a lovers' quarrel that escalated."

"Florina," said Bill Tilden, "I guess it's up to me to make the argument. He's had a very good record here - taught some prisoners how to fill out paperwork, became a reliable trusty, handling things with various assignments to downtown, never in trouble. So I vote yes.

Roger Kervich spoke up last. "Well, it is pretty early - at least one might think so, but, finally, I come down where Bill does. It does seem possible to me that he blacked out. There was that high school head injury..."

"Wait a minute, Roger," it was Carlson. "What doctor ever gave a diagnosis about that? Has he ever suffered another 'episode?'"

"None that we know about, but I..."

"Yeah - none."

Florina interrupted the debate amongst her male colleagues. "Look at your folders, gentlemen. The prosecutor declared that he was unable to conclude that a First Degree charge would stick, because he couldn't prove prior intent."

"Florina," said Martin, "I wouldn't bet a dime on a Black prisoner's chances of getting out so soon - or even getting a Second Degree plea accepted. Now, would you?"

Mrs. Seneca nodded in Martin's direction, a sort of recognition of his point. But then said, "I think we should vote now that everyone has had his say."

The vote was 3-2, with the chair casting the deciding vote. A little later in the meeting she also cast the deciding vote in the case of David Watkins. Both were recommended for parole.

§

Outside the room where the board had met, John Weiser had been waiting to hear from the guard inside what the decision had been.

"He's out," Kenneth Craig told Weiser. "Three to two."

Weiser hitched up his pants almost the way he'd seen it done in Westerns before the hero rode out to find the rustlers. "Yeah, I figured that." The first thing he needed to do was get a look at Stanson's file and see what happened to the information he had supplied the warden. The problem was how to do that. He had an idea.

CHAPTER EIGHT

BREAKING OUT

Before the appointed day of Robbie Stanson's release on November 1, 1963, the *Columbus Journal* ran a front-page story*: Trysting Trusty Granted Parole On First Try.* The story set out the details of how Stanson had been followed the several times that he took the penitentiary van on assigned errands and returned late each time. It did not name the person who had supplied the newspaper with such details. John Weiser was never named in the follow-up stories that detailed a scandal centered in Warden Allen's office.

At first, Allen tried to minimize the whole thing as a lot of to-do over nothing. "We didn't find anything really amiss," he claimed when reporters asked about the story, "the young man was a little late in returning, that's all."

But new questions kept appearing on a daily basis - and Robbie was back in the news, much to Governor Barney Rogers's distress.

It was clear that the *Journal*, no friend of the governor's, had been holding back the "best stuff." The following stories strung out the story as one of a prisoner enjoying the luxury of a sexual liaison while supposedly supplying the prison hospital and chapel with flowers. There were no real witnesses to such acts. But that only made things slightly less worrisome for the governor's office and was no help for the warden at his press conference.

"What did you do about this when you first heard about it?" he was asked.

"Well, we acted right away, took him off that assignment, and gave him a new job."

"What kind of new job?"

"He was a clerk in my office."

"Was that all you did - sounds almost like he got rewarded, sir."

The "sir" sounded almost sarcastic, and Warden Allen tried, alas, to recoup his position with disastrous results. "We sent him to the 'hole' for three days."

"Solitary Confinement."

"Yes. Look, this young man had an exemplary record here."

A day later one of the reporters having received an anonymous tip, asked the warden on the telephone: "Sir, could you tell me if anything was found on Mr. Stanson that connected him in an intimate way with the young woman he was seeing on these trips?"

"Well, that's not the way to put it, really, he was not 'seeing' anyone, just met her at the laundromat and drove around town a few times. That's all there was to it. You're making much too much out of this."

"Is it true that when he was finally asked about all these 'tardy' adventures, he had the woman's unlisted phone number on him?"

"Yes, that's so. But did that really mean -"

"Maybe you can tell us, then, whether it is also nothing much that he somehow purchased some items of clothing for her?"

"I have no idea where you're getting all this stuff to make it seem as bad as you can so you can sell newspapers."

"It's true then?"

"Yes, but -"

"Is it also true that the young woman's phone bills were being paid by a prison guard?"

"I don't know anything about that - but the whole incident has been dealt with properly - of that I can give you my full assurances."

§

Warden Allen's assurances did little to satisfy the press - or Governor Rogers, who called for a reconsideration of the decision to grant Stanson parole. Even as the board was trying to set up a new date for such a do-over, newspapers dropped a new bombshell. "It was learned today," read the latest article in the *Journal*, "that the information about Stanson's 'trysts' had not been in the files the Parole Board reviewed." One member, Ronald Carlson, told reporters that he had doubts before, but now this news of a violation of "all that was supposedly expected of inmates with special privileges had convinced him that no one over there in that brick building by the river had followed basic rules - or even common sense." Chairwoman Seneca told reporters that she had never seen anything in the files like what was now known to have been missing at the time of the discussion. And it certainly did not help when a former inmate told yet another reporter that, "Everyone knows you can get things taken out or put into the files for a pack of cigarettes."

Of course, that was not true. The "service" charge for "fixing" the files was a lot more - and in cash. But there was still worse to come. How this came to the attention of reporters was never explained, but the story got out that David Watkins and Mary Jane Austin had been "interrupted" in the warden's office late one Friday afternoon by the prison chaplain. The encounter turned into a shouting match that could be heard outside in the hall. And to top it off, Watkins had been granted parole at the very next board meeting.

"Allen," the governor shouted over the phone, "what in blazes is going on over there?"

"I'm really sorry, sir, we have fixed up all these problems just as soon as we could."

"Whatta mean 'fixed up'? You've just about destroyed the reputation of our penal system and screwed up my whole administration. I want your resignation letter, yesterday. Do you understand?"

Allen repeated he was really sorry for all the commotion that had arisen, but that only made the governor boil over.

"Commotion, my God man, do you still not see what you have done?"

§

The governor's next call was to Florina. "I don't want you to reverse your vote at the next meeting. Can you hold the other two in line who voted yes?"

"I think so - but why...?"

"Because that would make it look worse. If you messed up that badly, and the record was really altered that much, then you had no business letting him go."

"Yes, I see."

"Besides, aside from the 'romance' there wasn't anything bad in the record, was there. And Florina, you know how much I like you and the judge, your husband, because he was a loyal supporter - but I think you should probably resign. Let's clear the decks."

§

In the meantime, before a second meeting of the parole board and a new vote on Stanson's application, the newspapers kept up a steady drumbeat of bad news for

Allen, the board, and the governor. One state official didn't help matters by claiming that newspapers up north around Akron and Cleveland were being fed more juicy details. The anonymous state official said, "The papers are seeing things we didn't." Warden Allen, his back already to the wall, admitted that there were one or two "incidents" that were not in the file his office sent to the board - but there was much more material favorable to Robbie that they had considered.

The board itself was under heavy fire. It turned out they had approved Watkins' parole without there even being a letter in his file recommending release from the warden, who had written of Stanson that he was sure he could make a good adjustment - that his whole record - well, his whole record minus those incidents - had demonstrated he was ready to return to society and make something of himself.

Robbie's diligence in teaching his fellow prisoners was exemplary, the warden's letter had said, and he had indicated he planned to finish college. Curiously, the letter also said that Stanson was a "loner" while in prison, who always acted as though he were "a civilian." What that meant was not explained.

§

Reporters kept after the individual members of the board. Only one of the five claimed to have read the whole file - Ron Carlson, who told reporters that he felt that Stanson should have served at least three more years before it could possibly consider returning him to society. "What kind of message are we sending by freeing this man at the first go-around? I certainly don't think it's fair either to the girls' parents, or to the citizens of the state who expect justice to be served."

Then they went to the new prosecutor in Wyandot County. "No, he didn't see anything in his office files about whether his predecessor Tom Jackson had made any recommendation beyond accepting the guilty plea." Then on to Judge "Stony"

Kerwick. He was equally unhelpful. "I don't recall saying anything about parole during sentencing. If I did it would be in the record, wouldn't it?" And, then, worst of all, came a report from a former inmate challenging the idea that things could get pulled from files for a packet of cigarettes. "No, that's not true at all," quipped Maxie Simmons, "A friend will do it for free."

In a way that was even worse than exposing the fee Stanson and his cohorts charged for their services. The only thing the governor wanted to know now was how soon the parole board could meet to bring this "helluva stinking mess out of the newspapers and off the radio." A second vote was taken on November 6, 1953 - with the same outcome!

Robbie would be paroled to his parents' custody on November 27. A day or two after the vote, Florina Seneca announced that she was resigning from the board. Was this because of criticism of her decision, a reporter for the *Cleveland Beacon* asked? "Of course not," she replied. "it's just that the meetings sometimes go on so late, and my husband expects me home for dinner." It was about as frank an answer as anyone gave in the hullabaloo that accompanied Robbie Stanson's exit from prison.

As when he went in ten years before, reporters were there to greet him on the doorstep, so to speak. Robbie began this ad hoc press conference with a statement. "As long as I live what I did will be with me - I know that but now it is time for me to start a new life. I hope to show that I am no longer that person, but someone determined to contribute to society."

"What do you plan to do?" came the obvious first question. "Well, I had planned on the ministry. But after studying psychology, I think I would like to do something with the corrections side of social work." With a rueful smile, he added, "Of course, I probably won't be able to do that in Ohio." As for his plans to continue his college education in person, well, he hoped he would not be too hampered by the parole restriction that required him to live with his parents for an undetermined time. With that he walked to the waiting car his father had driven down to Columbus, still carrying the same books he had with him when he entered prison ten years earlier. He waved good-bye to the reporters and disappeared from sight as the car pulled away.

§

Governor Rogers was asked what he thought about the outcome of the "squabble," as he preferred to think of it. Reporters prompted him with another statement by Carlson: "Stanson - and the warden, mind you - just sugar-coated that bad stuff with the girl he was driving around in a state car."

"Oh, no protested Rogers," shaking his head, "that looks much worse in the newspapers than it really was." He smiled at the questioner. "The warden assured me it was just that - driving around doing some errands for the girl. She didn't have a car. Now that's all I'm going to say about it." The governor's security guards opened a path to his car, and he was whisked away to a luncheon at the annual state convention of local police chiefs.

In White Plains, New York, reporters searched out Mrs. Peters for her opinion on what had happened. "I hope and pray he doesn't enjoy another day of his life." Did she know this was coming? "I am terribly surprised. I had more faith in justice than this."

Russ Lewis read the brief news stories and both statements and breathed out a long sigh. He was no longer the youngest sheriff in Ohio. He was no longer a sheriff. He had become an investigator for Continental Insurance with offices around the state and in other states. But he had never believed he was quite finished with the "Red Slippers" case. Would it have made any difference if he had followed up on that detail concerning the suitcase that was found in the weeds outside the football stadium the morning after Robbie's confession? How had it got there? It would explain why only a few clothes were found. If Wendy had intended to make this her "wedding trip" – as Robbie had promised - why weren't there more clothes? The one suitcase in the river could not have held all her clothes she would need, surely? He had checked with the couple who rented the room to her, but they could not recall how many suitcases she had with her when she moved in during July. But certainly not just one.

He regretted failing to push very hard against Jackson's decision to accept the Second Degree plea, and he blamed himself for not speaking up. But, again, he was the youngest sheriff in the state, and going against an experienced prosecutor was not the easiest thing in the world to do.

Another reader of the news story of Robbie's parole who lived and worked in Columbus was Carl Peters. He blamed himself still for not protecting Wendy. He cut out the picture and text and pasted them in a new scrapbook besides two others that contained articles and letters – and copies of anonymous letters he had written. On the spine, he attached a piece of paper: **FINAL CHAPTER?**

And in Philadelphia yet another reader, new to the city, read a small item about the parole of the "Red Slippers" murderer and felt his stomach tighten as he rode in to work on a commuter train.

CHAPTER NINE

NEW BEGINNINGS

Robbie Stanson's parole conditions mandated that he live with his parents for an undetermined time. The decision about when he might be permitted to leave would be up to his parole officer, in the first instance, and then approval from the State Department of Corrections. Before the mandate could be lifted, Robbie had to show evidence not only of good behavior, but a plan for the next steps in his living arrangements. He promptly enrolled at Cleveland State University and began studying for a psychology degree with special attention to counseling. Living at home almost as a hermit provided plenty of time for study and his coursework went well. He kept to himself and it appeared that no one really paid much attention to him as he moved from class to class. There were mostly commuter students at the school who had their personal lives elsewhere, a situation that suited him fine.

When he met with his parole officer there was very little to report about his private life. He did not date and spent little time drinking coffee in the student union. Because he was a little older, and obviously stand-offish, some of those who encountered him in the library thought he might be a faculty member. Two years went by and he had finished the requirements for his degree. He applied to the University of Minnesota for graduate work in social psychology and was accepted. The parole officer congratulated him, and those above him voiced no objection to his new plans. He was supposed to maintain contacts with the office, and he did abide by this requirement without fail. His parents had agreed to pay tuition and board, but his undergraduate record and letters of recommendation from his professors earned him a one-year fellowship, which was followed the second year by a teaching assistantship.

§

He finished his coursework and Master's thesis. Deciding against Ph.D. work, and again with his parents' help, he established a counseling office in a Cleveland suburb, with the name, R. Carter Stanson. A few came to see him but did not return. It was hard starting out as an independent rather than joining a practice, he realized. Occasionally, moreover, he would get a letter in the mail, unsigned, with pictures of dormitories at Bashford, or country roads. After three years, he left the office for a job in a clinic.

The anonymous letters continued, now mailed to the clinic. He said nothing about them to his parents. Finally, officials of the clinic decided - after the letters became more frequent - that he had to go. "Carter," said his supervisor, "this just isn't going to work. I'm sorry, but I have no choice." Robbie nodded and left for good that afternoon. To his parents, he said he wished to see more of the country. At this point, everyone lost track of Robbie or R. Carter Stanson. The last card he wrote to his parents in 1971 told them not to worry he would be in touch when he returned from a hiking excursion in Yosemite National Park. The park covers an area of about 1200 square miles, he explained, with plenty of places to spend a night in the open or in one of the park-owned cabins. And then nothing more from Robbie for two years. His parents did not report him missing for fear of endangering his future. They did not believe something had happened to him, something bad. Rather, they believed, or hoped, that he had figured out a way to live with his past. They would wait they agreed until he felt comfortable with a new life. He will then reach out to them. The worst is over for Robbie – and for them. There was nothing else to do.

§

By this time Russell Lewis had long since left the sheriff's office for good. It was a dead-end job unless you planned it as a launching pad into something else. Electoral politics held no interests. He had his new career as an insurance investigator. He had not forgotten about the Peters case, of course, and his feelings that Wendy's family had been cheated by the plea deal. The years rolled on for Russ as he advanced to the position of senior investigator. He remained married, but things did not go entirely well on that front, and it became an off-again, on-again arrangement with his wife that seemed fine with her. They had one child, a girl, that he loved dearly, and who, as she grew up, started to understand her parents' decisions. Russ was out in the field so much that he was seldom at home, but he would come and stay for a couple of weeks at a time. His wife managed a small clothing store and joined numerous women's organizations.

§

On a Tuesday morning in October 1973, a large envelope addressed to "Russell Lewis, Esq." arrived at his office. He assumed it contained documents about some case he was working on and set it aside until he had completed paperwork on the most immediate case, a very suspicious car theft reported by a man who had defaulted on his payments two months earlier. When he opened the envelope inside was a 5" X 7" photograph of a professional office building, and the address in Trenton, New Jersey. Lewis looked at another sheet of paper folded inside:

"Dear Mr. Lewis," began the typed message,

We met years ago when my sister was murdered by Robbie Stanson. As you may know, he was released from prison nearly ten years ago. After finishing college and doing graduate work, Stanson set himself up as a 'Counselor'! Imagine that if you will. He did not succeed. But now he has disappeared. I hope you will agree to investigate that 'disappearance.' In the building pictured, there is the office of Stuart Freed. Freed is a psychological counselor – one who also studies old criminal cases looking for things that were missed and could shed entirely new light on the crimes. I hope you will agree to go to see Freed, and I am writing him today to expect at least a call, and hopefully a visit from you. For you – if I have judged correctly – it is unfinished business. For me, it is a matter of justice that the <u>whole</u> truth be known. Please be assured I am willing to cover your expenses in making such a trip and would be happy to discuss proper remuneration in case we should embark together on the full investigation that was owed to Wendy and never carried out.

Sincerely Yours,

Carl Peters

§

Carl hoped he had put the request in the right way to encourage Russ to get together with Freed, a surprise visitor who had been to see him to talk about his idea that there might have been an accomplice, and then, recently, had told him about a paper he planned to deliver to a Philadelphia seminar that studied old crimes looking for new clues. It was a bit of a gamble that anything would happen as a result of his letter to Russ, but he still remembered the sympathetic looks Lewis had given him the day sentence was pronounced. All he could do was wait and see. Was there a connection, he wondered, between the proposed Freed paper and Robbie's disappearance? He had followed Stanson's post-prison efforts and authored the "letters" that pursued him from private practice to the clinic. Russ knew nothing of this, or how obsessed Carl was in seeking "justice," but he admitted to himself that he was curious about what Freed might have discovered. He could shift his caseload around a bit and go to Trenton. There was no harm in that.

CHAPTER TEN

50 DUNCASTLE ROAD

Duncastle Road branched off Route 263 to Stockton, New Jersey. In places, it was barely wide enough for two cars, and sometimes drivers pulled off rather than risk sideswiping. A mile down the road was a stylish large house number 50, that reminded some people of one of the mansions dating to the Old South. This morning the owner, Stuart Freed, had rushed back to the house from the fields where his Arabian horses normally spent uneventful days in between the shows where they always attracted a large number of admirers. As he came into the house he had terrible news. "JoEllen," he called out, "Some damned hunter shot Jamilah. Call the vet. I'm going back to be with her and Sid. He's trying to keep her warm as best he can. I don't think it's too bad – but we really don't know."

With that, he went back out to his car parked in the circular driveway and drove down the lane to be with the mare and his groom. The vet arrived in a remarkably short time. But there was little he could do. Jamilah really could not be saved, and the decision was clear to all: it was best to end her suffering. She would be buried alongside the two others who had died over the ten years Freed and his wife had lived on Duncastle Road. Both very successful professionals, the Freeds had decided to raise Arabian horses when it became clear there would be no children. Instead, there was a large stable that had eight stalls. And was always fully occupied.

The Freeds entertained a lot. Guests to the house were usually taken to the stable first and encouraged to feed carrots or apples to the horses. Once that ritual was complete everyone returned to the house. One walked up a paved-stone path to a two-story classical American country manor with a verandah and rocking chairs across the front and a center double door with a sunburst transom. A cut-glass chandelier hung inside over a polished stone floor. Off the hexagonal foyer to the left three steps down was a reception room with a bar where Stuart and JoEllen provided guests with their choice of pre-dinner cocktails or aperitifs.

The room was book-lined on every wall. The Freeds obviously enjoyed reading here especially in summer with sunset views through the front windows of their fields and the horses sauntering away the hours. The books combined professional interests with classics – and there were also a large number of true crime books, especially, famous New Jersey crimes such as the supposedly still unsolved famous murder in the 1920s of an Episcopalian Minister and his mistress, the choir leader of his church. It was widely believed that the wife of the minister and her brothers, members of a prominent New Jersey family, were responsible for the murders one summer night in New Brunswick. Their bodies had been found near a New Brunswick city park with love letters strewn around them as indictments of their adulterous relationship. One of the widow's brothers was later prosecuted for the crime, but never convicted.

There were books as well about the "Crime of the Century," the kidnapping and murder of Charles Augustus Lindbergh, Jr. That crime was supposedly solved with the execution of Bruno Richard Hauptmann in 1935, but questions remained to tantalize authors and readers down to the present.

Stuart enjoyed showing guests his collection and encouraging them to think about possible alternative solutions to those famous crimes – and others. He liked to get his guests speculating about the nature of evidence, the reliability of witnesses, the supposed presence of the unknown shadowing accepted truth.

Freed managed these conversations so that they always ended with a question mark, always leaving guests impressed with their host's passion for revisiting old crimes. One time a guest joked at the door, "Stuart, I feel like we were playing 'Clue' with no solution about who did it." Freed was actually very happy with that comment.

§

Then one night, Stuart asked his guests if they had ever heard about another murder case: "The Red Slippers Mystery?" "Actually," he would begin, "it wasn't an unsolved case. The murderer confessed almost right away, agreed to a plea bargain, served time, was paroled after ten years – and then some years later disappears."

"How is that possible?" came the inevitable question.

"Well, the whole case is filled with strange twists, despite seeming so simple at first sight. He paused waiting until he had their absolute attention. It begins with a Dreiser-like 'American Tragedy' story about a young couple – college freshmen – at a small school. It appeared to be love at first sight – well, it was, to the extent that the couple locked onto one another – and moved around campus hand-in-hand the entire year. Her dorm mates occasionally noticed that sometimes she came in with bruises around her mouth – but they didn't report anything at the time. And, Wendy, that was her name, never complained."

At that point, Freed's guests would shake their heads in disbelief.

"But surely..."

"Ah, but that was hardly unknown behavior back in the 1950s – or for that matter even today. In any event, Wendy never complained to friends or dorm counselors and was apparently set on continuing the relationship after that first year in college, and so was her boyfriend, Robbie - or so she thought."

He paused to draw out their attention. "But now the situation has changed. Their plan – if it was their plan, because we only have Robbie's word for it – had worked. Wendy is pregnant and their parents could hardly object."

Freed paused and looked around the room, and then continued: "But there seems to be doubts now about Robbie's commitment. She talks to her landlady, and the landlady's minister. They advise her to seek help. But she only writes Robbie to tell him of the situation."

"And what does he say – I can only imagine," says one of the guests, a woman, shaking her head grimly.

"Yep, you're right. Robbie writes her that if the woman is older, the man cannot be forced to support the child. Of course, Robbie did not know that this letter would ever see the light of day – and then there was a final letter. To her pleadings that they carry out the original plan, he tells her to take a bus, bring all her clothes, all her money – everything and come to West River.

She obeys him – but not quite to the letter, so to speak, because she leaves behind those two crucial letters, one disclaiming his responsibility, the second instructing her to bring everything."

"I don't believe this," said another guest, throwing up her hands.

"Oh, it's true. Robbie just didn't know she left those behind."

"Do you think she did it on purpose?"

"Impossible to say. A detective found them in her room. The landlady did say, however, that she seemed really happy the day she took the bus down to see Robbie for the last time."

Freed paused again, milking the moment for full effect.

"When she arrived late at night, unseen by anyone, he supposedly took her to a shed on an athletic field where she stayed for the first night. The next day he brought food, they had sex, and then an argument after dark that ended with Robbie strangling her, loading her into his car, driving fifty miles from West River down a by-way, taking her into a woods and defacing her with a poker-like instrument."

No one spoke. He waited, then continued, "When the letters turned up it proved - or it could have proved – a real blow for Robbie's planned defense, which was eager after his confession to avoid a trial by pleading out to Second Degree murder."

"What happened then?

"Nothing more. His plea was accepted. Much to the relief, obviously, of college officials at Bashford who feared the impact of a murder trial on recruiting and alumni support. He then received a life sentence."

"And?"

"He got out ten years later on parole."

"What!" His guests looked at each other and then back at him in disbelief.

"Yep on his first try, by a 3-2 vote on the parole board. Wendy's family was not happy. They had been led to believe that a life sentence meant more than ten years. Robbie finishes college living at his parents' – then goes to graduate school in psychology."

Stuart stopped talking.

"And then?"

"And then a few years later he disappears from a national park in California – Yosemite. There are all sorts of rumors – but nothing ever led anywhere."

Stuart's guests were left with those thoughts to ponder. What he hadn't told them was he had given a talk in Philadelphia at a private seminar of invited guests only, dedicated to reviewing questions about famous crimes. The paper he presented on that night offered his preliminary findings on the question of whether there could have been an accomplice. Neither did he tell them that he had actually tried to communicate with Robbie Stanson years ago before he disappeared – and more recently had actually been in touch with Carl Peters, Wendy's brother. Stuart's research into the case had begun after Stanson disappeared and was presumed dead by accident or suicide – an outcome many who had followed his difficult post-prison years found reasonable and even just. He did not tell Carl Peters about his attempt to contact Stanson. But the visit to Wendy's guilt-ridden brother triggered the events that followed.

§

Stuart's talk at the seminar had gone well. He took many questions and, he thought, had handled them well. A couple of people had come up to him to pursue their questions in depth – a very gratifying response that these criminologists thought he was on the right track.

One man, a former judge, asked what his next step would be. Did he plan to pursue the matter with further inquiries?

Stuart responded that he was not sure, what did the judge think? Of course, Stuart had already decided that he was going to do a book, but he did not say that to the judge. "I'm not sure. There's a long road between a theory and finding the evidence, isn't there?"

"Quite so, but congratulations on your work so far and tonight's presentation. I have a hard time understanding why this wasn't pursued at the time."

"Yes, well there was the quick confession – and no one wanted to drag this matter out. That's the reason, and no one has wanted ever since to get dragged into what had been a shocking crime. Why involve anyone else? They had the self-confessed killer."

"Yes, well – thanks for a fine presentation. Good luck whatever you decide."

Two others were standing close by waiting to talk with Stuart. The first offered congratulations and left without asking anything more. The second offered congratulations and held Stuart's hand in his with a firm grip.

"Nice job, truly. I'm not a regular member just a guest. But I have something of a special interest in the case. I was a student at Bashford during this period. I never met Robbie – talk around campus was that he was pretty much a loner – nor Wendy either. There were about two thousand students back then. Hasn't changed much."

"Really, you were there. That's very interesting to me. We should talk even if you did not know Robbie or Wendy."

The man who joined the group around Stuart was a short, thin person wearing bifocals. He had a shy smile. "Well, maybe so. As I say I never met them." He paused thoughtfully. "And I'm not really all that convinced there was an accomplice. Just thought you gave us something to think about." He smiled again. Tilted his head slightly and then asked: "But just suppose there was one as you suggest. I guess he'd be pretty upset at the case being re-opened. I would I know."

One or two others standing close by nodded. "Yes, indeed," said a lawyer, "I was thinking the same thing, Dr. Freed." With a chuckle, he added, "Watch out now! You never know, do you."

The Bashford man who raised the point had moved off and was talking to another person. The two walked toward the cloakroom, and Stuart had to rush over to catch them up. "I didn't get your name quite, or how I can reach you. You could fill me in on the scene, so to speak."

"Oh, sorry, it's Kent – Kent Crider. I don't think I'd be much use to you. As I say, I didn't know them – maybe saw them around campus once or twice. But as I said a minute ago, I doubt you'll get very far. It's an interesting possibility, but not very likely is it? No one raised any doubts, and they had cops all over the place. I remember that – cops all over the campus for several days. And from what I heard at the time, Robbie had a real temper. Ah, well, people like to speculate about the mysterious unknown, even when there is a simple answer. You gave a nice talk. Thank you, lots to think about."

Before Stuart could say anything more, the chairman of the evening, grabbed his arm. "Over here, Dr. Freed, we need you to sign our book, and get your picture taken for our program write-up that stays here, of course, in our archives."

§

As Stuart was going through the formalities of picture taking and book signing, Kent Crider's comment stuck in his mind. Indeed, it gave him a funny feeling in his stomach. He would have to ask if someone knew how to reach him. And he thought about the encounter the morning his Arabian was shot. He had a foreboding that the person who did this had not been a hunter aiming at what he thought was something else, or a malicious teenager with a gun he found in his dad's study closet.

CHAPTER ELEVEN

FIRST MOVES

At 9:30 am the following day, Stuart Freed was in his Trenton Office preparing to meet his first appointment of the day. He looked again at the file his secretary had placed on his desk. It was a new patient; the referring physician, a friend, had little to say. "The patient is a forty-year-old, white man, who has developed a phobia about dogs that was interfering with his sleep. He kept seeing packs of dogs outside his house in his dreams." Besides the file, there was a note about a phone call from a Mr. Russell Lewis. "He asked when he might call to talk to you about an old case. That was all there was. He left a number of a local motel. Should I call him or do you wish to contact him yourself? Susan."

Stuart went into his secretary's office. This was another odd "coincidence." He had planned to contact Russell Lewis before he went any further with his re-investigation of the "case." Perhaps Lewis had somehow heard about his paper for the Philadelphia seminar? And wished to talk? If so, that was exciting. But how had he heard? "Susan, did you get any idea about how long he will be at this number?"

"No, sir, but he didn't seem to be in a great hurry."

"O.k., I'll try him this afternoon." He pocketed the phone message and asked Susan to send in his patient.

§

He called the number at 4:25 p.m. Lewis answered. "Yes, Dr. Freed, thank you for returning my call. I wonder if there is a time when we might meet in the next day or so. I'm here in town on some other business – and have an opportunity to clear up a little mystery."

"Oh, well if I can help, I will be glad to. What's this about?"

"Well, that's part of the mystery – I'm not sure."

"You want to talk about something that is bothering you?"

"No, not in that sense. I'm pretty uncomplicated, if wondering sometimes how in the world I wound up investigating insurance claims."

Freed was excited because he knew very well Lewis's connection to the Red Slippers murder. But he decided to play dumb for a minute. Was this a prank call? One of the seminar members having a little bit of fun. Freed replied, "So this has to do with one of my patients, and a false insurance claim of mental illness to get out of an obligation?"

"Nope again. I'm just trying to follow up on a letter I received from Carl Peters."

Freed was suddenly alert. "You're kidding. Carl is in touch with you? Well, I guess that answers a lot of questions – at least in one sense."

"Maybe it's best we just sit down somewhere, and I can talk to you about a letter I received from Carl."

"Sure, how about Friday, say about this same time. I should be finished with my patients then – and we can slip out for a coffee or beer somewhere close. I guess you know where my office is?

"Yep."

§

That night Stuart and his wife spent a long time in the stable. They talked with each of the remaining seven horses, commiserating with them and with themselves over the loss of Jamilah.

"She was a great beauty," said Stuart as he caressed the neck of the mare that occupied the stall next to where the deceased had stood, nodding her head and nuzzling Freed and his wife.

JoEllen smiled and rubbed Stuart's upper arm to support his sense of loss. "Do you think the police have any idea why someone shot our horse?"

He frowned, shaking his head as he continued patting the horse. "I also wonder what Lewis wants to talk about, how much Carl told him. I guess we'll find out soon enough."

Stuart had planned to talk to Lewis as soon as he had a chance to get away for a few days and try to find out more about the original investigation. He had long wondered whether the sheriff had ever entertained similar thoughts that there might have been an accomplice. What had Carl told him? Enough, apparently, to trigger a visit. Whatever, it now looked like he would soon find out.

§

After the phone call, Russ sat in his motel room wondering why he had set out on this trip to engage in detective magazine stuff. What was the point? How did it help resolve anything? Peters was obviously obsessed – perhaps to a dangerous point. He would meet Freed and call it quits – he told himself.

§

Friday afternoon Russ parked outside the office building and went in through the front entrance, opening it wide as he did to allow a wheelchair with an elderly woman to pass. Her aide smiled at him and he nodded back. One of the offices noted in the directory had listed an orthopedic surgeon. It was not a large building and there were only two floors of offices. "Stuart Freed," the listing on the plaque read, "Psychological Counseling." His office was on the second floor, next to a group practice of "Family Medicine" on one side, and a specialist in "Hypertension" on the other. Lewis smiled to himself: that might be a very reasonable location for a "shrink."

Stuart's receptionist greeted him warmly. "Please sit down, Mr. Freed is with his last patient – shouldn't be long."

Russ settled himself in a chair and picked up an old *Newsweek* from the table in front of the comfortable leather chair like those in doctors' offices everywhere. He thumbed through it, he thought, probably looking just like those waiting to begin a session always did. He was just as nervous, anyway, as he waited to find out what had brought him here all this way.

Stuart soon appeared at the door to his inner office with a woman who seemed to have been crying. He patted her on the shoulder, giving her a warm smile. "Next week, Mrs. Farahey, don't push it. You're really doing quite well."

He waited until she had exited the office and then turned to greet his visitor. "Mr. Lewis, just let me get my coat."

The former sheriff saw a balding light-haired man with a proper beard for a psychologist, who wore horned-rimmed glasses, also appropriate. He wore a tan sports coat over a dark blue turtle-neck sweater. He would guess his age at about fifty, one side or the other.

Freed had left his inner office door open, and Russ could see several prints of horses hanging on the walls opposite his desk. Freed picked up a briefcase and signaled to his secretary that they were about to leave.

"Susan, I'll be home all weekend. If Mrs. Farahey should call for any reason, make sure you let me know. I'm a little concerned."

"Yes, Dr. Freed. Will-do."

"Come on Russell there is a coffee shop down the street – unless you'd like something stronger to celebrate Friday?"

Russ was a little surprised at Freed's greeting as if to an old friend instead of someone he had never met but replied with a smile. "No, that's fine."

They walked about a block and a half and entered "The Big Cup." Freed seemed to know the owner and greeted her with a smile. Picking one of the three booths in the rear of the shop, he motioned for Lewis to sit down.

When they had been served Freed smiled in a doctor-like reassuring way. "Now Mr. Lewis what brings you here? I can guess, of course, but why don't you tell me." Stuart was not going to bring up details of the seminar paper or his research on his own, at least not until he discovered what Lewis knew.

§

Russ looked across the table and gave a little shrug of his shoulders. "You know, I'm not sure." He handed the letter to Stuart who read it quickly.

"Well, ok, I'll start, then. I went to see Carl Peters about my research – and then the disappearance of Robbie Stanson makes everything – well - that much more intriguing. And, also, it was my intention to get in touch with you, but he has pre-empted my – timetable, as it were."

Russ remained silent waiting to hear more.

"So, in this letter you received I guess Carl is pitching the idea he wants the two of us to link up Robbie's disappearance with my interest in pursuing the accomplice angle."

But Lewis only nodded and waited to hear more.

"What do you know about the paper I gave recently to a Philadelphia seminar on the murder?"

"That's easy to answer. Not much - in fact nothing. I have not heard anything specific about your paper and an accomplice. As you see, Carl simply wrote that you were looking at new angles at some seminar. But it explains a lot."

"Did he tell you we have been in touch? Well, more than just in touch?"

"No, his letter just urged me to contact you and go from there." Russ was more than a bit intrigued about the seeming assumption that Russ would drop everything and jump in on a likely goose chase. But he just sat there, waiting for Stuart to make his next play.

"I can see Carl has this desire to get us together."

Russ smiled, and nodded for Stuart to go on, curious about Stuart Freed's angle in pursuing a likely dead end.

"He may be right. Robbie's disappearance could be related to such fears, but he disappeared long before I even thought about the idea."

Lewis waited for more.

"What happened I think is that Robbie wanted to break free from Carl and start somewhere else. When he disappeared that spurred Carl to use my research as an added incentive to find out where he had gone - or maybe just to publicize the idea to satisfy his quest to show that the authorities had messed up in 1953. My research - and you supporting the search for Robbie would give Carl some satisfaction."

Russ had figured something like this had prompted Carl to write him. But he was not going to jump in, was he? What the hell! Yes, what the hell - still -   Stuart could see Russ wondered where things were going. He was now engaged along with Carl in trying to draw Russ into his effort to pursue the accomplice angle. That was clear. He thought he saw Russ trying to decide in his mind how to deal with all this from the past. He decided to push on the possibility to see what he might feel now, so many years later. "Despite the confession, Robbie offered," Stuart began, "there were some unsolved, or, better put, un-addressed, issues in what became known - as you of all people know - the Red Slippers Case."

Lewis shrugged. "It's all pointless, isn't it?"

"Come on, nobody *made* you call me. Carl's obsessed as we both know, but you're here. Are you planning to stay in the area for a while?

"That's a possibility, if I can arrange it. I'll admit I'm interested if only within limits."

"I'll write my home number on this card. Call me when you know your plans, what you decide."

Russ thanked him and put the card in his shirt pocket.

Stuart smiled. "Maybe we can arrange a visit to our 'farm'."

"I'd like that. If I can stay on a few days, maybe I'll see Philadelphia. The Liberty Bell and all that. Never had a chance, really."

Outside the coffee shop door, Russ shook hands with Stuart hesitating a second before letting go and gesturing with a nod.

Stuart stared after Russell Lewis, smiled at the turn of events, and then walked to where his car was in the office parking lot with a growing sense of excitement.

CHAPTER TWELVE
REVELATIONS

Stuart drove home thinking about how Carl had prompted Lewis to put aside everything and come to see him. No small achievement. Lewis was engaged – for sure. Where it would go from here was anyone's question, but he felt he was on the edge of a big story. Something he had wanted since settling in New Jersey besides raising horses, however much he enjoyed that aspect of his life.

Stuart and his wife had moved to New Jersey from Canada, in part because there were several well-known equestrian facilities not so far from Trenton where he and his new wife JoEllen could establish contacts with breeders and trainers. The availability also of large estate-size plots of land at reasonable prices seemed to confirm the plan as the right choice.

He had proved to be a successful counselor and the practice grew steadily. JoEllen, meanwhile, quickly found a place in banking. Their joint income with Jo Ellen's family money was enough to build the large house on Duncastle Road. And to provide the money for the horses they collected and showed at various events. But still, he feared being bored.

Stuart had included a "secret" room in their house. It was not really a secret because he sometimes showed it off to special dinner guests. Behind bookshelves on the first floor was a hidden door and steps that led up to a small "library," where Stuart kept his archive - books, articles, clippings, photographs - relating to the murder cases he explored with guests, hoping from their reactions to add to his own thoughts about what was germane to figuring out potential answers to questions left as yet unanswered by investigators.

He had only recently turned to a study of the Red Slippers Case. It excited him because it was relatively "untouched," in the sense that there were no books out about the case. He had immediately wondered *why*. Robbie had disappeared, and that added an exciting aspect to his research about why a pregnant Wendy had agreed to stay in that remote shack even for one night. There was something there, he felt sure of it. Robbie said he put her there when she arrived supposedly with all her belongings. But had she left other clues back in Cleveland? Perhaps former Sheriff Lewis would have something to tell him about these questions and other matters. What other things had he suspected at the time and ever since? Why else had he now followed Carl Peters' "instructions"?

§

Back at his motel, meanwhile, Russ Lewis stretched out on his bed to think about his first meeting with Dr. Freed. Carl had effectively set a stage, hadn't he, to produce what result? He smiled to himself at that thought. OK, he had bitten. What was next? His first impressions of Stuart Freed were of a successful counselor, with a well-run office that displayed competence and a welcoming environment. But he was surprised by Freed's investing so much about the "Red Slippers Case."

Who gave a damn anymore? Well, Carl Peters did - but anyone else? He lay there musing about their conversation. And again questioned what he was doing here. Was it because he still felt bad after all these years about his initial feelings when Carl came to identify Wendy? Hell, that was only a first reaction. And he had had no voice in what happened in court. He had no reason to feel guilty about that. "Guilty," for Christ's sake! What am I thinking? What was the point of all this? So Stanson had disappeared from Yosemite. Maybe he committed suicide. So what? To what end?

Russ was damned if he knew. On that basis, he decided he would call upon Dr. Freed at his home and let him (and Carl) down gently but for sure. Then he would get on with his life as an insurance investigator. Yes, that's what he would do.

But did he really believe himself?

§

So on the Sunday afternoon after their Friday coffee in Trenton, Russ called the phone number Freed had written on his printed business card:

"Hello."

"Dr. Freed?"

"Yes, is this Russ Lewis? And call me Stuart, please."

"I hope you don't mind the call so soon after our first meeting, but I wanted to say goodbye."

"No Russ, you can't leave without finishing our conversation, I absolutely forbid it. No, you must come to dinner - yes, come this evening. It so happens that we do not have plans, and we would be delighted to see you. I have a lot of questions to ask - that is if you don't mind. I know it's short notice, but we ought to talk whatever you finally decide."

Russ exhaled "Well, maybe we can help each other find out why Carl thinks we can work together – and to what end. I have real doubts this will lead anywhere."

"Indeed, so do I - but we ought to pool our thoughts and see where that leads. No commitments just say you'll come for dinner."

"That's really nice of you, but...

"No more arguments about it. Let us say 7 p.m., if that is ok."

Russ tried again to sound doubtful about possible collaboration on some future investigation. "Well, I wouldn't say there was too much mystery about the confession and a conviction. It was all there in front of us. All we had to do was convince Robbie to confess right away."

"Put all that aside for a minute. I'm offering you drinks and dinner. That's settled. But there were some questions about the disposition of the case I'm curious about. And if the state had not accepted the Second-Degree plea - well, the trial could have gone in some interesting directions - or would you disagree with me on that?"

"I don't know that I would, or that I wouldn't have."

"Well, we can talk about all this tonight. Look forward to our discussion."

Russ found himself surprised he had somehow agreed to come to dinner and at his next comment. "Right, so do I." He hung up feeling confused, not about his old doubts, but that he had allowed himself to yield to Stuart's coaching. He had to be careful where things were going, or this could end very badly indeed.

§

The directions Stuart gave him as they finished the conversation were simple and he had no trouble finding the house. Russ arrived just two minutes before seven. Stuart greeted him at the door and introduced JoEllen. "First, he said, let's drop the Dr. Freed. It's Stuart and JoEllen and I hope we will find out some things we both might be interested in. I've been thinking that maybe *you* might have an insight about what happened to Robbie Stanson."

Damn, Russ thought to himself. What am I doing.? What am I getting into? Has Carl plotted this all out?

CHAPTER THIRTEEN

A MEETING OF MINDS

"Now, Russ, what can I get you?" Russ felt like he had walked into a Hollywood movie set. It could be Nick and Nora Charles's apartment. All that was missing was Asta. What else was there to surprise him besides the period couches and chairs and low glass-topped coffee table?

"I'll just have a beer."

"Right, I've got a couple here. How about a Yuengling, very popular in these parts?"

"Fine."

"Bottle or glass?"

"Either."

Stuart poured the beer into an English-style pub glass. Then he fixed Rob Roys for JoEllen and himself, emptied cocktail nuts from a jar into a bowl, and sliced some salami onto a plate. Taking it all on a tray to a low coffee table, he raised his drink to offer a toast.

"To this evening's discussion. And more to come?"

Russ raised his beer with a non-committal smile.

§

Russ then asked about the horses he had seen as he drove up to the front of the house. "I saw a beautiful mare while driving down the lane to your house. It must give you a lot of pleasure being around those horses."

"Indeed, how much do you know about Arabians? We usually stable eight, but right now we're down one because some bastard shot one a few days before I heard from you. I'm trying to find out who it was and begin some sort of legal action. Another time, maybe, we'll take you out to the stable. The horses love company, particularly someone who might have an apple or carrot at hand. We supply these free of charge to our guests."

"I'd like that. How long have you been in the horse-raising business?"

"Well, it's just a hobby. This area has a lot of equestrian enthusiasts and professionals. So we had lots of help finding out where to begin. We started buying soon after we arrived here and got settled into this new house and our jobs. JoEllen's a banker in Princeton, or rather an investment counselor in a bank."

"She's Canadian, too?"

"Nope, grew up in your part of the states - Ohio. She can tell you about her buckeye background."

JoEllen took a sip of her drink and talked about Columbus and Ohio State University. "I majored in economics and finance. Luckily found a job in a bank that trained me to become an adviser - to the bank and to customers. Then they established a link with a Toronto bank and off I went - met Stuart, and here we are."

Russ nodded. "Well, that all worked out fine." Looking around the book-lined room, he asked with a smile, "Have you any special interests, besides famous murder cases?"

"Oh, yes, the usual collection of 'texts' one has to have for my work, but also lots of social history, along with books on the arts. I'm interested in how culture shapes our thinking - explains our actions maybe more than we psychologists suppose. Novels from Hawthorne to Phillip Roth about 'special people.' And of course, Scott Fitzgerald's doomed Gatsby."

He paused, watched Russ take some nuts from the bowl JoEllen passed him, then smiled in a self-deprecating way. "Maybe I'll write something one day about these cases we've talked about. When I find time, and JoEllen can support me."

"Would that include the Red Slippers? I have to admit that I've had a notion that maybe *you* pushed Carl to get me intrigued."

"No, I did not set Carl on you." He smiled. "I've met him a couple of times, and he is a determined man. Maybe too much so." Stuart frowned and repeated, "maybe too much so, yes, but he has reasons." He paused.

"Yeah, I had wondered also if you had talked with other people." Russ looked straight at Stuart. (It had somehow occurred to Russ, given what he knew about Robbie's attempt at a career as a counselor that – maybe he had talked with Robbie at some point) Russ went on. "But you haven't told me exactly what all you proposed in that seminar paper?"

"I argued for the presence of an accomplice. I haven't gone beyond that into possible planning of the crime."

"That sure might stir up someone."

"You were there on the scene, Russ. Who do you think that might be?"

"You mean besides Carl?"

"Well, Carl for sure... and the accomplice."

"Of course the accomplice. I met someone at the seminar who was in school with Stanson. And he almost warned me about that. Well, I don't know that he meant to warn me, exactly, but he did say if such a person existed, he'd be pretty upset at the possibility of being revealed after all these years of worrying about just that possibility - no matter how slightly involved he might of been in the actual crime."

§

"But," Stuart then shifted the topic trying to suggest another way of looking for other interested parties waiting for answers, "still, you were not entirely happy with the prosecutor's decision?"

"Not at the time, no. I thought Robbie was a pretty shrewd operator, with a very good defense attorney. But I thought we had a good case for premeditation."

"Especially if you had found evidence of an accomplice?"

"Yes"

"But you had no opportunity to investigate that angle, and no say in the decision to accept the plea?"

"No, but I hadn't found anything to confirm Robbie's version – absolutely no evidence the crime had been committed in that shack."

"So perhaps we have our answer to why you're here tonight?"

"What do you mean?"

"If I'm right in positing an accomplice – everyone would be interested, Carl for sure... the accomplice... and Robbie." So when you received Carl's letter in the mail, you were ready to follow-up after all these years. And that maybe, even, you believe Robbie Stanson is alive and having erased the past so-to-speak, has found a new life."

"Something like that, sure, but Stuart, please, I'm not looking to be psychoanalyzed - if that's what you're trying to do here." He went on. "Maybe Stuart it's you who has the biggest obsession with the case? I've moved on - a long time ago."

"But I've explained that it is part of my ongoing interest in unsolved murder cases. I treat them as I treat patients, as something to be explained that might help us to understand. And you came to me because you have been led to believe I have special knowledge by Carl. So it all comes together. We may be able to help one another - while avoiding the pitfalls of being led on by someone with an obvious obsession."

§

Russ put down his beer and stared at it for a second before replying. "You put it as if I shared some feeling with Carl that justice had not been done. That's putting it too strongly. I wasn't looking to get re-involved in the case. But ok, maybe I was startled, surprised might be the word - or puzzled. And a little interested, but not let's get ahead of ourselves. I'm not one to be manipulated about a situation that's likely bound to be a dead-end. And even if there is something out there to find, I'm not sure it's worth it. You can't go around seeking to right all the wrongs."

"Sure, agreed, Russ. But . . . Well, let's start with that day the court accepted Stanson's plea, and the judge handed down the sentence. Did anyone contact you that day, ask your opinion, criticize the outcome?"

"No."

"So no one contacted you at all about the case?"

"Nope."

"Not even Carl? And you haven't followed up on stories about Robbie's disappearance?"

"Well, sure I was curious for a while, especially – as you no doubt are thinking—the disappearance might be a convenient escape from the past. I thought about it a little, but no leads turned up so he is presumed dead."

"Yes, you could say a convenient escape for Robbie from Carl's wrath." What he thought but did not say was that Stuart's paper on an accomplice raised new issues – new dangers. – for Robbie, yes, a reason to stay disappeared, and – most intriguing of all! – for an accomplice to now start worrying his identity was about to be revealed. And who else knew that? Carl. If they did not work together, Carl was sure to pursue the idea. And then what?

Neither one said all this, whatever their thoughts. But they decided on one more meeting before Russ returned to his home base.

CHAPTER FOURTEEN

DECISIONS

Russ arrived the next Tuesday night at the Freed's precisely at 5:30. Stuart greeted him at the door and then they took a short ride to the stable in his pick-up. Inside, they walked from stall to stall and Russ could not but be impressed by his host's affection for each of the animals. He encouraged him to feed several of the horses the apples he had brought along for their tour. When they left for the house it seemed clear that he would have stayed longer if not for his guest.

"I sometimes feel I can communicate with the horses better than my patients," Freed quipped with a half-grin as they got back into the pick-up. But Russ took him seriously and noted it down in the back of his mind. When they got back to the front door, Stuart said that JoEllen was out with some clients but had left dinner to be warmed up whenever they wanted a break from crime to cuisine – as she had told her husband.

"But first," announced Stuart with a sly smile, "before even drinks – if you can wait a bit – I want to share with you a little secret, my special hideaway." He touched a wall light and a door in the wall swung open. Behind one of the bookcases in the large room where they had pre-dinner drinks the previous Sunday there was a stairway. Stuart led the way up these stairs to a room above the main floor. On all the walls were covers from old-style detective magazines. There were covers with photographs of two corpses – "The Minister and the Choir Lady." There was another with a man holding an infant on a ladder – "The Crime of the Century." Another depicted the gang assassination of New Jersey crime figure "Legs Diamond." In front of him was the last cover with a graphic artist's rendition of Wendy in a night dress shielding herself with an arm from an unseen assailant –"The Red Slippers."

"Wow," said Russ. "How'd you find all these?"

"Not too difficult, actually, there are specialty antique stores where lots of 'em turn up in collections."

"Another hobby, then. I expect it's cheaper than collecting Arabian horses."

"That's for sure. But all of these cases have, to a greater or lesser degree, an ongoing trail of would-be 'Sherlocks' or 'J. Edgars.' There's just as much or more mystery from true crime as fiction. And the legends that grow up in the stories about the crimes, even in these early depictions create their own 'reality.' People who imagine they know 'what really happened that night.' And it goes on without end. That's the main reason for collecting. It gets me inside the heads of people just like those who come to see me – not criminals – but seemingly cursed in one way or another."

"Well, that's a strange way of putting what you do. I never thought of psychiatrists that way."

"Well, how about the term 'shrinks.' Doesn't that imply what we do? Putting things in perspective might be another way of describing the effort to unburden people suffering all sorts of tortures mentally."

"But don't you encounter people who really did 'do it,' and just want some sort of self-justification?"

"Of course, but that gets us into other realms involving questions of crime and punishment, civic duties versus doctor-patient obligations and all the rest of it." Stuart seemed to be trying to convey what he had set out to do in the Red Slippers case as some sort of special counseling.

Whatever, it left Russ puzzled about who that was supposed to be. Still, he answered, "Yes, I can see that – and especially from my perspective. I suppose I'm both glad and sorry about the limits of my role in the case. I met Robbie. It was a vicious crime that would have come out in detail at a trial."

"It hasn't ended for Carl Peters." Stuart smiled at Russ. "He's pretty intense and sometimes uses unconventional means of getting attention." Stuart held out a hand and pointed him to a chair next to a roll-top desk. "This desk belonged to a private detective the defense hired in the Lindbergh Case."

§

"Another big find besides magazine covers, I guess."

"Russ, I've got lots else to show you. All those filing cabinets on that wall have documents and articles about the cases. They range from short notes to essay-length theories." He paused.

Russ nodded. "I suppose so."

Then Stuart continued. "I gave that paper at the Philadelphia seminar on old cases, some deemed solved, others not or only partially so." He left that hanging in the air, waiting for a response.

Russ took him up on what he seemed to be saying in a kind of code. "Do you know something about Stanson nobody else does?"

"Not really" - he hesitated. "Yes, might as well say what I think has caused Peters' effort to push us together. The paper was about an unnamed accomplice." He waited for a reaction. Then he went on. "And, I'm fishing here. From everything I've read the hurry to get the damned thing resolved stands out – the confession solved lots of people's problems. It ruled out an accomplice. I think you had some ideas." He paused again. "You couldn't do much once the prosecutor made his decision not to pursue the investigation."

"True, but I didn't see anything conclusive at the time. I keep telling you that. And besides what difference does it make if Robbie is dead or alive? He can't be punished anymore, can he?"

"Right, *he* can't be." Again a pause. "But even if such an accomplice could not be convicted after all these years, his life could be ruined." Another pause. "And Carl Peters would have some satisfaction."

"Whoa! This is all getting over-the-top speculative. And I'm not sure I want to go on a fishing expedition that might wind up with accusations (unfounded accusations) that could really mess up someone's life. What does 'accomplice' really mean here? I know from experience that unfounded accusations, or coerced cooperation, or - well lots of things - can play havoc with essentially innocent parties who have lived with such a mistake for decades. That might be the case and you will be messing with another person's life. Pretty serious stuff, Stuart."

He looked at Stuart like he sometimes looked at a dubious claimant, putting the onus on him to provide a satisfactory answer to his doubts.

Stuart shrugged, and smiled. "But that's what we're dealing with - speculations. Yes, at the time as well as now – but when you get to thinking about it?" Once again he paused. "And, Russ, this was your first murder case, right?"

"Go on."

"What about the forensics? What turned up in that old shack?"

"Well, it wasn't the best place to find any prints, especially given the methods then."

"But did you find any forensic evidence *at all* that proved or even indicated Wendy spent a night in that shack and was actually killed there - after having had sex remember?"

"No, still..."

"And no one - no one - saw them there for two days? Even in Robbie's statement, there was just a someone - but likely, I think, made up."

Russ demurred and waited, and Stuart accepted the challenge: "Was that likely? What made you think - and accept - that premise?"

Still there was no response, but Stuart was hitting hard on points that had bothered Russ from the start. The only thing he had was that one student who was "making out" in a car parked on the road and recalled seeing some lights like a flashlight.

"And you had put the idea into Robbie's head by taking him there, right?"

Russ hated hearing all his doubts thrown back at him this way.

Stuart went on. "But you had the confession that was going to preempt the defense from launching a plea of temporary insanity, right?"

"Yes, O.K."

"Could not there be someone else today who has learned about my paper and ongoing research? But unlike Peters he wants me to stop my researches."

"You mean an accomplice fearing being revealed all these years. And I suppose you think killing your horse was to warn you that he was on watch. Another big speculation, Stuart. My God. I don't think that is at all clear."

"Of course not, but the timing's right. If Peters knew that I was pursuing the question of an accomplice, so could someone else, despite all the promises of confidentiality at the seminar."

There was a funny feeling creeping around Russ's stomach that this was going in a strange direction. What did he know about Stuart Freed? Did he really believe

Stanson disappeared because he feared disclosure after all these years about an accomplice or for some other reason? The case had left him dissatisfied, but he was far from eager to see it re-opened; besides, he told himself, things could end up in a worse way for everyone still alive - including Carl Peters. He also began to think - of all things! - that maybe Stuart was manipulating *Peters* in a cruel way.

Russ was right - up to a point. Stuart was holding back two things in this narrative, one, he had been in constant communication with Carl Peters when he started serious research, and two, he had actually once tried to contact Robbie. At that time Stuart had said in a letter that he simply wanted an interview, crazy as that might sound now – or then. But maybe now someone else knew all about his "speculations" and intentions.

§

Russ had been looking at Stuart for several seconds, then decided to play along with the warning signal idea. "I would take the shooting of your horse seriously – but I don't know if it has anything to do with your researches or any plans you might have to publish it."

"Oh, I think that is the case."

"Well," continued Russ still playing down the coincidence. "Perhaps then you should bring in the State Police. The horse shooting would certainly come under some issue of law enforcement, wouldn't it? And they would have resources that you and I don't."

"Yes, but where would that rank amidst all the stuff they have to deal with? I can't see them putting too much effort – even if they agreed to try – into finding out what this is really about. And how would one even prove that the shooter was sending a message at this stage? You aren't at all convinced, and I admit I am getting pretty far ahead. Just a feeling, I admit. But stranger things have happened."

Russ remained unconvinced. But he would continue to play along -up to a point. "People don't usually kill beautiful horses simply by mistake, I will agree. It would appear, if you are right, there are people -or only one person- seeking to discourage you."

"Well, maybe that's a good reason for you to stay with me on this until we know a little more about where it's all supposed to lead."

"Maybe, by the same token, it's time for me to exit."

"Don't be too hasty about that. I think there's a good chance we can work together. Give it a couple of days at least until we see if there is a next move. Then decide. If or when that happens we can have another conversation, or you can bow out."

Russ looked at one of the pictures on the wall behind Stuart's desk for several seconds. Then he nodded and rose from his chair.

"We'll leave it at that. You know where I am staying."

"I'll show you the way out."

Russ smiled at the (maybe) unintended message in that comment. He was not going to 'play along' with something Carl Peters and Stuart Freed might have been working up in secret, something that they would spring on him. He was very uneasy where this was all leading. He hated his sense of being manipulated.

CHAPTER FIFTEEN

A LETTER TO STUART FREED

A letter arrived two days later at Stuart's office. There was no return address. It had been mailed from New Brunswick.

Mr. Freed,

I think it is time for us to negotiate about the future. Before you go any further.

I will be in touch!

Stuart stared at the letter for a long time. It might not be connected to the shooting of his horse and might be a hoax. Yet, hadn't one of his listeners at the seminar asked if he weren't afraid that the supposed accomplice might wish to take action to stop him from pursuing his research? That had been why he had pushed Russ on the shooting coincidence. The questioner had raised it in a somewhat joking manner, but now Stuart wondered if that might not be so, indeed if the questioner might have special knowledge. What was his name? He couldn't remember his name. It had been a large meeting that night, over twenty showed up. He had not spoken with them all.

This was serious. If Stuart had found out the name of the supposed accomplice (which he hadn't yet) the full danger to that person was one of exposure for a man likely with a family and successful career, all put in peril, a life ruined after years of worry about that very possibility Had the accomplice himself written this note, and what did he mean to do next?

There was yet another possibility. This correspondent, he speculated, might even be Robbie himself! Not likely, of course, but he had not been found. If alive he might (or certainly, would) not want the case re-opened. But how would he have known about the seminar? The permutations were almost endless, leading off to infinity like sitting in the barber chair when he was a youngster, staring into a mirror across the room which reflected not only him facing the mirror, but a mirror in the back of his head which reflected his face and on and on.

But most likely it was the accomplice or someone associated with him. This person (the accomplice) might *even have killed Robbie himself* - to get rid of one threat of exposure. Now, that was something to consider! This man had lived all these years fearing exposure. Now he wanted, actually was desperate, to get out from under that danger even if Robbie was dead – and, of course, - especially, if he had killed him.

While he was scared, he had to admit he was excited at what his research had - or might have - stimulated. But how to handle this new communication? The first thing to do was to contact Russ, explain that he had received a message. And try to find out if someone had contacted him as well. He didn't think that was likely, but... nothing was likely, and yet it happened, and was happening.

§

Lewis, on the other hand, had almost concluded that Freed knew something about what had happened to Robbie, or something else that would be dangerous to someone. But to whom? He would have to wait to see what that might be. Clearly, there were things Russ did not know. He sure as hell wasn't going to get deeper into this production until he understood a lot more about who was behind the controls.

This was a strange outcome for something that had called him from his office on a Saturday morning two decades earlier. A new ending? Was he now being forced to protect Stuart from an accomplice, or even Robbie? The only way to start finding out what was real was to set up another meeting and force some answers out of Stuart. Yet it was also possible there weren't any answers – just Carl Peters' ongoing anguish.

§

"Stuart, it's Russ."

"Yes, Russ, have you heard anything?"

"No, how about you?"

"I got an anonymous note yesterday. And I think we should meet to talk about what to do. Doesn't that make the shooting of my horse more suspicious?"

"Maybe. That was pretty quick - almost too quick, Stuart." He did not try to hide the skeptical feeling he had about the psychologist's "tales" of mysterious communications. Did he send the letter to himself?

"Yes, I would have to agree - but there it is. Do you want to see me or not?"

"Oh, yes, I agree we need to sort out a lot of things."

§

At four-thirty that afternoon they met in the same coffee shop where they had initiated their conversations about the murder. Russ wondered what the other customers might be thinking about these two men who sat in a back booth. It seemed like a long time after the waitress had put down their coffee before either spoke - at least it did to Russ. Then he sat back, putting his cup down on the saucer and looked up at Stuart with a slight nod.

Stuart began. "I think I better tell you some more things, probably some things you might have guessed, and maybe some you have not."

Russ knitted his brows just slightly in anticipation of what was coming next. "I have a little confession to make, Russ."

CHAPTER SIXTEEN

THE WHOLE STORY?

"Here's the whole story," began Stuart. "I never actually met Robbie Stanson, but I corresponded briefly with him after he got out of prison- that is, I wrote asking for an interview. I could not be sure about the 'Red Slippers' case. It seemed to have elements of both a crime of passion in the moment and something planned ahead. The question of an accomplice had occurred to me. I admit that I did not tell Robbie my whole purpose in the letter, only that I hoped I could gain his trust enough so that he would at least be willing to write to me, and maybe meet me."

"Why in the world would he want to do that – especially so soon after he got out of prison?"

"Yes, well that was the question, wasn't it? From what I had learned about the case in the articles – it was pretty well covered across the nation for a short time – I knew that Stanson had been a pre-theological student before the crime, or claimed that he was, and that when he left prison ten years later he planned on finishing his undergraduate degree and going to graduate school in psychology. I wondered, of course, how he was going to get into any American graduate school. And being Canadian, I guess I thought I might have some good advice to offer."

"Oh, how was that?" Russ could hardly believe what he was hearing. "Did you suggest he change his name? Create a new identity? That would take some doing. And you were offering your help. Didn't that put your own career in danger?"

"Well, maybe so - we didn't get that far. We didn't get anywhere, in fact, but now he knew about my interest and had my address."

"How did you know where to write?"

"I wrote him at his parents' address, offering advice on graduate school and maybe implying *(he winced at this confession)* I would try to help find him a position afterwards."

"But there was some connection – later?"

"Yes, he wrote me from Yosemite years later. He said he wanted to see me out there if I could make it. He signed the letter with another name. Roger Sullivan. It said nothing about the case, just a note saying he would be pleased to see me and leaving his address at the lodge."

Russ waited for what he thought would come next. Stuart looked at him for several seconds. "I never got the letter – at least not in time. I was away that summer, and by the time I received his response, it was too late. I wrote back to the lodge where he had been staying. But my letter got bounced back."

Russ did not think for a minute that Freed had completely leveled with him. There was no way to tell – not yet, at least. "Jesus," he said, shaking his head. "OK, let's go from there. What did you have to offer him at that point? Better put, if he was planning to disappear, why in the world would he write you?"

"I have no idea - but people go back and forth about such decisions, don't they? My old offer of help might somehow have triggered an idea in his mind."

§

Freed's next statement leaped ahead in a sort of confession. "Probably I hoped to get a book out of Robbie's story. The psychological angle on a real-life story about a teen romance that ended in tragedy. By all accounts Robbie had been a normal teenager, the only thing his defense lawyer brought up when he thought that they would send him for a mental evaluation to the state hospital was that he had been hit in the head playing baseball. It never came to that when the prosecution agreed to accept the guilty plea to Second Degree murder. I wondered from the beginning about outside pressure. Did you think about that possibility? You probably had more contact with Robbie and his lawyer and family than anyone during this period?"

"I said I always thought Robbie was a very clever guy. Not quite clever enough maybe, and maybe more self-deceived than he realized."

Russ was thinking that Stuart was way out of his league. He had no idea about what Robbie was capable of. "Other students who had a chance to observe him told me that he had a very hot temper. But no one talked about black-outs, or anything like that. I did think our prosecutor could have dealt with the temporary incapacity stuff – had he really wanted to. So I don't put the outcome down to Robbie's cleverness. He had a good lawyer. It was over before it began, which is what the folks at Bashford College wanted. But look, he was young..."

Stuart could not resist interrupting. "Why didn't he then? I mean the prosecutor, why didn't he choose to battle it out - in your opinion."

"I just said. They didn't want a murder one trial, none of them. For a lot of reasons. And among them near the top was a concern it would hurt the college's reputation."

§

Despite his frustration with Stuart's problematic theorizing about the past, Russ even picked up the thread. "I still remember Robbie posing for pictures at the door of the prison, his arms full of books, talking about how much time he would have to study. Hell, he acted for all the world as if he had already redeemed himself in the eyes of the court – and even public opinion – and was, therefore, only waiting for everyone to 'forgive' him his trespasses. I drove away from the prison that day thinking Robbie believed he was a celebrity on a long road tour. And even when he got caught driving around Columbus in the prison van – even then – even after he spent time in solitary and was 'fired' from his flower-gathering job – his parole went through on the first try."

"Well," said Stuart, "I think we are dealing with someone who may be the accomplice or a friend, someone who wants to protect his identity. Someone who could have been there at the seminar even!"

They sat there staring at one another with Russ marveling at Stuart's agility, like a bullfrog leaping from one lily pad to the next. But he had to admit that some of it made sense.

"Yes, the accomplice would not want you to write anything that might expose what he had believed had been forever buried."

"I talked to Wendy's brother" Stuart now began on a yet a new path. "Several months ago I contacted him. He didn't seem upset about any plans I had, indeed encouraged them and he told me he had later hired an investigator to find out what had happened out at Yosemite. She came back with a report that the trail had gone dead at that point."

"Obviously, he's engaged. That's why he wrote me about you." Russ went on. "The new letter writer obviously has a different purpose - to discourage any more speculation."

CHAPTER SEVENTEEN
KENT'S SOLILOQUY

Kent Crider sat in his office looking out over the Schuykill river. The last few weeks had been a terrible strain, ever since that night of the seminar. He was not an official member, God forbid, and had only been invited a few times by a lawyer friend, Sterling Wheeler. He had often said no, because he had no wish to hear anybody re-open old cases. But his friend kept after him, apparently with the notion that he needed to get out of the rut of corporate mergers.

"Oh, c'mon, Kent," Sterling had argued, "get into something exciting for a few hours." Sterling kept pushing. "You went to Bashford, didn't you? Freed's supposed to talk about a murder on campus. Hell, you probably met the killer! Not a very big school is it?" Kent could not say no, now could he? "You should meet this guy, really. He wants to do a book apparently. Maybe you could help him with background."

Help him with background! Kent had only one desire now: to discourage Freed from writing anything about the Red Slippers case that suggested the idea of an accomplice. But how? Robbie had promised him – many times – that he would never get mentioned, let alone identified. The last time was when Robbie told him about letters from a psychologist trying to pump him for information just before he was fired from the clinic and went to Yosemite. Carl Peters had never stopped chasing him, and now this other person. So that was Stuart Freed? And was the *information* he wanted from Robbie about an accomplice, the subject of his seminar paper. That had been some time ago.

He had not contacted Kent for a long time. But he doubted Robbie was dead. What a strange turn of events. Kent had now seen for himself the threat Stuart Freed posed. Jesus! As he sat there that night, he looked around the room as if searching to know if these would be Sherlocks realized who was actually there sitting right beside them.

Some were taking notes and adding exclamation points and question marks. He tried hard not to look too carefully at what any of them was writing down. One man had uncapped a fountain pen, a relic from old trials surely, and Kent could not help staring. He even wondered if his face was red.

His mind leapt to the aftermath – the possible aftermath of this evening. What if Robbie's body was now found somewhere? Would that set off a new round of speculations? And Freed would be more than ready to join in the fun.

He also had to consider the possibility that Freed had contacted Russ Lewis. In fact, someone asked in the question period if Freed had tried to contact the man who had taken down Stanson's words whether the sheriff had suspected there was an accomplice? "Not yet," came the answer, "but of course I will – soon." Freed then told the questioner he had always thought that Lewis, who had talked with Robbie more than anyone else, might be the key to unlocking the final mystery of the missing accomplice. He ended the evening with that tantalizing "clue" to strong applause.

§

Kent had seen Lewis in town during the investigation corralling groups of students. He tried to guess what was going through his mind. But there was no outward sign during those days he was hunting for an accomplice. But what if he had it figured wrong? Then and now? After all, Lewis could add stuff to Dr. Freed's proposed book – authentic conversations with Robbie. He could even make stuff up if he wanted. But he doubted if Lewis was that kind of person. Still, the former sheriff might like it if a book came out featuring him as the man who got Robbie to confess - and suspected all along an accomplice? He did not know if any of this was so, but now he had to worry.

He had kept watch as best he could on Freed's office after that night at the seminar and lucked out - if that was the right word - and was shocked to see Russ Lewis with Freed leave Freed's office and go together to that coffee shop. He had been just outside trying to get up the courage to confront Freed with a story about the supposed harm re-opening old wounds with a publication about some supposed accomplice that more than likely was not true and how it could harm an innocent person accused of aiding and abetting a horrible crime decades ago. If Robbie was dead that might work. What would he have said, though? He would have had to admit more than he had just been a student at Bashford. Lewis hadn't changed all that much since he had last seen him so long ago, and Kent quickly dodged out of sight when they came out of the elevator.

He had not planned out what to say, in any event. He certainly did not want to make a threat, but what was his option? Therefore, it was lucky he had not seen Freed alone and said something stupid. It gave him time to think about a better plan than open confrontation. He had been a fool to even think about confronting Freed in person.

But there was something else: when Robbie disappeared, Wendy's brother had hired an investigator. Stuart talked about that briefly in his paper, without saying anything more. He had put it very cleverly something like he "had heard" Wendy's brother was following out some new lines of inquiry with a professional investigator. He did not know if that person was still looking. He was concerned that "brief" fraternity connection to Robbie at Bashford College might eventually – if it had not already happened – put that investigator on his trail. He could only hope on that score that his old fraternity brothers would take seriously their obligations to the brotherhood in the YITB stuff. "Yours in the Bond." Well, how many of them even remembered he had been Robbie's "Little Brother"? It had only been for a short time, for Christ's sake, just September - one month. If they did remember, would they want to talk about it now to a stranger and bring down a scandal on the house? Of course not. Well maybe someone would. It all looked problematic - if not worse. And he was the one with the most - hell, everything to lose.

How did he really plan to prevent any of this? His friend who told him about the seminar and invited him to come had no idea of his connection to the case, or even that he had ever known Robbie in college.

§

He could not stop thinking about what could happen. It might even be worse if Robbie were dead – and Freed knew that for sure! He could say all sorts of things about the "true" history of the case and make Kent central to the murder. He might. So, had Robbie communicated with Freed? He had told Kent he had not responded to his overture. Maybe so. He was not sure he knew.

Once again it all came back. That night was the worst six hours of his life. When he came back to the dorm room there Robbie was. Wendy was on the bed in her nightgown, not moving. Robbie was sitting with his head in his hands. He wasn't crying. Just sitting there.

Kent had gone over and over every word that they said time and again over the years. Robbie had begun as if he didn't know:

"Is she dead, Is she dead?"

"Robbie, I don't know. What happened?"

"She said she was going to tell my parents."

"Tell them what."

"That she was pregnant, and that we had planned all this so that they would have to allow us to get married."

I just looked at him. Then Robbie put his hand on my arm:

"Don't worry, Kent, we'll get out of this."

I was stunned:

"We'll get out of this, we'll get out of this? What the Hell do you mean?"

"This is your room. All we have to do is to get her out of here."

"What do you mean! Where are you going to put her? She's dead."

"Yes, but no one knows she came to see me."

"What are you talking about – how do you know that?"

"I told her not to tell anyone. It was part of 'our' plan."

"Plan? You didn't tell me anything about a plan – just that Wendy was coming down to see you – and you were planning to let her down gently that it was time for both of you to move on. I wondered about that, but you didn't seem worried about how she would take it. Holy Jesus! Now I think you were planning on this all the time – and expecting I would help you get rid of the body. And you don't even know whether she really kept the trip a secret."

"Of course she did. Didn't I just tell you?"

"You told me, but I don't believe it for a second, and I damned sure don't believe she came down here without letting someone in on her plans – especially if she was pregnant."

"Well, that's not the immediate issue we have to deal with tonight. We have to get her somewhere that she won't be found."

"You really are crazy. What do you mean 'We have to get her somewhere'? I didn't do this. I don't want anything to do with it. All I said was you could have my room for a couple of nights and I would stay at the fraternity house. That's all I said. Christ, that's all I said. I just helped you pick her up downtown when she came. I did wonder about where you told her to meet you.

Little brother you are going to have to help me now, and I promise I won't say anything, if trouble does come, about how you helped out."

"If trouble comes – if trouble comes? You really are nuts."

"What choice do you have? As you said this is your room. Maybe we both had sex with her, who knows? But I promise I won't say anything. I'll say she stayed somewhere else – if it comes to that – and I got mad when she told me she'd been seen and just lost my head. No one will know she stayed here. I promise. But you've got to help me now."

All these years had passed since that night, but he never forgot every word from that conversation, or what followed after they got Wendy to the car. Oh, my God, what happened then.

But he could not think about that right now. He had to think what to do next to ward off disaster.

This much was clear: Robbie was still threatening his life, if from beyond the grave. What now?

Clearly, he must stop Freed one way or another.

CHAPTER EIGHTEEN

A NEW LETTER

The next letter to Freed arrived at the end of the week. It was typewritten in bold letters. There was no salutation.

I am writing to you at this time to make clear the dangers ahead should you decide to go ahead with any project connected to the 'Red Slippers' case. Perhaps you believe that justice was not done with the sentence handed down by the court. You may also feel that a shocking injustice was done when Stanson was granted parole. I might feel the same way. Or you may believe there were other questions left unanswered. Or you simply wonder what else there is to learn about what happened. I suspect you hope to profit – one way or another from bringing this story 'up to date.' You should be aware that I am not the only one that you need to be concerned about.

I will call your office Tuesday at four p.m. giving the name James Polk. We can discuss what to do about this situation. I am also prepared to offer you a financial settlement to, as it were, cease and desist.

§

Freed read this letter and now realized more than he had ever admitted to himself that he had gotten into a very deep situation. There were numerous studies available about hidden violent tendencies in young adults and the Red Slippers murder seemed to offer another fine case study of how they manifest themselves under pressure The thought that there might have been a third party present had not come to him immediately as he had looked into the circumstances surrounding Wendy Peters' murder. It emerged only as he tried to figure out Wendy's complete trust in Robbie, as if she had been comfortable engaging in sex with him that last time, and certainly not as if she had been stuck in a shack for all that time with no drinking water or toilet facilities. She certainly would have resisted such a plan. Of course, that was only what he had concluded. He had no inside info about her state of mind.

Yet it was only Robbie's self-serving statements to the press after he confessed that suggested her willingness to do that. Had Lewis gotten the whole truth? There had been no trial, no testimony, no cross-examination. And Robbie could not be tried again, whether dead or alive. But someone who was near, someone who agreed to allow Robbie a place for comfortable sex, would have calmed her down once she had reached West River. Stuart had hinted at that in the paper he presented - and more than hinted in the discussion afterwards. If still alive Robbie was beyond prosecution, if not free from Carl Peters' determination to seek justice according to his ideas of retribution. Someone who was there that night, however, or heard about the paper was in much greater danger of exposure and what would follow, perhaps actually from Carl Peters, obviously, but equally or more so from public shame if not from actual legal action.

§

And there were some things that Stuart had kept to himself, or even kept from himself might be a better way of saying it. He had long suspected that Robbie's difficulty in setting up a practice was all to do with Carl Peters. He had no proof that Peters was doing this, but he fully suspected that might be the case.

When Freed had contacted Carl Peters, after Robbie's disappearance, he found Wendy's brother full of suspicion that he was another of those who - to his way of thinking - almost blamed the victim for putting herself in harm's way. But over the course of the conversation Stuart had convinced him that he was on to something,

Stuart had sent him a copy, when it was ready, of his planned talk at the Philadelphia seminar.

First the response to the seminar, and now Carl's letter to Russ had brought together a surprising new urgency in the quest for answers - and alarmed someone enough to propose a "buyout."

§

Stuart had canceled all appointments for Tuesday afternoon and sent his secretary home saying he had some case files to review before they got out of hand. The phone rang at precisely four p.m. Stuart picked it up on the second ring. "Good afternoon, Dr. Freed."

Stuart replied curtly as if it was a nuisance call, "I'm not at all sure we have anything to say to each other. You killed one of my horses, and …."

"Oh, but we do. We can settle that strange notion, because I didn't kill anything of yours. Compared to your real problems that is a minor incident. You must be really scared about where your actions have led to think me guilty of doing such a thing. You should be concerned about what you are doing, because you have no idea of the consequences for innocent persons. I intended to get your attention, but not that way."

The caller went on. "You are right about one thing we are at only the beginning if you choose to pursue your unwise plan. Please believe me when I say we are both in a precarious position."

The caller paused. Then decided he would try to make Freed understand how it had all happened, and the possible consequences for his "friend, someone totally innocent of wishing to do harm - or hold up punishment for Wendy's killer."

Stuart said nothing, waiting.

"Well, I could go on but obviously you wish me to put the matter in simple, easy to understand, terms. I am going to appeal to your sense of justice. I know that sounds funny, perhaps, but you are a trained counselor and should understand the uncertainties of college life to a person three months out of high school, with nobody close to talk to. How much do you know about the college fraternity system, Dr. Freed?"

"I know generally, of course, but I assume you are talking about Bashford College in the early 1950s. And, you will not be surprised that I had wondered about some connection. There was Robbie's confession statement that he had been driving around with a friend hours before Wendy arrived in West River. And then there was the suitcase outside the stadium."

"Correct, and some fraternity relations among the 'brothers' were, to put it simply, 'coercive.' This was especially true of the system of 'little brothers.' Most often, or at least very often, new pledges – those on a sort of provisional membership, the not-yet initiated, mostly first-year students, had no voice as to who would be their 'big brothers.' Little brothers were expected to treat their big brothers with deference and a sense of obligation. Big brothers were not so much protectors, because all the pledges were subject to general hazing. Do you get the situation so far?"

"Yes."

"Well now add to it that the early 1950s were a transition period in lots of ways. When Robbie came to Bashford there were still seniors who were World War II vets studying there with funding from the GI Bill of Rights. Do you know about that?"

"Yes, generally. A government payback for having served in the war."

"Right, and you should also understand that these veteran students remained somewhat aggrieved about the 'youngsters' who had just started college – boys who had not spent two or three years risking their lives overseas. In fact, the pledge master at Robbie's fraternity – a kind of hazer-in-chief – was one of these veterans. In a few more years that would die down, and then in the 1960s things began to change rapidly. But at the time I was in college some pretty strange things happened. Really strange."

"So this is all leading up to your involvement, right?"

"I didn't say that, and I think you should be very careful about what you say from now on."

"So that's a threat."

"Understand it as you may, an appeal or something else."

§

Stuart took a deep breath. "I don't see where you are going with all this except that you are really afraid that I will identify *you* as an unindicted accomplice."

"That's one conclusion. I don't say it's true. But if it were you should understand the dangerous situation you find yourself in."

"But, surely, you must have thought someone sooner or later would postulate an accomplice. There were – or better put, are - plenty of reasons to think so. Surely some professional, like the person Wendy's brother has hired would start asking himself the questions that weren't asked in 1953. I gather you must know about that?"

He hoped this last comment would indicate that the caller had been there that night at the seminar, and that he at least knew what he looked like.

183

"Possibly so."

Freed was now sure that his caller had been there the night of the seminar, because that information had come in the question period! "Yes, all right, but with Robbie missing – likely dead – anything a 'third' party might write would only be speculation, and I had no intention of mentioning names. Certainly, there would be no case in law."

"I can't decide, Stuart, whether you are really that obtuse, or whether you think I am some sort of fool. I don't think it actually is either one. But what other choice is there? Let me be plain. However your plan to write a sensational new take on a decades-old murder case took shape, it would be bad for a presumed accomplice. Suspicion could fall on anyone - not just a 'Little Brother.' And now that Robbie is missing you can say anything you want about that person's role." All of a sudden, the caller dropped the hypothetical accomplice language, and laid claim to being the person. "Truth was, if it mattered then (or now), I was a fall guy. I now know that - actually knew it at the time. I fell for Robbie's display of anguish and regret. He just needed me to help him get rid of the body."

"Why didn't you say that at the time?"

"Oh, for God's sake! How is it you have any patients? I really think you may be an obtuse idiot. What was I going to say? I wasn't going to ruin my future. I didn't kill anybody. Robbie had no incentive to bring me into the courtroom scene, as I already explained, because it would destroy his post-confession plea. He wanted nothing to do with exposing my role."

"You mean you really think your secret was safe with him?"

"How many times do I have to tell you that Robbie could not expose me without bringing down real trouble for himself."

"But you can't be tried twice for the same crime."

"We're going in circles, Freed, let's stop and figure out what we are going to do. The first thing is that you are *not* going to write anything about the case."

Freed continued to play it like the caller was his patient. "Someone else might come along and decide to do it. Someone who was there that night at the seminar. You can't intimidate everyone who might be curious. And besides, another person has become involved, and brought in-Russ Lewis."

"If that is the case, and if Carl Peters is messing around, the only person I can imagine who would mess around in this way - you need to discourage him. At this point in my life, I simply can't tolerate any questioning of what I did or didn't do that night. Have I made it clear enough?"

"Perhaps I should turn everything over to the police, including now your threats. I'm sure Russ would agree with that."

"No, no. That is exactly why I think you really have to consider what I might be capable of if you put me in an exposed position. I am willing to pay you a fair sum, say $25,000 not to publish."

"Well, that's a new take on blackmail!"

"It doesn't matter what you or I call it."

"How do you know I haven't recorded this conversation?"

"I don't but think about everything and all that you have to lose. I'll be in touch."

§

When Stuart put down the phone it came home to him really for the first time how deeply involved he had become. Of course, the caller might not even have been the supposed accomplice postulated in his seminar presentation. Indeed, there might not even have been such a person! Somebody could be playing with him – like straight out of a movie thriller. Stuart had not gotten far in his researching of Robbie's friends back at Bashford. He had not expected to be able to name anyone in his re-examination of the case. But now he understood that didn't make any difference. All the other cases he had explored were old, too old for anyone alive to be put at risk. There were people still around who would certainly remember and put a name to the mystery accomplice. It gave him a thrill to think about that. But... if the accomplice was scared enough, then? But how could he dare risk exposure by doing something to stop Stuart? Killing Stuart might only increase "X's" chances of exposure, but did he think much beyond eliminating an immediate threat? Then he realized that psychoanalysis of his phone caller wasn't much use.

§

The first question was what to tell Russ about the phone call. There was this: the caller was obviously not as smooth an operator as he sounded, or tried to sound, on the telephone. He had sounded scared. Whatever he did now would make it very difficult to keep his identity a secret for long. Wouldn't it? But did he think that way. There, Stuart told himself, he was doing it again! Trying to analyze a desperate man.

But he still did not know what to do about confiding his fears to Russ.

CHAPTER NINETEEN

FOLLOW-UPS

Stuart left a message for Russ at his motel. He said that he had heard from their more recent correspondent, and he believed that they needed to talk again. Russ picked the message up with his key late in the afternoon. He had already decided that he would leave the next day. They had not decided on any code for their messages, but clearly, it could be read to mean there was a real threat.

When he called Freed at home, Stuart simply said that he was welcome to drop by that evening to discuss their present situation.

They sat for a time in the large library. Russ waited for Stuart to begin. "Well, I heard from our Mr. X., I guess we call him." Russ nodded, and continued to wait. "He is quite determined that I not publish anything about the case. He told me readers would figure out he had been there that terrible night, and eventually even who he was. I think maybe he is playing a game with me. He might want to step forward and prove he was nowhere near the room where Wendy was killed and make me out a fool. I just don't know. And then," he paused, "this could all be a hoax, couldn't it? Someone who was at the seminar is playing with me."

"How far have you gone with this – how many people have you told about your ideas?"

So now Freed had to talk in more detail about the Philadelphia seminar. "I spoke about how unlikely the whole scenario of Wendy's last trip really was – no matter how desperate, or infatuated (take your pick), she was."

"No, I don't think you can make that a premise beyond a doubt. She had moved to Cleveland, after all, to be close to Robbie. She had almost cut off contact with her parents and brother. I always thought that was strange, but you're someone who must have come in contact with some really strange behavior."

Stuart nodded. "Yes, there was nothing about Wendy to cause parental concern before she went to Cleveland. Do you think she had made it clear that she intended to force the issue of marriage by getting pregnant?"

"Now we're trying to solve a question we can't about why in the world she would cut off everything and take that fatal step. She went. And, face it, she might have stayed in that shack. I had no real reason - or evidence - to think otherwise, but apparently, your suggestion of a possible accomplice stirred someone up at that seminar."

"He is going to contact me again, presumably with some details of a proposal."

"Well, the only thing to do is to wait for his next steps. Russ, how concerned should I be that he might do something really dramatic?"

"I don't know, Stuart, I don't have any kind of handle on Mr. X."

§

The next day Stuart received a brief message brought to the office by a message service. It read:

"Enclosed you will find an open ticket on New Jersey Transit from Trenton to New Brunswick. Take the 9:35 train Wednesday and wait for me at the station. Do not tell Mr. Lewis about this trip. You can be sure that I will know if you are followed. There is a newsstand at the station. The man selling papers will have a message for you. Tell him you are Mr. Jordan. It's time we met to talk over our future dealings."

Stuart did not know what to do about talking to Russ. If anything happened to him and he hadn't told him about this "invitation," it could make things worse. He told his wife, who was adamant that he not go.

"But how can I do that."

"Report it to the police. Let them pick up the message for Mr. Jordan and take it from there. This guy is a dangerous lunatic – you must know that."

"Maybe, but what if he simply fades away and comes back later – in some more awful way."

"My God, you are not thinking straight. Stay away, please."

"But he knows about the Philadelphia seminar – he knows from that where we live. That's what started all this, and there's nothing to be done about that."

"You can't do this – you just can't. Just tell the police. Why are you holding back? "

"He hasn't actually threatened anything – at least not in writing. What would the charge be?"

She stared at him in disbelief. "I'm amazed you would say that. Intimidation, for one thing. Surely there are laws about this kind of creepy harassment."

"Suppose it's all a fraud. Suppose it's someone from the seminar who thinks it's funny to scare people."

"Oh, sure, you don't really think that."

"No, what I think is the police won't really do anything, and Mr. X will make a different move."

"So, are you going to tell him that you've abandoned the idea? You think he will believe that."

"I think I have to go and pick up the message he's supposed to leave, but not do anything else like meeting him on a bridge over the Raritan River or something crazy."

"Had you thought he might have killed Robbie himself to insure nothing comes out about his role? He's been afraid of that happening for twenty years. Now you've come along and are his worst nightmare. He'll never think you won't pursue the accomplice idea to the end – not now, not when he knows you think it is the road to a big pay-off professionally – not the $25,000 he's offering but the prestige that comes from writing one of these True Crime exposes."

"Jo, we are living in some sort of fantasy world - whoever it is is not going to risk killing me in a train station."

§

Stuart canceled all his Wednesday appointments and went to the Trenton Station a half-hour before 9:35 to look around to see if anyone seemed to be following him. He knew it was probably a futile gesture because there were numerous stops before New Brunswick. Someone trailing him could get on at any one of those without him seeing a follower. When he got to New Brunswick that would be the time, but, then, of course, there were bound to be many people getting off there.

Not as many people got on the train as Stuart expected there might, but then it was after rush hour. The train arrived shortly after 10:15 and a few younger people, perhaps Rutgers University students got off and walked down the stairs ahead of him from the platform to the level where the magazine stand stood - by itself at the end of the hall. They exited quickly and he was alone. The station seemed strangely silent. He could not even see if there was someone there behind the racks selling newspapers or cigarettes. The feeling - the atmosphere - was hardly like a train station in a metro area. It was more like a dream where one walked on and on until it ended and you woke up feeling uneasy that you were all alone. He could feel his heartbeats speed up as he approached the stand and could read the headlines on the newspapers.

As he got close, he could finally see a man sitting behind the board counter to the stand, drinking a cup of coffee and reading a magazine. He did not lift his head until Stuart stood directly in front of him. And then he seemed to frown as if upset that he had been interrupted. He was a small man, with a red-apple sort of face, and missing teeth. He just kept looking at Stuart.

"I'm sorry," Stuart finally said, "I was told you might have a message for Mr. Jordan."

"I was promised $10," he said, rubbing the front of his neck with his left hand while he continued to stare at Stuart.

"You have a message, then, to give me, I am Mr. Jordan."

"I was promised $10," he repeated.

Stuart reached for his wallet. He had two fives and some ones. He handed over the fives. The man took them and put them in his shirt pocket, still without taking his eyes off Stuart. Then he grunted softly, turned around and reached under a stack of Time magazines. He found an envelope there and faced Stuart again. This time with a smirk.

"Something secret, huh! Probably I should get a lot more, case someone asks me about 'Mr. Jordan.' Don't ya think?"

Stuart looked puzzled.

The man went on holding onto the envelope in a teasing manner. "I know where that train comes from, don't I. Might help me forget what you look like, 'Mr. Jordan.'"

Stuart shivered. He had to pull the envelope out of the newsman's hand.

"Careful," the man laughed, "you don't want to tear it open out here in front of everyone." He looked around the room with wide eyes.

Stuart could have said there was no one around, but his only thought was to get out of the station before anything more was said. He walked out the door and down the few steps to the sidewalk, where a single taxi was waiting for passengers. The cabbie looked at him as if he were somehow 'in on it,' whatever 'it' was. By now, Stuart had the awful feeling that everyone knew about 'Mr. Jordan' and the envelope bearing his name. He walked past the taxi looking for someplace where he could open the envelope in peace.

§

As he looked around on the street he had the impression that everyone was watching him. Finally, he saw a restaurant across the street on Albany Street. He entered and a young woman directed him to a table. There were students and a large number of business-dressed men and women. They ignored him. That was a relief. And he began to think no one was watching him, and he exhaled.

He almost didn't notice as a menu was shoved onto the table by a passing waitress, who then came back a moment later. Probably a student.

"Help you?" she said.

"Oh, yes, coffee, black, and a Danish." He had remembered that he left home without having breakfast. Well, he had filled up a bowl with cereal and poured milk on it. But he dumped it out in the kitchen sink before leaving to drive to the Trenton station to take the train to New Brunswick.

He waited until the coffee and pastry arrived. The girl smiled at him and left the check. He nodded a smile back. Then he took out the envelope with its "MR. JORDAN" hand-printed on the front.

He opened the envelope and there was a folded piece of paper inside. And inside that were strips of paper cut out of a yellow-ruled legal tablet. He spread these out on the table. Fitted together they spelled out, again in capital letters. BUCCLEUCH PARK TENNIS COURTS NOON. It was now 11:45. He had stupidly left home with only the two fives and some ones. He called the waitress over and gave her a credit card, asking her to hurry up with the bill. He would be at the door. She nodded and met him with his card as he stood there and waited to sign the charge, adding a $5 tip.

Across the street, back at the station it looked like the same taxi was waiting. Was the driver part of the "game"? He was leaning against the door reading a newspaper. But Stuart had the feeling that he was waiting for him - just the way he smiled as he approached.

"Are you free?"

"Looks like it. Where do you want to go?"

"Buccleuch Park tennis courts."

"Meeting someone?"

"I might be. Put it that way, not that it's any of your business."

"Whoa. I was just saying I could wait for you if you needed transportation afterwards."

Stuart narrowed his eyes and looked hard at the cabbie.

"Just trying to help. You might need someone."

"OK, sorry I took it the wrong way. We'll see."

§

The tennis courts were almost empty when the cab stopped. One pair were hitting on the last court closest to the street entrance to the park.

"This do?" the cabbie asked.

"Yes, sure. Why don't you come back in fifteen minutes or so?" He walked towards the courts seeing no one around except the two players and stopped at the fence. Then he began walking down the length of the courts. Behind him, a boy on a bicycle rode up close, passed him, and then turned the bike around.

"You Mr. Jordan?"

"Yes, I'm Mr. Jordan, do you have anything for me?"

The boy reached inside his windbreaker and pulled out an envelope. Like the one at the train station it had MR. JORDAN written in caps on the front. Stuart took the envelope and, unlike the news dealer, the boy showed no interest in teasing him and pedaled off not looking back.

Stuart saw a bench and walked over. He could still barely hear the players hitting the ball, but they did not look his way even once and there was no one else to be seen. He opened the envelope carefully, for the first time thinking it might be "evidence" of some sort. But he had no intention of going to the police so what did that really matter?

Inside there was a picture of his house, his wife was coming out the front door. A piece of paper was under the picture. On it was written, again in capitals: "YOU CAN'T ALWAYS BE THERE."

Stuart's heart started skipping beats. This was madness. "X" was a deranged fantasist who might do anything. Now he would have to go to the police. But would that only postpone some sort of fatal encounter? It seemed his only interest was in stopping Stuart from writing anything that might lead to his discovery. But how could he know that it was not already written? That's it, there was the solution - and so simple. He would wait for X to contact him again. He would have to contact him again. When he did so "X" must be told that if something happened to him, an article would be published anyway. He would have to tell him that. Yes, that was the best way to handle it. For a moment he felt great relief. Then he thought again. Oh, God, what he meant by this photo is that he was ready to kill his wife. Was that why he thought a $25,000 fee would work. It would presumably provide one reason for him not to publish - *but the real threat was to his wife!*

But that made no sense, either. Because, surely, he could not wait around forever to see if Stuart took his threat seriously and gave up the idea of publishing anything. On the other hand, he couldn't really do anything against either one of them because then the whole story would come out. He would make sure to tell this madman his article would reach the newspapers after his death or if anything happened his wife. But that assumed the blackmailer was rational and had figured out everything. It also assumed he would contact him again, either about the $25,000, or to follow up the threat with another offer. But Stuart had no reason to think that. He could keep ticking off the scenarios he imagined his tormentor had in mind, when the real issue was whether he had reasoned out any sort of a plan at all. *That might be the worst thing of all: that the writer was operating in a spur-of-the-moment panic.*

As he sat there almost in a daze, the cab returned, and Stuart directed him to take him back to the train station. Had it been some sort of test to see if he would follow instructions – or something else? And what would come next.

CHAPTER TWENTY

THE WAITING

For several days nothing happened. Each morning Stuart looked out the windows before he left for the office and dropped off his wife at her bank, searching for - what? Surely the man would not show himself. But what difference did that make? Stuart could not count on rational behavior. It appeared that they were now bound together in some sort of "contest of wills," even though nothing new had developed since his trip to New Brunswick. It continued to grow on him that his "adversary" (What else to call him?) had no plan and was simply improvising without a plan. Maybe it was all a bluff. But he could not count on that.

Stuart found himself staring at strangers on the street whether he was near his office or any other place around town. They left the house together now - always - even for short errands. Stuart hesitated even to see new male patients. He became convinced that there would be more messages sent to the office and tried to be there before his secretary to go over the mail, but that did not work because his wife's schedule was not the same and he would not allow her to drive alone.

But no new letters arrived. No phone calls.

§

Then, three weeks after the trip to New Brunswick Russ called him at home. "Anything new?"

"No," Stuart sighed into the phone. "Maybe it was all just a bluff, or even a terrible game by someone with a sick sense of humor. I'm halfway convinced that's the case."

"I don't think so," replied Russ. "Remember I'm ready to come back if something else happens. Problem is there has been no real threat, so even if you tell the police about the Philadelphia seminar and what you make of all's that happened since, there's not likely to be much of an investigation - especially now that you've not heard anything more for quite a while."

He waited but Stuart said nothing more.

Russ went on. "Have you heard from anyone else? Now is not the time to hold out."

Stuart said nothing. Russ went on: "It's for sure Carl is now in a full-throated search for the accomplice you speculate about. You can claim credit for that!" He could not resist twisting that knife in Stuart's fears, even though he was not happy about tormenting him at this point. "Robbie's disappearance is another trigger. Everyone could be speculating about his finding a new identity."

Russ waited for a response. Hearing none he then went on. "And can you see as well that you might appear to Carl as a key player in all that has happened."

"I suppose I might. Carl thinks he needs me just as Mr. X has an interest in stopping my work on the case."

§

After the seminar, Kent had relived the whole scene many times. He had not imagined Robbie capable of such scheming at the time of Wendy's "death,"- but then he read in the newspapers about those fatal instructions - the letters telling Wendy to bring everything with her, and read his "confession" about where he planned for her to stay until they could go to Kentucky to marry. All lies, of course.

And once more he heard in his mind the introduction by the seminar program chair: "Tonight, our speaker brings our attention to a lesser-known case. Hardly anything has been written about it over the twenty years since it happened. I do not know exactly what he is going to tell us this evening - but I gather it is pretty startling. Apparently, there was someone else there the night it happened. Someone who has never been placed at the scene of the crime. So, I'm sure we will all listen with eager ears to the story of the Red Slippers murder case – was it solved or not?"

As Stuart began to speak, Kent recalled in his mind Robbie's first words about Wendy's coming "visit":

"Hey, little brother. I need some help. Wendy's coming to town and I need to find a place for her to stay for a night or two. She's coming for a visit."

§

All a lie! Robbie had not said anything about a plan for them to scoot off to Kentucky to get married. Of course not. Lies, all lies. He had just wanted to make it seem to Kent that he didn't want to put out the money for a motel room when his girlfriend came to town. Kent had wanted to say no. But before he did, Robbie had put his hand on his shoulder like he was conveying a close secret. He couldn't put her in the fraternity house, obviously, so the way he then explained things made a kind of sense, even if it was not convenient for him. Robbie promised that he would get her out of the room by early morning. Kent could go to the Delt house for the night and stay in his room. It was just for a night or maybe two after all. Put that way he would have had a hard time refusing, even if the big brother-little brother thing was not the main hold Robbie had on him.

He remembered Robbie's sly smile, as if he was being let in on a secret they both could enjoy afterwards about how they got around all the fussiness of college rules. Oh, did he remember it? His life had been shaped forever by that mocking snicker. During the first days of the investigation the strain was almost unbearable.

As Freed talked on about Robbie's planned deception, Kent was back there once again entering his dorm room reliving it yet one more time: *There was Wendy either unconscious or dead and Robbie looking stricken in the chair. He almost said something out loud - God forbid! He must not do that.*

Freed came to his dramatic conclusion: "There is no convincing evidence that Wendy was ever in that shack," Freed ended, "and furthermore," he paused for effect - looking around the room, "I believe he had help getting that poor girl's body out of town that night."

There was loud applause, and immediately hands went up to ask questions.

§

Kent saw it all happening again:

Robbie was sitting in his chair across the room at Kent's desk. He looked up at Kent, making and holding eye contact, then brushed his hair back in a swift gesture. "We need to get her out of here." There was no other explanation. Kent had not understood at first: "What do you mean? She's sick - or - or - WHAT HAVE YOU DONE, ROBBIE? WHAT HAVE YOU DONE?

"Shut up, you fool! We have to get her to my car."

He had prayed that was it, getting Wendy into the car. He could not imagine anything worse as they carried her to the car. He was sobbing and repeating over and over.

"Forgive me, dear God, forgive me."

"Shut up," Robbie had hissed as they struggled with Wendy's body and reached the car. Way down the street they could see two couples getting into a car parked at a curb alongside the athletic field with the equipment shack Robbie would

then tell the police he had kept her for a night and a day. "Just shut up. Somebody will hear."

With one hand Robbie opened the door keeping his other arm under Wendy's shoulders. Then the two pushed her body onto the back seat. He had drawn back in horror as Robbie shut the car door, and her nightgown was caught.

Robbie opened the door and pulled it free, shutting it again so that nothing showed. "Get in."

"What - I'm done."

"Oh, no, you're not. Get in the passenger seat."

"I can't do that. No, no, no!"

"I said get in. You have to help me finish this or we're both in deep shit."

Robbie's voice had a menace in it he had never heard any time before in his life. And his eyes looked like those he had seen in some horror movie - staring at him. He felt weak inside. His stomach hurt. His mouth was dry when he tried to lick his lips and say something,

"Get in - now! We can't be caught out here."

"I'm done, Robbie."

"Think that do you? Well think again, because if I'm caught - you're caught."

Kent knew Robbie's threat had been real - at least at that moment. He had believed that if he had walked away Robbie would pull him back in if he was arrested. When he confessed using the idea that he had flown into a rage, of course, pulling someone else in as an accomplice wouldn't help him. It would make matters worse. But the threat had never completely gone away. And now, suddenly it was back in a worse way than at the beginning. It had come back because some psychologist wanted to write a story about a crime that happened twenty years ago.

At the seminar, the question period had begun.

But what he heard was Robbie's harsh whisper just as it was that night as he opened the car door and slid in beside Robbie.

"We're going to the Delt house."

"What, with her spread out on the back seat like that. You're crazy."

"I have to get something."

"But what about all her things back in my room?"

"Yeah, well that comes later. First I have to get something."

They had driven to the fraternity house where freshman "rush" was in full swing. At first, Robbie drove by slowly continuing on two blocks before he doubled back passing the house illuminated with spotlights on a Greek letter flag hanging from a second-floor window, and loud music pouring out the front door onto the porch where it mixed with a babble of louder voices in a haze of cigarette smoke. Just below the fraternity house at the corner, he turned right and then right again into an alley that ran back of the brick building and provided access for the town's garbage trucks. He parked and shut off the lights. He waited until he could see in the near darkness keeping his hands on the steering wheel. Sitting beside Robbie Kent listened to his own breathing. Once or twice Robbie moved one hand to his forehead to brush back some threads of hair. Kent could see that he was sweating, the only sign of what had happened - what they had done! -was bothering him.

"Move over to the driver's seat. Stay here. If anyone comes out of the house towards the car but me, drive away and come back in ten minutes. But don't stop in the alley. Go on to the next block and park a few feet along."

Robbie got out of the car, went to the trunk and took out a raincoat. He draped it over his arm and headed for the rear entrance. There was no one there, but Kent could glimpse through the window the kitchen and people moving around carrying plates of sandwiches and salad dishes with stuff he couldn't see on them. He looked at his watch a couple of times. Then Robbie emerged from the door, carefully shutting it behind him, and came down the five steps to the concrete path that led out to the alley.

This time he was wearing the coat. Re-opening the trunk lid he took something from under the coat and placed it inside so quietly he did not make a sound. He was listening hard and barely heard the trunk door lock in place.

Robbie came around to the passenger side and got in before the inside light went out and turned as if he were checking on Wendy to see if she was still asleep!

"You drive."

"Back to my room, right?"

"No, you drive where I tell you. We're not going to stay in town with Wendy back there dummy! What's wrong with you. We have to find a place."

Kent turned away from the look in Robbie's eyes, trying hard not to show him the tears in his eyes. He turned on the motor, but forgot to shift gears down to first, and the car jerked and bucked. He thought they were finished right there. He eased up on the accelerator and the car engine finally calmed down.

"For Christ's sake Kent. Do you even have a license?"

"Of course I do, dammit. But what the hell - what are we doing? The best thing would be to go to the police and tell them exactly what you told me. That you were just rough-housing."

"Oh, sure, my man. Would you really like that? I don't think so." Robbie even laughed as Kent choked out a sob. "You're in this as deep as I am, and you best remember that. From now on what happens to you depends on what happens to me."

Freed had just asked if there were any more questions. "Did Robbie intend to deface her from the start?" "He must have," was Freed's answer. Kent's jaws clenched.

§

They drove back to the center of town and he heard Robbie say drive north on the main state highway out of town.

"Just stay on this road until I tell you where to turn."

His eyes on the road he could only think which was worse. Was she really dead, or not? What would Robbie do if she was still alive? He hadn't felt for any pulse, and had no idea if Robbie actually knew. Awful as it seemed, he decided it would be worse if she were still alive. After an hour or so Robbie started giving directions until they were driving down a little used county road. There were no cars on the road. But when Robbie ordered him to stop and get out, he could hear music. At first, he thought it was his imagination, but then he could see lights far off across the road and beyond fields of corn. When the breeze blew their way he definitely heard music. It was not his imagination. A carnival? Maybe. Or a county fair, more likely that.

Robbie said nothing, went to the trunk and pulled out a long pipe-like thing. It was too large to be a furnace poker. Then he saw it had an eye on the end. He stood still - waiting.

The seminar questioners were still asking about the decision to transport Wendy to this remote place as Kent again heard Robbie's command:

"Get her out."

He did not hesitate. By this time he was completely in thrall to Robbie.

His only doubt was about whether Robbie intended to kill him, too, or tell authorities that he was the killer!

No one around. The moon was bright enough to see Wendy's face. She looked like hell, her face contorted into an accusing grimace. He kept thinking about the earlier scene when he returned to his room and found them, Wendy on the bed with only a nightgown and red slippers, Robbie moving from the chair and sitting beside her his head in his hands. When he looked up at Kent, his eyes seemed to be pleading for understanding. Now Robbie's face showed only determination to finish with an unpleasant task. He could see no sign of doubt or remorse, standing there with that thing in his hands.

"Get her out - and help me carry her."

They managed to maneuver Wendy through the underbrush at the side of the road. Later Kent would pull off burrs stuck to his trousers and actually squeeze them as if to feel some pain in order to make what he had done seem real. But in those moments he had lost any sense of where he was, or what he had done already.

"Go back to the car. Wait for me. I won't be long."

Kent had turned around and pushed through the weeds and got to the car. Very soon Robbie was back. He had already taken the keys and unlocked the trunk. He heard the pipe thing rattle around when Robbie threw it in the trunk and slammed down the lid.

"I'll drive now," Robbie had said. "Get some music on the radio." Then he actually winked at Kent. "Maybe we'll see some townie girls out for a late date when we get back. That'd help if we get asked where we were tonight, don't cha think."

Kent just sat staring ahead out the window at the white line down the center of the road.

"Did you hear me? We've got to have some answers if anybody starts asking. I don't think they will, but you never know. Wendy wasn't supposed to tell anyone where she was going. But once she turns up missing, there's bound to be questions. So we need to plan this out."

"Why do you keep saying 'we,' I didn't do anything."

Robbie had laughed at Kent and hit him a nudging blow to his leg. "C'mon, man, you know damned well we're in this together."

§

Kent did not take his eyes off the road. They returned to town with no more conversation. *"Let's take care of Wendy's stuff,"* Robbie had said. *"I was afraid it might blow around up there if some animal got her suitcases open. There's one in my trunk and the other is in your room."* They parked outside the dorm but did not go in for a minute. Two guys were heading for the door.

"You get rid of the one in your room," said Robbie pushing him towards the door. *"I've still got some things to do. I'll meet you at The Dive for a late breakfast at nine, and we can talk about things, ya' know."* The Dive was a favorite college restaurant. Everyone went there.

Kent had gotten out of the car and pushed the door shut. Ever since that moment, he had been waiting for something to happen to drag him back. And now it had.

CHAPTER TWENTY-ONE

THE RETURN OF THE INVESTIGATOR

Miriam Stronge had left Carl Peters with her report and returned to her home in suburban Columbus, where she and her husband, Larry had lived since she had left the Police Department ten years earlier. Her private investigations firm had not done too badly, but there were few big paydays like the one she had just scored. Yet she was her own boss and it sure beat chasing after burglars and car thieves, what she did mostly in that section of the detective bureau. She had hated to go to work many mornings because it quite quickly became apparent that there was no future for her there - just routine. The promotion list always found her at least halfway down. She had a good record, but no real friends at the top. She was never sure why that was so, but it was, and leaving the department had not been a hard choice. Well, it was true she was a woman in a man's world. She supposed that was part of it.

Miriam was the name of a prophetess in the Bible. Her brothers were Joshua and Solomon, and, as the names suggested, hers was a "fundamentalist" family. Still, she had managed to break away just a bit by going to college in far off Wooster, where she majored in psychology and anthropology. She proved herself more than once in solving disappearing persons cases. But there weren't that many, after all, on police case files – beyond, that is, runaway kids and disappearing dads.

They gave her a going away party - five guys and a couple of beers in The Bauhaus over in the Germantown section of the city. And that was it. Larry, a contractor, had not been opposed to the move and actually helped her with setting up her new office, rented space in North Columbus where she could afford a couple of rooms in a prewar brick building above a dry cleaner. The outside door to the offices on the second floor was a wooden frame with the top half smoked glass. On it were three listings, *"Stronge Investigations,"* an accountant's firm and an insurance broker. There was not a lot of traffic up and down those stairs. Sometimes Miriam wondered if the others were making a decent living, but she had enough to worry herself about when she started up as a one-woman operation.

Maybe she was lucky. But maybe also her contacts with the police department gave her a bit of an edge, because she started getting referrals from people who had had no success with regular authorities, and who were then told about her. So it stood to reason, perhaps, that she had made an impression on somebody or more than one. Now it was also true that her rate of success was also not very high - if you thought of success as full customer satisfaction. But her clients seemed to feel they got their money's worth, and that they had tried all reasonable avenues. She also promised them to "stay on the case" and pursue any new lead. Once in a while that paid off for both her and the client - as when she found the body of a missing woman who had been killed by a lover and left in a long-closed family mausoleum in an old cemetery near Marion, Ohio. She had come up with the idea of looking there because the man's family lived in that town. It had led to a conviction, and lots of good publicity.

Probably the similarity was why Carl Peters had asked her to find Robbie Stanson, although it had been a bit of a surprise happening when she got the call asking for an appointment. There wasn't anything, obviously that could happen in terms of more prison time for Wendy's killer, but her brother was apparently determined find out where Robbie had gone in search of a new life. He did not accept the idea that he had died in Yosemite. But why her, there were larger agencies who had the resources to mount a thorough investigation? It became apparent when they met that Peters valued discreetness above all else. A bigger firm might mean too much attention, too great a chance of leaks - or so it apparently seemed. She could think of no other reason.

"Mrs. Stronge," Peters had told her when he came to the office, "you have been recommended to me as a person with a more than usual sense about missing persons. Do you know the history of the 'Red Slippers' Case?"

Miriam frowned. "I might have heard about it a long time ago, but not in any serious way. The details don't come to mind."

"The victim was my sister, Wendy Peters. Her boyfriend strangled her and then dumped her body in a wooded area off a county road near Massillon." He paused, the hurt appearing in red blotches across his face. "Then he took a poker-like instrument and defaced her." Peters waited for her reaction, looked at her with a steady gaze that was full of hurt and long nurtured anger. "I did not do my duty then and keep watch over her when she went to Bashford in the fall of 1952, or when she moved to Cleveland the next summer to be close to Robbie. I did not realize the awful hold he had over her."

His eyes filled with tears as he related all the details. He took out a handkerchief and blew his nose. Hurt turned to disgust as he swiped away the tears.

"Then there was that prosecutor who accepted a Second Degree plea. I don't blame the judge at that time. He sentenced him to twenty-five years to life. What none of us could imagine was that the parole board would let him out only ten years into the sentence – " He let out a deep breath "and even after all that dirty business about a 'girlfriend' he had when he was driving the prison truck on his own. My God – my God! How could they do that."

Stronge nodded along as Carl continued the history of the aftermath of the "Red Slippers" case, pressing her lips together waiting to hear what she was going to be asked to do.

"When he got out he was supposed to live with his family. He did for a couple of years then he went to the University of Minnesota and got into graduate studies in psychology. Apparently, he got his master's degree plus some additional course work. I followed all this best I could because I was determined he was not going to set up a practice somewhere and live the life of a respected counselor."

Miriam shook her head. "But you had no right to pursue him in such a way after he got out of prison – no matter how vicious the crime."

"When he got out my Mom was devastated. I'm sure it caused her death – well not in a direct way, but she just sorta gave up living any kind of life. Dad died a few years later. But you're right I couldn't follow him around everywhere. I didn't, but I kept tabs as best I could on his whereabouts because I just thought something would happen. And it did, didn't it?

Stronge nodded – in sympathy for Carl's feelings, but not as if she approved shadowing someone who had been released from prison. Besides she did not know exactly what Peters was talking about.

"He supposedly disappeared forever out in Yosemite. Maybe he did fall into some crevice or other, I don't know. But it's pretty hard to believe."

"Yes, but maybe justice was served that way? – I just worry about you getting stuck in some futile search. I know it's difficult after all the family's suffering, but …"

"There's something else. Maybe Robbie had help. Back then, I mean."

§

Miriam raised her eyebrows and picked up a pencil on her desk, leaning forward a few inches and waited for Peters to continue as if she were back at her police desk hearing a report about new evidence in a cold case, ready to dismiss the story. But still intrigued.

"I had always wondered about his story of how Wendy stayed overnight in that shack on the athletic field," Peters went on. "Do you know about that?"

"No, I don't know very much. What's your idea?"

"Despite Wendy's deep infatuation with Robbie – even if she did think it was love – she was supposed to have stayed in a bare shack on an athletic field, following his orders that she shouldn't be seen because it would spoil their plans to elope and get married." He stopped there and then leaned forward for emphasis. "There's only Stanson's confession for this account, obviously, and why believe that? No, I can't see her being willing to stay overnight by herself in some old shack – worse than a prison cell, which would at least have had a bed. No, she would have protested."

"But what good would that have done, Carl, where could she have turned for help?"

"Yes, well I will concede that she must have felt trapped – and I thought about that in the sense that the coroner's report said she had sex with him hours before he killed her. She might have thought that would soften him up. The story he gave out about an argument they had over her being seen that day was all Robbie wasn't it. Clever bastard. The only way it fits is this: Wendy thought that after sex he would listen to her and that's when she said she wouldn't stay another night there."

He looked hard at Miriam for her reaction.

"Yes, I could follow that." She nodded for emphasis.

"And he killed her not because he was mad that she had been seen by some wandering fisherman who passed the shack – but because now it was put up or shut up time. What he doesn't say in that 'confession' is that he really had no intention of marrying Wendy. We know from the other letters he wrote that turned up that he had pretended to another girl that they were no longer together. Imagine that prosecutor ignoring all this stuff - just for a quick exit. And he wasn't...."

"Let's skip that for a moment."

" O.K. So now he has the choice of actually doing what he told Wendy they would do – slip off to Kentucky and get married – or eliminate this 'threat' to his future plans. Which had been the real reason he invited her to come down to the college town."

"So you don't credit his story at all."

"Of course not!"

He sighed again. "That was what he put out there when he was gaming for either temporary insanity or a something like a manslaughter charge. There's no evidence anyone confronted him with these letters after his confession. Or if there is, it was not presented at the time of his 'trial,' which was nothing but a formality. Why was the prosecutor afraid of pursuing a First Degree murder charge? Oh there were reasons why, none of them in the name of justice."

He went on, keeping steady eye contact with Stronge. "There's one more thing. She was pregnant."

He paused for that to sink in. "Here's what I think happened. After Wendy told him she was pregnant, she said she wanted to get married, but Robbie must have told her no and maybe said he really agreed now with their parents, on both sides. They were too young. And he must of made sure she hadn't told her parents about the baby. I don't know, probably she had told him about the baby earlier."

He looked away for a moment and then went on. "So Robbie wanted her to come down not to slip off to Kentucky but to someone who could help them out... in another way. You know, an abortion. I'm sure he must have hinted at that. And she tried to stall him or simply refused. Either way he lost it. Or, as I think, he knew exactly what he would do in that case."

"Yeah, ok, I follow your reasoning, but you said something about help he might have had."

"Right, what I just told you was the way everyone saw at the time - treating Robbie's story as the real framework. But suppose it did not happen that way at all."

"Whatever different way could it have happened?"

"Suppose Robbie got Wendy into a dorm room."

"What?" She shook her head.

"That seems pretty unlikely in the 1950s."

"Well that's true, but consider this, the shack was on a field just south of the football stadium, where, in the aftermath of the war extra dorm rooms for men were created under the stadium. This special dorm did not have the close supervision like the women's dorms, or even very much supervision at all. Less than at a fraternity house, even. Besides, no one at the time saw Robbie carrying *anything* to that shack - or from that shack, least of all a young woman. Yet he supposedly visited twice (at least) the next day. There were people parked along that road or street day and night."

"But that would suggest someone aided and abetted the crime – again making Robbie's defense plea useless."

"Exactly."

"But no evidence of such a person ever turned up."

"It might have."

"Meaning?"

"There was an empty suitcase found in the bushes beside the dorm."

Miriam sat back in her chair, twisting her pencil in her fingers.

"Yes, that's what I said – but by the time Robbie took Sheriff Lewis to the river to fish out Wendy's belongings and that awful instrument he used... well, no one was interested in learning any more about the case. They had their confession. Exactly what Bashford wanted – and - No More."

He paused and took several deep breaths. "Bashford College wanted it over asap. Our family was coaxed, or better put, cajoled into accepting the decision to drop efforts at a First Degree prosecution. The school paid for Robbie's defense attorney - how about that? And there was no jury; all the judge wanted to do at that point was to deliver a little sermon and pronounce a sentence. Almost, for Christ's sake like making a blessing after confession like a priest. Well that's unfair, but I heard later that Sheriff Lewis was upset by the rush and wanted to explore some other things. But he was given to understand in no uncertain terms that his part in the Red Slippers Case was over. Period."

Another deep breath. "But there were those letters Wendy left behind, especially the one instructing her to bring everything, tell no one, and meet him blocks away from the bus station. Remember a Cleveland detective found them before the case was to go to trial. And on top of that the letters found in Robbie's room to the other girl saying he was no longer dating Wendy and asking *her* if she knew how she was doing. Jesus, what absolute gall. I don't know how they got there but it was plain he was putting up a long term alibi."

Stronge had stopped playing with the pencil.

"Well, you know what Miriam? I think she had a premonition. I think that no matter how much she was in love, or under Robbie's spell – she knew. Somewhere down deep she knew this was not right and she was going to leave a trail. That may sound too much out of a movie or something, but I feel that way."

"OK, I can see that is a red flag."

§

Miriam decided it was worth looking into, not re-opening the case, but Stanson's disappearance. If she discovered that he had actually died, Carl Peters could feel some satisfaction. But she felt down deep that she agreed with his unstated belief that Robbie Stanson had managed the whole scene. And she was repulsed by the story she had just heard, enough so to join forces with Carl. Up to a point, she told herself. But what would happen - if... Stop it she said to herself, she would know when to pull back. "So where do you want me to start?"

"Well, if you can find out any more about Robbie's last trip to Yosemite. Did he leave any luggage anywhere – I doubt there is much of a trail there. But maybe someone remembers seeing him with another person, or there are phone call records – anything to tell us about the disappearance. A few people disappear out there every year, and I don't think they look very hard."

"OK."

"I know it was some time ago, but fresh eyes might pick up on some leads. I'm sure in my mind that there was an accomplice or more than one in his career of evading a just ending. Maybe Robbie has had help in finding a new life. And, then, also maybe the place to start there would be with Robbie's fraternity. What do you know about the Greek letter societies?

"Very little. I never joined anything like that at Wooster. My parents wouldn't approve, anyway."

"Well, Bashford was over ninety percent Greek, as they said in those days. You belonged to a fraternity or sorority, or you were a social outcast. Well, not quite that bad, but you get the idea."

"I do."

"Yes, well the fraternity system with its pledges and big brothers was big time scary for many first-year students away from home for the first time. Once you pledged a fraternity all those first days of wooing and big handshakes were gone – for the year - until you were initiated. You had a Big Brother, theoretically to help with it all, but you did not choose your big brother. He chose you and he had control. And his reports to the chapter were what mattered. And there was always the "Blackball" threat. You could be put adrift any time – almost for any reason – if your big brother could find a reason to do it. If for example he called upon you to help him, and you failed to respond. Now – there were great differences, obviously, about how pledges got treated. And few actual "Blackball" occurrences. But there was always the threat. More often "Little Brothers" actually became quite close to their big brothers, so either way, you see."

"I think I do, but surely something would have surfaced."

"Think so? I would say the opposite. Once Robbie's little brother became involved some way, say by letting Wendy stay in his room, that was it. Even if that was all there was to it. He was stuck with being an accomplice. Hell, what happened out in Yosemite might even have been that the accomplice at Bashford killed Robbie to be rid of the threat of exposure that he posed to him all those years! Yes, I can see that as a possibility. They were hostages to one another, a continuing threat."

Carl looked at a spot on the wall behind Miriam's desk, as if he were thinking it all out for the first time. She put up her hands in protest at where this was all going. "Whoa down. You're really stretching here. Now you have two improbabilities going on."

"Yes, but I've thought a lot about this - as you might imagine. It haunts me that I failed Wendy. And you might be able to clear up some of it. I'll pay for your investigation, and you won't regret doing it. I'm pretty damn sure of that!"

"Let's be clear here. Why do you want me to do this?"

Peters nodded. "I understand what you're getting at. I can't undo what happened to Wendy, or the resulting treatment Robbie got – while I'd like to say, got away with. No. I just feel like I have to know the whole story."

"But then what? I'm not going to finger someone for an act of retribution." She frowned and waited for more, concerned about what she might hear. Maybe she had given Peters too much leeway - that she had reached the point...

Peters shook his head and went on. "I'm not a violent man. There are other things."

They sat there looking at one another, seemingly waiting for the other to complete the interview. "Look," said Peters finally, "if you find something, I'll simply notify the authorities, or, maybe that former sheriff, Lewis. I'm sure he'd like to know what happened."

"OK, that's a good idea – a working outline."

"And I'll pay your fee, and, of course, all travel expenses. You won't regret it."

That comment jolted her. It was often said too easily to ease fears - but maybe she was being alarmist.

§

Stronge put aside her doubts, and told herself that, hey, maybe she could find out what really happened to Robbie. She would be helping the authorities, then, she told herself. Wouldn't she? It was a close call, admittedly. Peters was acting simply as an avenging angel. Did she want to be part of this? It was a big case – or at least could be. If she didn't accept the assignment, somebody else would. He had said he wasn't a violent man.

She looked at Peters and said, "OK, you had years to do something bad after he got out of prison and didn't. I guess I can accept that you are only interested in the truth." She said this aloud as if trying to convince herself – which she was, without complete success.

He nodded and they shook hands.

§

They stood up. Carl looked even more grim and determined. "Lest you think I'm loco there's something else – something that can really shake the truth out of this net of lies and cover-ups Bashford threw over the murder. There's a researcher working on the accomplice angle right now. We can talk about that later." Peters left that hanging in the air, smiling at her stunned look.

She decided that the first place to look was Yosemite, obviously, the last known location where Stanson was seen. She booked a flight the next day. When she got there, none of the rangers still around had much to say. There were records at the lodge where he had signed in under an alias, but nothing in the room. He had kept to himself. Told the desk clerk one day he was going out on the trails, checked out, and said that he had camping equipment in his car. And then he was gone. No one remembered seeing him on any of the trails.

"I know about the case," one ranger told her. "But we didn't have the manpower to keep up much of a search. Truth be told, people sometimes come here with that in mind."

"Suicide?"

"Nope, well maybe but more likely just disappearing for one reason or another. There's lotsa reasons for that. I bet you can think of a bunch yourself." The ranger smiled in a knowing look. "In your line of work, I mean."

"O.K., but you don't know anyone in any of the eating places or shops who might be able to help? I'm prepared to offer a 'reward' so to speak, to anyone with genuine knowledge about Stanson's visit in 1972."

"Maybe I do. But it's a long time ago in terms of the turnover here."

"This help you to remember." Stronge took two twenties out of her wallet and waited.

"You might ask Julie at the Ahwahnee. That's where he checked in. She's been here a while."

"Thanks." Stronge handed the ranger the money and turned to look at the map on the office wall. "Thanks, again, Jim," she smiled, and gave the ranger a slight nod. Jim watched her leave and wondered if maybe he should have been a bit more coy before he gave Stronge those names. Well, too late now

§

She decided to try to find Julie at the Ahwahnee. The lodge had a classic, upscale Western lodge look. She walked in the front door between the rough stone pillars. At the front desk she asked if she might see Julie. The woman behind the counter was not friendly at all, showing irritation at being interrupted from the reservation forms she was studying.

"Yes?" she said still staring at the forms. Miriam remained silent. Finally, she looked up with a frown: "How can I help you this morning?"

"I'm looking for Julie. A ranger told me she has worked here quite a while."

"Is this for some particular reason? We don't hand out information about someone who might have worked here at one time."

"So, she's no longer here."

"I didn't say that. I said we don't hand out information about our personnel - without a very good reason."

"Hey. I'm not here to give her a summons or something. I just need some information about whether she ever saw a person who stayed here."

"And how is that better?"

"Look, let's start over. My name is Miriam Stronge, and I've been asked to locate a missing person. I'm not the law or a debt collector. I'm just interested in talking with her to see if our man ever stayed here or anything."

"I'm Julie."

"Oh, I thought from what the ranger said that Julie might be a waitress or something."

"Or something? What does that mean?"

"I really am sorry. We seem to be off on the wrong foot. I'm just looking for information. And I can offer you a fee for your help - if that doesn't sound awfully sordid."

Julie smiled a little at the corners of her mouth. "Sorry, but you know how it is. Give me a name and I'll look at our records. Can't promise anything. How long ago would that have been?"

"1972 - summer."

"OK. I'm pretty busy right now. Come back around four and I will have any information we might have. About?"

"Stanson, Robbie Stanson. He might have registered under a different name.".

§

When Miriam returned precisely at four, Julie met her at the reception desk.

"I want to apologize for this morning," Miriam began. "It was rude of me to just announce myself that way."

She grinned. "No, I just wanted to give you a bit of a hard time. Sometimes I feel like doing stuff like that, especially when I get really wrought up with all the calls for rooms coming at once. Why don't we go to the coffee shop."

Pointing the way, Julie stepped out quickly ahead of her. She walked with a bit of swagger that demonstrated her self-confidence. She wondered how long she would settle for her current position. But, then, she really did not know what her position was. Clearly, however, she must be in a managerial situation.

Finding a table near a window, Julie sat down. A waitress appeared immediately. They both ordered black coffee.

"Now, what was it you wanted to ask?" Julie began.

"Well, right. I'm here on a mission trying to find out for an interested party what might have happened to someone who supposedly disappeared from Yosemite a few months ago."

"Oh, and who could that be? The person who wants to find out. Or..."

"I can't tell you that," Miriam smiled, almost apologetically, "but it's not the law or the IRS. I promise you."

"But someone wants to find this person, obviously."

"Yes."

"And this someone is paying a good deal of money?"

"Yes, again."

"So how do I know this someone means Mr. Stanson , or whoever, no harm; even if I knew something, why should I tell you?"

"No reason, except I don't work for that kind of client."

It was clear Julie did not believe her from the way she looked at her without blinking or nodding. But Miriam looked down at her coffee as if searching for the right answer. "I'm willing to pay you for any information."

Julie knitted her brows:

"I don't remember anyone by that name," she said. "And it was a while ago."

"I have a photograph. That might help." Miriam reached into her coat and pulled out a photo Carl Peters had given her. Peters had first wanted to give her a newspaper photo from the time of Robbie's release, but Miriam had said that would raise too many questions for any would-be informant, even if a different photograph would now be twenty years or more old.

Julie looked at the picture. She handed it back to her. "Maybe. He reminds me vaguely of someone who stayed here once for a few days, but I'm not sure if it was 1972. And the person had a different name."

"Well, did this person leave any unclaimed baggage, a suitcase or something?"

"I don't remember anything like that. And without a name there aren't any records we have that I could check."

"Let me ask this. Did someone come to visit him. Did you see him in the dining room with anyone else."

"Now, you're really pushing me into fantasy-land. If there was someone like that how could I remember. After all," she grinned, " we already decided I wasn't a waitress, ever."

But she reached for the picture. "Let me keep this for a day and ask around." Then grinned again. "Why don't you treat me for dinner tomorrow night and we can see what has turned up?"

She nodded. "Here?"

"No, check back sometime in the late morning." She handed her a note with a phone number.

"Right."

§

At ten the next morning Miriam called the number and Julie told her to meet her at Mountain View at 8. "I might have some information for you."

She showed up right at 8 and Julie came in the door five minutes later. "Hi there Miriam," she nodded. The hostess showed them a table.

After drinks were ordered Julie opened her purse and gave Miriam back the picture. " I asked around, not much luck, but one person thinks someone who looks like your Robbie was here for a couple of days and had lunch with another man about his age a couple of times. Then she didn't see him anymore. They paid cash so there was no name on a credit card."

"Does she remember them or him driving away?"

"No, but they did leave the bar together both times. She was busy with other people."

"What made her remember him, then?"

"I don't know. But there were no reports of a missing tourist around that time, so he must not have left luggage in a room, or a bill unpaid. We don't even know if he stayed in the hotel."

"Anything on the other guy?"

"Not on him specifically - except she thinks she saw him at a gas station one day later."

"Well, is there some way I can talk to her?"

"Maybe, she only comes in half-days anymore."

"Tomorrow?"

"No, but she might see you at Degnan's coffee shop."

"Yes?"

"But you have to understand she needs compensation."

"Yes, I get that."

Miriam looked steadily at Julie, who kept her eyes focused on her the whole time. "She needs $500."

"What!"

"Yes, she needs the money really badly. Her husband's sick. That's why she can't work full time. And I want to help her all I can."

"And what would I get for that sum."

"A license plate."

"How will that help? "

" She thinks it will because it was out of state."

"And what about you?"

"I don't want any money. I still don't think this is right, but I'm willing to put my fears in that regard aside to help Consuela."

"Sure?"

"I am, but if you keep talking this way, I may change my mind."

"O.K., what time do I meet her?"

"Eleven. She'll recognize you. Just as everybody knows you're not from around here, and that you don't look at all like a normal tourist."

With that Julie picked up her menu and ordered dinner.

§

The rest of the meal went well, as Julie treated her to a running account of why she continued to work at the hotel. She liked being in the Park, she told her, and the hours were pretty good. Not too much stress except at certain periods of the day. And she and her boyfriend didn't really want for much. It was hard for Julie to tell her age, but she seemed just a bit cavalier for saying she didn't want for much?

Yet Miriam listened to all this and thought it might be 'catching,' this lifestyle - at least the way she described it. Meal over, Julie got up pushed her chair back to the table and said goodnight. "I don't imagine I'll see you again, and I don't know whether to wish you luck in your search or not. But, in any event, have a good trip back to wherever you're going. I don't think you ever said?"

"No, I didn't. And, like you, I'm not sure what I might do with the information."

She thought she saw a reaction, a blink, but Julie covered it well - if there was anything to cover. "Yes, well I guess we both have reasons. Bye-bye, Ms. Stronge, *whoever you are.*"

That last comment seemed to communicate a message, but Miriam smiled and nodded. Julie turned and walked straight out the door to a car in the parking lot, and her boyfriend waiting there. She got into the car on the passenger side and they drove away without saying anything.

"Well," he finally said.

"Consuela will give her a lead - or mislead. And we'll get Mr. Stanson out of town safely."

§

The next morning Miriam showed up a few minutes early at Degnan's. Precisely at 11:00, a small woman entered the coffee shop and walked directly to the booth where she was sitting.

"Ms. Stronge," she said with a big smile, "I believe you wish to talk with me about something I seen a long time ago."

"Yes, Consuela, I am looking for information about a visitor to the park several months ago, and I understand you might be able to help me."

'Mebbe, mebbe not."

Miriam reached into her coat pocket and pulled out a long envelope, obviously thicker than if it held a letter or bill. Consuela took it and put it into her purse.

"You trust me?"

"Why shouldn't I. Julie say you're ok. That's enough."

"What about this man - what made you notice him?"

"I seen him with the other man, arguing. The one in the photo."

"What did the other man look like?"

"Like the photo, I told you!"

"Oh, yes. I'm sorry, I am most interested in the man in the photo. So did you see the one in the photo with this other man?"

"No, I didna see him with anyone else that day."

"Please, let's get clear. You saw two men one day together, arguing, and the next day you saw one man, not the man in the photo, the other man get into a car."

"Yes."

"Where?"

"At the gas station. He seemed nervous."

"O.K., What kind of car was he driving - did you notice?"

"It was a rental car, that I know."

"How do you know that?"

"It had an Avis sticker on the rear bumper."

"And the license plate?"

"Out of state, but I only see a coupla numbers."

"OK, do you remember the date?"

"Monday, for sure, because I always go to filling station on Mondays, when I have the day off."

"Right, and it was July?"

"Yes."

"Did you notice anything else about him that makes you remember him especially?"

"He seem nervous, like I say, looking all around him."

"But that could be just because he was a tourist - taking it all in."

Consuela shrugged, and gave Miriam a long look. "Yes, could be. But I think I see someone in passenger seat." She looked for Miriam's reaction for a second too long. Then she got up and left, leaving Miriam alone with her coffee.

What had she learned? Next to nothing, not even the make of the car. Miriam was not happy. She felt she had been played by Consuela - and maybe Julie as well.

§

Back at her motel Miriam pondered what to tell Carl Peters. If Consuela was telling the truth Robbie had a visitor - maybe - that he argued with, someone who left on a Monday morning, maybe with Robbie. It was not clear why no one had apparently followed the lead - except that he had apparently left no unpaid bills or luggage anywhere. Consuela had supposedly seen two men having lunch, and arguing, and later saw one and maybe two at a gas station. So much for this first search. Nothing, Nada. She was not going to waste time hunting around for hidden valleys or other places. It was time now to get back to home base in Columbus and start thinking about what Carl had said about someone who might have been an accessory and who would be most concerned about Robbie - and the possibility that the whole story might come out. Might that account for what Consuela had seen? And might it be that Robbie's disappearance had to do with the "other" man. Maybe, indeed, the real question was how to find the "other" man, not Robbie? So, in that case, what was she going to report to Carl?

Perhaps the place to start was Bashford College.

CHAPTER TWENTY-TWO

SEEING THINGS CLEARLY

On a rainy morning Miriam reported to Carl back in Columbus that the trail at Yosemite had run out - that Robbie had left no trace, and after a perfunctory search the "authorities" had given up without so much as a sigh. Peters grunted. "I've been thinking," he said. "It's surprising that no one back here seemed interested, no one related to Robbie or any former friends." He could understand that old friends might not wish to have anything to do with him after the murder. But what about his family? To start with, of course, Miriam explained, he was an only child.

Not much going there anyway, she concluded. If Robbie had used his 'disappearance' to start a new life they were not going to spoil that. And besides - as I said at the time his father was now dead, his mother was in a nursing home about to die... And that was more or less where things were, Miriam told Carl Peters. She told him about the person who had called upon Robbie days before he disappeared. Carl could not understand why that lead had not been followed up at the time. Consuela had demanded money. The more he thought about Julie not asking Miriam for money - maybe that meant she had been paid off by someone else? Miriam nodded at that suggestion but said nothing about any follow-up worth pursuing.

He paid Miriam but made no motion to indicate the conference was over. As Carl sat there the more he thought about it, he figured Julie at least knew something. If so, there appeared two alternatives: Julie had worked her own scheme with Consuela, and there was no lead, no man at the filling station, no rental car; or, two, Julie was working with a third person, and this unknown person had planned out a scenario that whoever showed up was to be told about an argument and a rental car to send them off on an endless search for Robbie some place away from the disappearance site. The scheme would also cover the mystery of an accomplice to the killing. When Carl then suggested that she had been "duped," Miriam reacted with a laugh. "Of course, that is a real possibility." But it was also possible Julie had played it straight. The search had several possible endings, she said, and their problem now was to find which one promised the greatest reward.

Carl was intrigued by the accomplice angle she had raised at the end of the conversation that morning when she made her report, the mystery man at the gas station. It fit the idea of an accomplice. She had seemed impressed more than before about that possibility. He had not at first told her about his contacts with Stuart Freed, or what he had learned about his paper at that seminar. But now they both agreed that was a line worth following. For Peters it was much more than that, but he would not confide anything more to Miriam just yet.

§

Where should she go next, Miriam asked? That forced Carl to talk about Stuart Freed's theories. After hearing him explain this angle, she agreed that was a logical place to start, even if she had doubts it would produce results. Fortunately, it would seem to him, Carl told her, that should not be too hard, despite the passage of years. The 1950s Bashford College yearbook, *The Emerald*, like most in those days carried photographs of all the "Greek" fraternities and sororities. All those students back then in coats and ties, smiling for the photographer as if auditioning for roles in musical comedies.

Before they had parted that morning, Carl, who did not entirely expect Stuart to follow up his paper had decided to make his move by sending contact information to Russ Lewis, hoping he would be intrigued. He knew, or at least thought he knew, that Lewis, now out of law enforcement, would not automatically respond to a message from him urging him to see Freed and go from there. It was a tricky maneuver, but one that might work. And now he had Miriam working this other angle. At some point he would try to call them all together.

§

Robbie's fraternity was one of the larger ones - Delta Chi Psi. The best place to look for the 1952 *Emerald* was in the library at Bashford College. That was no problem, the 1952 yearbook was readily available. The problem at the outset was that Robbie was in the 1952 Emerald, of course, but there was no indication of a "Little" brother there because he was a freshman, and in the next year, 1953, he would be sent to the Ohio pen. Robbie would most definitely not be in that year's *Emerald*, nor, for the same reason, would there be any reference to a "Little Brother." So, it was fair to say, it was not going to be all that easy to find the person, if there was one.

She reported back to Peters periodically on the state of the search- that she had contacted five of the pledge mates of 1953 without results and had little hope about the rest, at least in the short term. She had managed to get the addresses of the "brothers," but so far none had responded to her letters. She talked on the phone with a few all of whom professed not to remember anything about Stanson's connection to the fraternity. Why should they? She also tried to contact other students there at the time, but they did not have any reason to remember who Stanson's close pals at the fraternity were, or who his little brother might have been. Not all the members had little brothers in any given year. It would take some time for all this to boil down, and when it did there might not be anything there. "Should she offer some money?" Peters accepted the situation without dismay and sent Stronge a large check for expenses to Yosemite and 'related matters.' "There are other ways of going after the truth," he said. Now Peters began in serious the task of drawing all his threads together. He had already "introduced" Lewis to Freed. "Why don't you look up

Sheriff Lewis?" he told her. "I understand he is now a private investigator for an insurance company, but he might have some interest in the case still. He was the only person our family ever really thought treated us fairly."

"Do you know the company?"

"Continental, last I knew."

He had not told her all the details about how he had moved to secure a connection between Lewis and Freed, or where that matter stood, because he did not know.

§

Miriam wrote that down on a pad. Continental was a huge company with lots of agents and investigators. She wanted to wait a couple of days to think about the best way to approach Lewis. She did not have to wait long for something to happen that changed things around again. Peters sent her a clipping about *The Franklin Club,* describing it as a private monthly gathering of mystery buffs, where papers were presented to a select group of experts of various backgrounds and talents. A psychologist named Stuart Freed, he told her, had presented a paper about the case at a recent meeting. That was another lead to pursue.

It would take Miriam almost a week to find out much about *The Franklin Club*. The problem was she had no credentials - or knowledge of any member. All she could learn was that the "club" met in Philadelphia in one of the old buildings that dated back to the Revolution.

Miriam decided first to take Carl's suggestion and pursue Lewis to see if he had anything to say about the possibility of an accomplice, or the mysterious *Franklin* outfit. Finding him at Continental turned out to be a bit harder than she thought, because the company was not at all eager to reveal anything about its investigators, some of whom worked undercover. Using contacts from her old Columbus Police Department friends, she found out that Russell Lewis worked out of Cleveland.

She called the Cleveland office and was told that the company did not give out information about investigators. But that was a pretty obvious dodge, she thought. "Well," Miriam said on the phone with the operator, "I represent a client who believes he has some information to offer about an old investigation and I would like just to sit down for a quiet talk with someone who might have some knowledge of Mr. Lewis. Would you see that this message gets sent to the right person there? I would hate to be a public nuisance."

After a brief silence, the voice at the other end replied, "I will tell my superior about this call."

"Well, I'm going to leave my number just in case."

§

Five days later Miriam received a phone call. "Am I speaking to the person who was trying to find a Russell Lewis?"

"Yes."

"I might be able to help you with that connection."

"Oh, ok, anything you might be able to do would be appreciated. Perhaps you know the person who has suggested I try to get in touch with Lewis?"

"Yes, that would be a good idea."

"His name is Peters, Carl Peters. I think you knew him a long time ago, well, pretty long, twenty years. His sister was Wendy Peters. Does that help?"

"Look, why don't we set up a meeting someplace convenient for both of us."

"Sure, any suggestions?"

"I was thinking of the Fort Hayes hotel in Columbus. Do you know it?"

"That's fine - when?"

"How about Wednesday, say at 12:30? There's a small private dining room I sometimes book there during my trips around the state."

"Great, who shall I ask for?"

"Oh, no cloak and dagger, just Russ Lewis. We don't really have secrets at the company, just want to keep our folks from being pestered too much. I'll see you then."

§

On Wednesday Miriam drove down Route 23 and found her way to the Fort Hayes. She spoke to the hostess at the hotel restaurant who pointed her to the wide stairs leading to a heavily carpeted hall with elegant wallpaper depicting 19th Century scenes along the Scioto River.

One of the doors along the hall was slightly ajar. So she figured that would be her destination. Inside the small room with the letter "C" on the door sat Russ Lewis.

"Good afternoon Ms. Stronge. How is Carl? I haven't seen him in a long time - not since he watched me put a passenger in my cruiser headed for a place not very far from here."

"He still speaks well of you, of course, suggesting that probably you were the only one who questioned the outcome of that case."

"Well, that's going a bit too far. I had some lingering questions, that's all."

"About the evidence in the case, or the sentence?"

"I guess you could say both."

Here were two ex-cops thought Stronge, both talking around the point trying to figure out what the deal was.

Lewis smiled. "Suppose we just start by ordering lunch and then you tell me why Carl Peters hired you after all these years, and what it is that he wants you to find out from me."

"Well, did you know that Robbie Stanson seemingly disappeared while hanging out - I guess that's the right way to put it - in Yosemite? Actually, he had registered at the hotel under a different name. It was only after that person disappeared that the investigation revealed it was Stanson who had gone missing. At least I found that out from some questions I asked on a recent trip out there."

"Yes, there was some little notice of it because of the case I would imagine."

"Did you think there was anything really odd about that?"

"Maybe." Lewis looked at Stronge with an expression that said he was waiting to hear more, but with no promises of agreement. "I have to imagine he had planned at least that part, and maybe did a very good job of 'What's in a Name?' He was always pretty good at that sort of thing." Russ gave a little smile.

"You know, then, that no body was ever found."

"I did, but that's a big place."

"Maybe they didn't look very hard." Miriam put this as a sort of challenge to Lewis's seeming complacency.

"True, that happens."

Stronge pursued the point in police fashion. "Don't you think it was odd that at least someone didn't want to find out what had happened?"

Lewis shrugged. "Maybe. I gather you know for sure someone who does now, Carl Peters, and that's why we're here."

Stronge was trying to put a purpose to Robbie's disappearance, again waiting for Lewis to take up the idea. But there was no immediate response, so she began again. "Or maybe something else happened - maybe he had "help" disappearing like that so smoothly."

"That's always possible."

"So, there are at least two other possibilities. Right?"

"One, he had help disappearing; two, he *really* had help disappearing."

"Supposing a second party either way, then."

"Yes. I went out there and found a lead to someone who saw Robbie under his other name with another man, and then saw the other man at a gas station as he was leaving. My informant couldn't say if the person who looked like Stanson was in the car when it drove away."

"Really. Well, why didn't anyone out there follow up."

"I'm not sure. May have been they did without any luck. No pictures were available to help people identify the guy. No one took down the license plate, etc. I asked around but it would appear, I stress appear, that all the trails ran out with that other man leaving the park. There'd been no reason to detain him because Robbie had not yet been missed- to put it another way."

"What about luggage?"

"Well, there wasn't any. Which was kinda funny also. "

She waited for the reaction. "The person I talked with in the lodge said he registered under a different name. Another hotel employee saw a conversation between the Robbie alias and a second man. The Robbie figure might have been seated in the passenger seat with the man driving away from the gas station the next day. So what happened to him? All very hazy."

"I guess what you're driving at is that Robbie might have had a plan and maybe an 'assistant' to help him out of Yosemite - and out of his identity."

Miriam spread her hands. "Does look that way, doesn't it."

Stronge waited to see how that sank in, then went on. "Did you ever really wonder about Robbie's confession?" Miriam tilted her head to one side so as to look skeptical and waited for that to sink in as Lewis's eyes stayed on her and he nodded slightly as if hearing all this for the first time.

Then she went on. "But you accepted all his, 'confession' bull about elopement plans - just a tragic end to a college romance."

"And why shouldn't I have?" Lewis gave a little smile suggesting he might have an idea of what was coming next.

"You never thought, then, at that time about whether Robbie had help, not to do the killing, maybe, but to provide a place for her to stay where she wouldn't be alarmed?"

"Maybe I did think about that. But when I went down to Bashford to question Robbie's classmates, and a whole bunch of other students who I hoped might have seen something that night - nothing turned up, nada, zip. Oh, there was sight of a flashlight - maybe - but nothing solider than that."

"But you did give it some thought?"

"I did, but there was nothing to find out - least not from any possible witness."

"And when you fished around in that river with Robbie looking on from the bridge, you thought that one suitcase was all she had when she arrived in town?"

"Well, I thought Robbie didn't care to tell us any more at that point, and what difference did it make if something else got lost in the river - besides, remember, I found the murder weapon - or what he used to deface her."

"And you settled for that? You were *sure* that was the weapon?"

"Yes."

"Even though a few days later another suitcase turned up outside the stadium?"

"Yes. It was never proved that was Wendy's. Nobody saw what she was carrying when she came into town."

"But did you ask her landlady up in Cleveland about any of this - or the detective who found the letters from Robbie, claiming he didn't have any responsibility for the child she was carrying? He, at least, thought that all spelled premeditation, didn't he? And now are you also telling me Robbie could have found that instrument right away – if he hadn't planned on using it from the beginning?"

" You've done your research. Carl Peters hired you, right?'

Miriam nodded.

"Look, by then things had moved on. We had the confession, the prosecutor wasn't going to push for First Degree - for two reasons - first, because the defense was planning on a plea of temporary insanity, and urging a psychiatric exam that would have stretched out the process and maybe - even likely - ended with him getting away just with treatment and a nice room at one of the state hospitals for a couple of years. And, second...

"Yeah I'm anxious to hear that one."

"Robbie's youth."

Miriam grimaced. Russ waited a second. "And, o. k., third, I was being pushed aside by the prosecutor who, I guessed at the time, was under pressure from Bashford to get the thing over and done with, with the least delay to shut down the continuing bad publicity."

"So, you did have bad feelings about that?" She waited for a reaction, but then went on "and, now, after Robbie's strange disappearance it still didn't occur to you there was more to the case to be found out?"

"Which one, the murder, or his disappearance? No, I thought he might have committed suicide."

"But it could also suggest he had a plan to disappear. "

Russ did not respond. Miriam went on. "Here's what I think, and why. I'll start by saying that I have tried to contact Robbie's fraternity brothers, starting with his pledge class, to find out about his "Little Brother." You know about that system?"

"Yes, sure."

"But do you know how binding that can be - and I use the word in both senses."

"I think I might 'of heard of that - of course." Lewis did not hide his sarcasm.

"Back then it was something like 'blood brothers' even if the intensity varied from school to school and fraternity to fraternity."

"Yeah."

"I have tried to find out who his little brother was in 1953. Remember this all occurs in the early part of the year, so whoever was 'assigned' to him really hadn't had much time to figure out exactly how far he was to respond - or better put - yield to Robbie's desires. So there are really two groups of possible interested parties. First there were Robbie's classmates, the sophomores, and then there were the freshmen pledges. Right?"

"If you say so. So, what did you find out about Robbie's little brother? Anything?"

"Not yet, I tried to contact all of the - seventeen pledges - but so far I've only seen five."

"And?"

"And they aren't telling me anything. But there's something else."

"Always is, or I don't think you would've come to me quite so fast or at all."

"*The Franklin Club*. Carl told me that this man who is a student of old crimes gave a paper there about the Red Slippers murder. I looked this organization up and it's a semi-secret society in Philadelphia, apparently devoted to old cases."

"Really, well that changes things a bit."

Then Russ went on as if the idea was new to him. "At the time no one wanted to go beyond Robbie's confession. It was a helluva messy case - with everyone, *everyone*, just wanting to lock him up and forget."

"Oh, not everyone Russ. You know that." Miriam stared straight at Lewis. "Carl Peters and his family wanted more - and did not forget. They did not like it at all when he got out - and that's driving Peters mad now that Robbie's 'disappeared.' He would get a measure of satisfaction by knowing if he is dead, and - unlikely of course - if someone did him in."

"Yeah. I get the drift. But how do I fit in?"

"Suppose I get someone to really open up to me about the Franklin Club? Then maybe we'll have an idea how this could work out."

"You mean what to tell Carl Peters." Russ's thoughts were racing ahead. Should he tell her all he knew about Stuart Freed and Mr. X's threats? All that he already knew about the paper.

Miriam straightened up in her chair a sign Russ took to mean that she had some sort of proposition to offer but was being very deliberate. " Let us say just to begin with, that the people in the hotel out in Yosemite were not being entirely straight with me."

"Yes?"

"I don't *know* that was the case. I don't *know* that the women I spoke to, Julie and Consuela, had deliberately misled me. It's possible, always, that Consuela did not see anyone with Robbie out there, and that what she told me was just a form of a scam to get $500."

She went on. "Then there's The Franklin Club connection - it could be - crazy as it sounds that this mysterious paper I heard about has stirred up a whole lot of fear in someone besides Carl Peters. Something has triggered a lot of interest in the whole thing, and someone who is pursuing answers to whether Robbie had any help has been energized - or - really scared. Now, what's far-fetched (but maybe worth thinking about) is the possibility that this person Consuela supposedly saw killed Robbie out there because if he *were* caught out as an accessory it would re-open the case. I know, I know, this is truly farfetched. But imagine for a moment if you have lived all these years under the threat of being exposed."

Russ did not say anything. He was wondering about Miriam Stronge and how much she really knew about Stuart Freed's role in setting off this new interest in the case. He decided to wait before talking more about his meetings with Stuart.

§

Then he picked up his napkin in a gesture that might mean the conversation was over, stopped for a second, and decided to play it cautiously.

"But look at everything, Miriam, Robbie was paroled. He's not liable to any more prison time, and, according to the law, allowed to live his own life by this time - if, again, he is alive."

"But what if some new threat has appeared in his life? That's why he has 'disappeared.' Maybe Carl would be interested in how that might be. Aren't you?"

"Not really. Why make trouble for someone else at this point?"

"Well, what if that person wants to make trouble?"

Russ spent a full minute deciding what to tell Miriam, and his own doubts about getting trapped. "Suppose he already has - or someone has."

Now they were down to it. What she was really worried about was that Carl might try to do something desperate at some point, and it would be best to have some ground rules laid out that would cover all eventualities.

So it would now appear, did Russ. And he proceeded to fill her in on all the Mr. X contacts and threats. She sat back and felt a funny feeling in her stomach.

§

She feared where it was all going. This was turning into a game with shifting alliances - secrets within secrets - and likely no satisfactory outcome. Russ and Miriam were the most experienced with this game. But, in the end, could they really trust one another?

CHAPTER TWENTY-THREE
SEARCHING FOR A PLAN

Russ asked the waitress for more coffee, asking Miriam if she wanted anything else.

"No, I'm fine."

He had decided that, for the moment at least, they needed to work together. When the coffee came, he outlined in more detail what had happened in the last few weeks, starting with the letter from Carl that led to him meeting Stuart Freed. "I still don't know quite what to make of him. I don't think he's told me everything. And I certainly don't know exactly why Carl has thrown us together, as it were, but there is no other likely explanation. What does he think we can do? Maybe determine if Robbie is dead, or in hiding."

Miriam said nothing, waiting,

He nodded at her reaction. "Then there is this second person who doesn't want Freed to write anything more. If he wanted to discourage Freed from writing about the case, all he has accomplished with threats is to make it more likely, in fact almost inevitable. Freed is scared, of course, but not enough to drop everything. Besides, now someone else will pick up where he left off."

"You're sure Freed isn't bamboozling you into believing there really was (or is) someone out there threatening him?"

"Why would he do that?"

"To make sure that he gets credit for 'solving' a troubling aspect of the Red Slippers case. Maybe that's it? "

"Well, that's a thought."

§

Miriam continued sketching out a scenario to test Russ's degree of involvement with Freed. "X is Freed's invention to lure you, and Carl Peters, who jumped at the notion, and a whole bunch of people into believing in some accomplice theory. He doesn't have to prove it, does he to become famous."

"But, Hell, Miriam, you went out to Yosemite and came back with a story about Robbie's apparent disappearance and this strange other fellow. You're the one who's got me half-convinced to pursue this nutty idea - because there might be something in it."

"Yes, and you are the one who's been meeting with Dr. Freed - or should I say Freud - the way this thing is going it looks like we might need a shrink to figure it all out."

"Maybe we do."

§

They left the room agreeing to stay in touch. Miriam planned a trip to Philadelphia to see what more she could learn about the mysterious mystery seminar, and who might have been in attendance that night. It was not listed in any phone book, so she decided to try a local historian - one who specialized in secret societies. And to make that contact she started out with a phone call to the public library as a place where such a person might have been a regular doing research.

"There is a man," the library specialist on local publications told her," but I don't know whether he would be willing to talk about his research, especially if this is a secret society of some sort. He teaches at a local high school."

"Can you give me his name and suggest the best way to contact him?"

"Well, he's not the nervous type and he's pretty friendly to all the staff here, so I don't think he would mind. But let me check with him first and either he or I will get back to you."

"That's great," and Miriam gave the librarian her phone number.

Two days later she got a call. "Miriam Stronge?" asked the caller in a friendly sounding voice.

"Yes."

"My name is Frank Warren. And I teach history at one of our high schools. I understand you are interested in some of our special interest groups here in Philadelphia.'"

"Yes sir, I am particularly interested in 'The Franklin Club.' About all I can find out is that it is a secret society dedicated to studying unsolved cases."

"Well, that's a little strong - they may have 'solved' one or two over the years, but mostly they just have presentations and talk about possible solutions. In most all of the instances it ends there. But they do have some prominent folks, specialists in various ways, lawyers, forensic specialists, a couple of novelists, and so on. Well, I should start off by saying it's not really a secret society, just a private seminar that gets together once a month or so."

"Do they have a regular organization, so I can get in touch with them - or, better put, some individual in the group? I have a couple of things I'd like to talk about and maybe show such a person. I think they might be interested."

"Oh, really now. It must have to do with one of the seminar presentations, I would imagine. Can you talk to me about it?

"I have no objection to talking to you, Mr. Warren, but maybe we should think about a get together with someone who could represent the group. If I say it has to do with the Red Slippers murder case, you'll find out if there's any interest. Then I'll make a trip out to Philly and get a feel for the best way to proceed."

"Very well, I'll see if there is any interest in Red Slippers."

§

A few days later Miriam received the phone call she needed in order to spend the money and time on a trip to Philadelphia. She contacted Russ about the communication, but they agreed it was "premature" to inform Carl Peters - they had privately reached an understanding it was now apparent that perhaps their interests were not entirely parallel with those of Wendy's family. That was one way of putting it. And beyond that Russ had still not filled in Miriam Stronge with all of his information about Stuart Freed's starring role in stirring up this whole new "line of inquiry."

She made an arrangement with George Warren to meet at the Wyndam Hotel in the historic district. This place was neither upscale nor filled with "old treasures" as its location and publicity might have suggested. It was renovated mid-20th Century. Plain rooms and a pleasant enough with booths where, Warren had suggested, they might meet without causing much attention.

This last implied to Miriam that there was something to talk about. She hoped so because she wasn't at all sure how she was going to recover the expenses for the trip since it had been agreed that they would not tell Peters anything - yet.

Miriam had been told that George Warren would meet her in the bar/restaurant at the second booth to the right at 4:30 on Friday, October 22, the earliest he could get away from the school where he taught, the Friends Select School not far from

Rittenhouse Square. So there she sat that afternoon looking over one of the hotel's copies of tourist events, sipping a cup of Earl Grey tea.

"Ms. Stronge," announced the tall man who had come to the booth and stood smiling down at her with a friendly smile. "I am George Warren, at your service. Sorry I am a few minutes late. A student had a bit of a problem with an assignment. I say a bit of a problem, but I am afraid it was little bigger than that. He misplaced a book I had loaned him. But all's well that ends well - he went back to his locker and there it was!"

Miriam noted right away the British accent that may or may not have been exaggerated for her benefit, perhaps to establish his credentials in opening a serious conversation that had to do with very weighty matters. "That's perfectly all right," said Miriam with a gesture for George Warren to join her. "What will you have to drink?"

"Oh, thank-you. Just coffee, I think."

"Not tea, Mr. Warren," said Miriam.

"No, I seldom drink tea. I guess that surprises you."

"Well, yes, but it's a good warning not to stereotype." Miriam signaled the waitress and the coffee was delivered.

"You want to know about the Franklin Club seminars, Ms. Stronge?"

"I do, but it is Miriam, please."

"Very good, well there is nothing terribly secret about what it does. As I said on the phone, the membership is made up of lawyers, forensic specialists, and others with an interest in old unsolved or partly solved crimes. Usually murders, of course."

"Yes, I figured that out. A very impressive bunch, I guess. Now what I'm interested in is one particular murder, known as the 'Red Slippers' case. Goes back to 1953."

"Occasionally, very occasionally, I have been invited to attend one of its meetings. And as it happens, I did hear a paper delivered on that case by a psychologist, Stuart Freed."

"I had hoped so. Were there any other guests - or members - who took a particular interest in the paper - and its presenter - that night. Someone you might have noticed?"

"Not at first blush. You have to remember that I am not a regular. And the 'social hour' that attends along with these meetings does not last long at all. The members come, there is a drink (never more than one round), and the chair introduces the speaker - or turns it over to the evening's program organizer who then introduces the speaker."

"So you have no real idea about guests that evening?"

"Sorry, no - I couldn't say from memory more than half of those who were there - if indeed that many, I fear."

"Is there someone I could contact who might help."

"Well, I'm not sure there is, Miriam, because first of all the Franklin Club seminar works on a trust basis. Some of these cases they study have contemporary issues and implications attached. True, sometimes, if they actually contribute to 'solving' a case, there might be a bit of publicity. But even then... It could hardly be otherwise."

"So there is no list of participants and invited guests at the seminar for any given meeting?"

"'Fraid not. Sorry. Not an attendance sheet, but, of course if someone spoke up that would be noted in the minutes."

"There's no one, then, who would be able to give me a list of the members and guests the night of Freed's paper?

"No, sorry, again."

"Well, I guess that ends this trip."

"But perhaps not. Have you spoken to Stuart Freed about the seminar? He might remember the participants and be willing to talk to you. But, you know, you have not informed me about why you are pursuing the 'Red Slippers'"?

"I am a private investigator hired to find out all I can about what happened to the original murderer, Robbie Stanson, who served ten years for the crime, was paroled, finished college, went on in graduate studies and became a practicing therapist. He disappeared not too long ago while on a trip to Yosemite National Park. And I am employed to find out what I can. More than that I cannot really tell you - except to say that there is not much more I could tell you anyway."

"No new theory, then?"

"Well, I wouldn't..."

"Oh, please!"

"If I were to tell you there was some inkling of an idea to pursue, would that help your memory about that night?"

"I don't know."

"What did Freed's paper say about an accomplice."

Warren stirred his coffee. "It suggested there might have been."

§

Kent Crider had ceased communicating with Stuart Freed - at least for the time being. He decided to take some time to think more about what had led Freed to write about the case. Was it some recent idea he got somewhere? It could be, of course, that Freed had simply looked at the record of the investigation and Robbie's confession and guessed at what might have happened. Had Robbie told him?

No one supposedly knew what had happened to Robbie. If he was dead, the corpse was missing. It mattered little. The danger to Kent now was Stuart Freed's desire to "cash-in" on the old murder. How to stop that? Threatening Freed had been a freaked out response to reliving that terrible night. Made matters more dangerous for him. Another way? He had to think about that. He really did. No more cockamamie stunts.

CHAPTER TWENTY-FOUR
GAME PLANNING

Miriam Stronge decided she had to meet with Dr. Stuart Freed. He was at the center of this maze. Getting an appointment with him proved easy. His secretary found a time on his calendar in two days. When she came to his office at 9:00 on Wednesday, she was the only one present besides the secretary who sat at her typewriter apparently transcribing notes from the previous day's sessions with patients.

"Take a seat, please, Mr. Freed will be with you in a short while."

She looked around the waiting room at the pictures Freed had selected. Doctor's offices had interested her since she was a kid tagging along with her mother. She had just begun reading a story in *Time* about President Nixon's troubles when a door next to the secretary's desk opened and Freed appeared. He wore a brown jacket over a tan turtleneck sweater.

"Good-morning, come in, please. Would you like some coffee, or maybe tea?"

"Thanks, I'm fine."

Freed's office had the expected desk and couch and chair of someone who fit the bill of a "shrink," along with a box of Kleenex, also expected as standard "consultation" room furnishings. There were the framed diplomas as usual. Freed pulled his desk chair out into the room from behind his desk, in an opening gesture of equality, and motioned for Miriam to sit in the chair nearest the couch, making the scene as close to neutral as possible, and suggesting that the psychologist had no intention of playing doctor-patient games.

He began. "Now, I understand we have a mutual friend, Russ Lewis, someone you have met with recently and discussed matters of interest to all three of us, and, I now gather to Carl Peters – perhaps especially to Mr. Peters."

She said nothing, so he continued.

"Apparently my talk, and it was very preliminary, very sketchy, has set off a surprising number of reactions. I assure you at this point it is still largely conjecture, but apparently some people who learned about it - are feeling anxious."

He stopped at that point and shifted in his chair before going on in a new tone accented by folding his hands together fingers interlocking. "How much has Russ told you? I gather you had something of a surprising luncheon with him recently."

Miriam nodded. "Yes, you could certainly say that, and I suppose then he told you that Carl Peters has hired me to find out what happened to Robbie Stanson, who apparently disappeared a few months ago in Yosemite? And that he pointed me to Lewis?"

Stuart nodded.

"So you met, learned about my research and have come to me to see where this all meets – if it does?"

"That would seem to be it, yes."

Freed nodded.

"Well, there is something else," Stronge looked at Freed in a way to suggest *her* investigation had gone beyond simple conjecture. "I have been trying to find out who such an accomplice could have been – and no luck so far in trying to reach out to the fraternity brothers. Have you thought that your paper has simply kicked up a dust cloud? That there's no accomplice there? Just someone pulling your chain?"

Stuart looked at Miriam Stronge, and picked up a pencil, pursing his lips, and touching the eraser end to his nose before he answered. "Yes, when I started this I thought I might be wrong – well not really – because I actually wanted it to be right, that maybe the upshot would bring me a publication. Perhaps Russ has told you about my hobby? I have a sort of collection dedicated to unsolved cases."

Miriam nodded.

"He also told me, however, that you'd been in touch or tried to be in touch - with Robbie a long time ago when he got out of prison. That's right isn't it?"

§

Stuart smiled. "Yes, he told you that did he?"

Miriam was determined not to be "tag-teamed" by Russ and Stuart. "Ok, then, this is a lot more than a hobby to you."

"Yes, of course, I didn't mean to sound supercilious – sorry. Let's start over. If we are going to work together, a reasonable idea, I believe, I owe you a better statement of where matters stand. I read about the Red Slippers Case in a couple of magazines and went back over the details. When Robbie got out of prison, I tried to set up a meeting. And, yes, at one point I even entertained a notion of helping him get a restart. And that was pretty stupid…"

"Excuse me – but do you think Robbie thought it was pretty stupid? Did he think that maybe you were playing him for some reason?"

"Well, I don't know – I just suggested off the cuff in a letter he never answered that maybe we could get together and talk about things."

"He had a graduate degree in psych now?"

"Yes."

"What were you going to do? Analyze him or what?"

"I know it sounds really dumb."

"Wow, I can't believe this!"

"Russ said some of the same things to me, so I'm getting used to being lectured about my presumptions."

"Did you think what your real 'clients' would feel about your stuff on the side? I sure as hell wouldn't want to be one of your patients Dr. Freed. I would sue you for malpractice."

"Yes, I have agreed it was dumb – but it never led anywhere."

"Who broke it off?"

"There wasn't anything to 'break off.' I merely suggested we get together. But I didn't hear anything from him. And then…"

"Yeah, I think I know where this is going. You got serious about the case and started thinking about the 'accomplice' angle."

"That's true."

"But you didn't tell Robbie?"

"No."

"And then years later he disappeared – maybe dead – so he couldn't object, supposedly, to you blowing up his confession 'story.'"

"I thought about that, yes."

"But whether he was gone for good or not, there could be someone else who did not want the lid opened – if you were right."

"Yes, I certainly see that possibility, especially now."

"Bullshit, Dr. Freed, it's very hard for me to see what you thought might happen in playing around this way."

" I hadn't gotten beyond the suggestion he might have had help."

"But if your life, the life you had lived all these years since that one night, had come under threat suddenly, what would you do?"

Freed threw up his hands, and Miriam went on: "We don't know, I agree. But then Carl Peters, had a purpose in sending Russ to you."

"Yes, and you've no doubt learned from Russ that there has been a strange sort of blackmail threat as well from someone who wants me to cease and desist."

"Lewis mentioned that to me. Didn't this Mr. X lead you on a bit of a wild goose chase a while ago?"

"He did."

"And you haven't heard anything more about a money offer? Or anything else?"

"No."

"Well, you appear to be in a holding pattern, then, right?"

"It would seem so, yes."

Miriam got up to leave. "I'll talk to Russ and see if we can all get together." Stuart rose and held out his hand. "Yes, I think that would be the next logical step." When Stronge was gone, he sat back down, brooding about the complications that had brought about this strange alliance.

§

After Miriam returned to her hotel, she took the piece of paper with Russ's phone number. He had said he would wait to hear from her.

She dialed the number and waited. "Russ, I just left Stuart Freed's inner office. Have you ever been there?"

"No, we talked in a coffee shop both times we met. Why?"

"He's been lying to you."

"What are you saying?"

"He doesn't have a Ph.D in psychology – he has a master's in social work."

"What?"

"That's right. But you know that there are lots of people who set themselves up as counselors. And his diplomas are right there on the wall, so he wasn't deceiving anyone - at least not purposely. Well, I take that back. He's hardly a model for the good doctors on TV, is he? I was a little put out that he didn't stop me calling him 'doctor.' But never mind all that."

"Well," Russ mused. "What do you think our next step should be - meet with *Dr.* Freed or something else?"

"I need to think."

§

Miriam believed that there were too many loose ends. She smiled at that phrase, because the great danger was that a meeting of the three would only end by tying them in knots. But it was the only way to proceed that she could think of. Usually, when Miriam had sat in on police examinations, the person being quizzed had few options to answering questions. But this was different. Stuart Freed was not suspected of committing a crime - indeed, he was closer to becoming a victim if someone was threatening him. But was he really being threatened? The starting point was Robbie's disappearance. So that's where they should begin with Stuart. What did he know, or suspect had happened out in Yosemite?

She and Russ were going to have to be careful not to give Stuart an easy way to explain everything. But there was Carl Peters' passionate interest. Did Carl hope to use Freed to flush out an accomplice? Whether he intended things to go this way, Stuart Freed now appeared at the center of this circle of events.

The first thing to do was to call Russ and plan out a strategy.

§

Russ had waited to hear from Miriam about the next moves. Was he at all sure he could trust Stronge? So far they had met only once and had a few telephone calls. She had said that she is working for Carl Peters. Is she also freelancing? And they had not yet talked about the end game. Where does all this come out? What is the point now, anyway? Is it to destroy someone else's life? Why didn't he just wash his hands and go home? What had happened back then happened. Who was to say that Robbie had not paid fully enough for what he did? Still, Russ could not forget that morning in the woods and what he saw there. If someone else had been with Robbie that night, to what degree was he guilty? He kept thinking also, in the back of his head, that maybe it was his duty (funny word when he wasn't 'on duty' anymore) to try to prevent something else from happening - but what might that be?

CHAPTER TWENTY-FIVE
CHOICES

Russ took the initiative suggesting that they - Miriam, Stuart - and himself should meet together, after which the two former law officers would hold their own confab to discuss the next steps. The best place, he had insisted, was his motel room. And so they gathered there on Saturday morning. Russ sat on the bed, Miriam in the standard motel easy chair, and Stuart at the desk with the motel letterhead stationery in a tray. He immediately picked up a ballpoint pen near the tray and began doodling cursive alphabets. Miriam looked annoyed.

Russ began. "As I see it we need to pursue again the Yosemite angle. Miriam, you went out there and talked to a couple of people, who – I gathered – you were not sure if they told you all they knew. Right?"

"Yep. That was Julie, who works as a receptionist and sort of general manager, I guess, though I never got her exact title, and Consuela, who apparently saw Robbie's visitor as he was driving out of town. Whether Robbie was in the car also, she can't say. All she knew was it was an out-of-state car."

"O.K. So Stuart, did you ever hear from Robbie?"

"No, I wrote him a couple of times at his parents' address, as I said before but no letters back."

"So," Miriam said, "you were in touch with Robbie much more recently than you let on."

"Well, that's not so. My letters were not answered. I keep saying that."

(Actually that was not so, or only half-true. Robbie had tried to correspond once, but Stuart had been on vacation and did not see the letter until Robbie was presumed missing or dead.)

"How in Hell then did you know he was headed there?"

"I didn't say that. You're trying to trick me. I think I read about someone whose picture looked like him going missing. And that was confirmed at least by his parents."

Miriam glared at him. "Okay, we'll let that go for the moment."

"And you don't know if any letters were found in his room?" Russ asked Miriam.

"Honestly, I didn't ask, I didn't inquire. Should have. But remember this person went out one morning and never came back. So anything he threw away that day would have been gone by the time he went missing."

"Yes," Russ said. "Unless someone was watching."

Stuart picked up the line. "Are you suggesting someone might have followed him to Yosemite?"

Miriam replied, "Could be, Stuart, I don't rule out anything." She looked hard at him, and he stared back. Then she turned to Russ. "And it could also be that Consuela had been clued in by somebody, perhaps Julie, to pay special attention to anyone asking around. They may have played me. Can't be sure of anything or anybody."

Russ held up his hands. "Let's take this back a step or two."

He went on, "Miriam, did you see anyone out there who knew of a visitor, besides that one instance with Consuela? And what did she actually see?"

"I'm not sure. All Julie told me was Consuela saw someone at a filling station that she had seen talking to someone who looked like Robbie at lunch, and then that person filling his car with gas.

"Well, maybe," Stuart said. "But then, again, suppose there was no person at the gas station. That Julie simply told her to say that so as to throw you off."

Russ felt the conversation was going nowhere, simply back and forth over ploughed ground.

§

"I think, Stuart, that Miriam and I need to talk about the next steps."

Russ's dismissal statement made clear Stuart was not invited to the follow-up conversation. But he nodded and left with a smile on his face to suggest he understood that the other two would call the shots on what came next. He smiled to himself as well, because he suspected they did not tell one another, either, all their thoughts. That was fine, too. "I'll wait to hear what you decide."

After a few moments, Russ picked up a piece of motel stationery and the ballpoint pen. "I think we have to take Stuart out to Yosemite - just to see if he is the person who Consuela saw. We can't pinpoint all the dates from this end, and a facial recognition is the best start – if we're going anywhere anyhow." He wrote "SY" on the paper. "We need to have Julie and Consuela see him and take it from there."

"Yeah, ok, who's paying for this? So far there's a big nothing out there – just Carl Peters' interest in finding out what happened to Robbie and a possible accomplice per Stuart's seminar paper – about which he found out some way – and his plan to write an article. Why should Stuart bite? He has no reason to go - unless we play on his vanity about his 'project.'"

"Carl already paid you, right, for your report?"

"Yes."

"And he sent you to Philadelphia."

"Yes."

"So presumably you're still on the case, and he's paying (or at least promised to pay) expenses and a fee?"

"Yes."

"Well, you can tell Carl what the plan now is, can't you? He's playing his own game with you."

"I'm willing to sign on to Yosemite," said Miriam. "I need to have a talk now with Carl, bring him up to speed – about the need for another trip to California – to show Stuart around. But not too explicit, because I'm a bit leery of getting too close to a possibly unstable guy who thinks he is calling all the shots. At some point we may have to find a straitjacket, and I'm only half-kidding!"

Russ nodded that he understood.

§

When Miriam called Carl Peters about the plan to take Stuart out to Yosemite to gauge reactions - he thought the "plan" was worth a try. He approved everything, tickets, hotel, per diem, and a $5000 fee for each. Getting Stuart to close down his office for a week on short notice proved not to be a problem. Indeed, he seemed more than eager to accompany the 'investigators' on this quest. Here was a chance to test out the theme of his planned article. The dangerous Mr. X had not been in touch again. The truth was, of course, he simply didn't know. But he felt safe with them and Carl Peters even called him to say he had high hopes for finding the trail. What Carl did not say was he also had plans to join the trio.

§

So Stuart was happy to be involved in the search for "clues.'" He took a couple of days to re-arrange his scheduled appointments. None were all that pressing at the moment, routine anxiety and depression cases. The only one that seemed a bit iffy was a woman who had talked in one of their sessions about suicidal thoughts. But that was months ago, and he gave her the name of someone to call if she felt really bad while he was gone. Actually, this schedule fit what Miriam and Russ wanted to do, anyway. They hoped to get to Yosemite and look up Julie before Stuart arrived. They would inform her that they had found someone who knew Robbie (maybe not a lie – who knew for sure?) at one time and they wished to talk with Consuela along with this person. Stuart might – probably would – figure out at some point that he was being used or tested. But that really didn't matter.

§

Their plan never got started anyway, because Julie had left her job weeks ago. She was no longer at the hotel – no longer in Yosemite so far as anyone knew. She had left a note telling the manager she would be traveling for a while but would write soon as she got settled. The manager, Robert Seedloe, was not happy, both angry and sad at the same time. "She just pulled up and whoosh – was gone. Left me to scramble to find people to cover for her while we looked for someone else."

"Didn't tell anyone where she was going, then," Miriam asked?

"Nope, she was a good hotel person. Be hard to replace her. Knew how to handle unhappy guests. Kept the reservation entries in good order. All of it. I figured if she left it would be for a top managerial place somewhere like here, only better paying. Actually, we would have tried to meet an offer."

He would have gone on talking about the many talented Julie, but Russ interrupted: "What about the maid, Consuela? According to Julie she knew something about a man seen around the hotel with Robbie Stanson."

"Don't know about that. I don't even know the name. Not that I know everybody on the payroll, of course. Some people come in for work, then stay for a few months, or even just weeks - or days! If you were to test me on any given day about all the staff here, I couldn't possibly tell you all of 'em. Now if it was the chef, or the bartender – especially the night bartender – now he's very popular..."

Russ raised a palm in surrender. "I get it, but would you mind if we asked around?"

"Sure, go ahead. I'd like to know myself about someone who knew Julie and where she might have gone."

§

"So what do we do now?" Miriam said to Russ later in the bar. "Stuart's arriving tomorrow and we don't have anyone to show him to. We don't even have a picture of either one."

"No, but I'll bet the hotel personnel files has one of Julie, at least. I'll go to the airport to meet Stuart while you check around for a decent enough photo. Just don't get bogged down with Seedloe."

The interim manager was happy to provide a photo as well as the picture of Julie on the advertising brochure. He even looked for some record of the hiring of a maid named Consuela or a name like that.

Leaving his office a few minutes later, he handed the materials over to Russ. "Like to have the photo back when you finish with it - just don't take it when you leave."

"We won't, I promise, I'm just going to look around a bit, ask a few questions in a low-key manner. You don't mind that, do you?"

For the first time Seedloe frowned. "Maybe I responded too quick. I don't think I can give you permission to just walk around among the guests or stopping members of staff - doesn't look exactly right. And you're not policemen on a manhunt, are you."

Russ looked apologetic. "No, no, I understand, of course, but could you ask a couple of people who might have known Julie, if they would be willing to talk to us?"

"Now, I'm not sure I feel comfortable about this, either – the more I think about it. She has a right to privacy. And I may already of stepped over the line a little bit. I think I'm going to ask for the photo back. I made a mistake."

"Well, I still have the brochure."

"That you do, but I hope you aren't going to wave that around, stopping people."

The more Seedloe talked it became clear he was regretting ever having said anything at all about Julie's abrupt departure. He was especially sorry now he had even emphasized how sudden it had been. "How long are you guys going to stay around, anyways?"

"Not long, two or three days."

"OK, but I need those rooms by Friday – latest." He walked back into his office not slamming the door but shutting it firmly.

§

Russ let out the breath he had been holding. Wow, I blew this one, he thought to himself. I shoulda just tried to navigate – maybe I should've let Miriam handle Seedloe. He went into the bar, sat on one of the stools, and asked for a Bud.

"Draft or bottle?" the bartender asked.

"Draft's fine."

When it was put down in front of him, he smiled, and put an Andrew Jackson on the bar. "You miss Julie?" he asked, touching the bill.

The bartender smiled back at Russ –" a little bit, well, like just between us she had a fine style." He was almost a caricature out of a Saturday afternoon Western, like those he had seen every week back in Massillon as a pre-teen, with a handle-bar mustache and garters on his arms. He brought Russ's change back from the register. "Didn't know her much – I usually came on after she left for the day."

"Oh, ok," Russ said, starting to pick up the money. The bartender put a finger down on the bills and waited. Russ pulled out another Jackson and put it on top.

The bills disappeared. "She came in a couple of nights to see how business was, what the guests were having, you know, just casual stuff."

"Yeah?"

"Yeah. Chatted 'em up a little."

"Anyone in particular you notice?"

"Not really. But there was one night she brought a guy with her and sat down for a few minutes with him and someone in a booth over there." He gestured towards the area with a slight arm bend.

"See that guy again?"

"By himself, you mean?"

"Or with someone else."

"No."

"That's all then?"

The bartender looked at him.

Russ opened his wallet again and pulled out a third bill. "I'd like another beer," he said putting the twenty on the bar between them.

The bartender took the bill and came back with the beer. "There was one time I saw her out in the parking lot on my way in. She was with a shorter woman, dressed and looked like a Mex or something."

"Yes?"

"They seemed to be talking about something serious. She gave Julie a piece of paper – but then I was already past them, couldn't see anything else."

"Suppose I bring a couple of people in here tonight. How late are you here?"

"Depends."

"Depends?"

"What night it is."

"Is tomorrow a night you'll be here.?"

"Could be, depends."

"Depends?"

"Yeah, you know how busy we are, stuff like that."

"And maybe you might have seen one of them before, you know."

"I might remember if I did – hard to say. Lot of people pass by here."

"Make it after seven."

"Right, after seven."

§

Stuart's plane was on time, and Miriam met him at the gate. It was an almost two-hour drive then from Fresno Airport to the national park. They finally got to the lodge about nine in the evening. At a late dinner in the lodge's main dining room, Russ filled them in with what he had learned from the bartender.

"That woman Julie was seen talking to might be Consuela," Miriam suggested.

"Yeah, but I don't think that's anything to count on, given the bartender only saw her for a few seconds. And even if that is who it was, might not mean anything."

"Right," said Russ. He did not tell them about the man Julie talked to in the bar, not until he had a chance to talk to Miriam alone first.

§

Stuart was happy to rest up after the flight and go to bed watching tv. Miriam called Carl to fill him in with the latest developments.

"Great," he told her. "That bartender may prove very helpful. But the news that Julie has suddenly quit her job is even more important. How much background do we have on her?"

"Not a lot, but we'll keep looking here, and Russ gave me a copy of a brochure with her picture. I'll fax it to my old buddy at the Columbus police department, see if they have anything on a Julie Fowler."

"Why them?"

"Suppose she's tied up some way with Robbie. Just a chance." But she had little hope of a positive reply.

CHAPTER TWENTY-SIX

IDENTITIES

They all met the next morning for breakfast. Russ had talked a bit to Miriam about the bartender's willingness to talk about Julie's 'acquaintances.' Now he elaborated. It bothered him a little that the man came up with information so readily, and whether any of it was made up for a "tip." But Miriam had seen Consuela supposedly, as well as Julie. Maybe the bartender's description of the other woman in the parking lot might be enough for him to recognize who Julie met outside. Probably not. Never could tell. But maybe he would recognize Stuart. Russ remained convinced that Stuart had not told them everything about his connections to Robbie. He realized (too late, alas) that he had not asked the man how long he had worked here. He was not even sure Miriam had told him everything she had found out on her trip out here.

Miriam had no trouble allowing Russ to be the "team captain," as it were as they began by talking once again to the ranger station, this time with Stuart in tow. But once again nobody there claimed to have seen Robbie Stanson or anyone who resembled him in 1972.

There were dozens and dozens of mountains, they were reminded: El Capitan, one of the steepest, or Mount Hoffman, and there were deep valleys all around, they were told. "Lots of 'em. It's not surprising no sign of Mr. Stanson had ever turned up. There were places and places not seen for years by hikers."

Russ looked at one of the park brochures with a picture of a log cabin overlooking mountains off at a distance in a blue haze. The caption read, "Escape to a Perfect Cabin Getaway in Yosemite National Park." He smiled to himself, "So you did, Robbie, so you did. Why'd you come out here, anyway?" He turned to the others. "Let's go back to the lodge. We've lost our one lead – or two if you count the mysterious Consuela. We'll have dinner, a drink in the bar and see if we can change our tickets."

§

But there was still the bartender. He smiled at them as they entered. Russ arranged seating so that Stuart was facing the bar as he went up to order the drinks. "Don't think I know that slim fellow. I do remember the other one – she was out here asking questions a few weeks ago about that man who disappeared – but I couldn't help her."

Russ nodded and took the drinks back to his companions. Another disappointment. So far the trip had been a total waste of time and Carl Peters' money. He himself had been ambiguous about the search. Miriam had been hired by Peters supposedly to find out if Stanson was still alive, and if so where. Why should he get involved in what was getting to look like some sort of lost cause - and maybe better that way?

They said goodnight. Russ returned to his room and his phone message light was blinking. It was a call from Carl. He would return it in the morning.

§

Miriam and Stuart stayed a while in the bar. Miriam had wanted time to talk with Stuart alone. "You know," she began, "Carl Peters is very interested in your research into a possible accomplice. He sent me to Philadelphia. And now we're out here trying to chase down a lead I found – and nobody's around, apparently, who knows anything about that. You find that odd?"

"Yeah. But people change jobs pretty often in the resort business."

"Oh, well, yeah, but it's still pretty interesting, don't ya think that, well that, it almost seems like someone knew we were heading out here? Julie seemed pretty set in her job – a good job, so she indicated to me. And Consuela – well she supposedly has a sick husband, or something. Seems strange to me. How 'bout you?"

"I don't really think much about it."

"Ok, doc – only I guess you aren't really a doc."

"No, patients sometimes call their therapists that out of their expectations, I guess."

"And your master's degree – that's actually in social work."

"Yes, but I think you'll agree there's a lot of overlap, and I think you'll also find there's quite a number of people – good people – working in therapy, with patients that benefit a lot from our help. I have never pretended to be anything other than what I am."

"But you're not really qualified in criminal psych are you?"

"No, of course not – anything that comes close to that in my practice, I immediately refer to someone trained that way."

"Yet you have a big interest in 'unsolved,' or partially solved cases. Right."

"Yes, but you know all that already."

"Yes, I know all that from you and from what Russ has told me. What I don't know is how you came to think Robbie Stanson had an accomplice. Simple deductions, I guess you'd say. Pretty good – cause it seemed to hit home."

Stuart just nodded and took a drink.

"Well, what made you first think about an accomplice, then?"

Stuart put down his drink and looked at Miriam as if seeing her in a new light. Miriam merely smiled back.

"I don't think I'm one of those people you used to interrogate in Columbus, Mrs. Stronge," Stuart said, getting up and sliding out from the booth. "I think I'll say goodnight now. See you at breakfast."

"Sure. Goodnight, sleep well. We'll talk about some of these things – sooner or later."

§

Stuart returned to his room and locked both locks on his door. He went over to the desk that held hotel stationery, pulled out a couple of sheets, and sat down to write. But he decided instead to watch TV. It was Sunday night, and a segment recorded broadcast of an old *What's My Line* was on, part of a Fifty Years of Quiz Shows special. That show, thought Stuart was on when Robbie watched television – if he did, back in college. But it was on at a time when he was probably with Wendy. Stuart switched channels. He knew he was going to have a tough time going to sleep. He would call his wife in the morning. She would be worried, but no sense calling so late – he told himself. He knew he should have called earlier but had really been distracted by the news that Julie was no longer around. What if he had recognized her? Seemed unlikely, of course – she hadn't been here that long, or had she? There was no connection - except the thought that had occurred to them all that Julie and Robbie might have linked up some time ago. Well, he had enough to think about with the matter of an accomplice.

§

Miriam thought about calling Russ up for a talk about their next steps. The more she talked with Stuart, the more she was convinced that he was holding back more information. His insistence that his talk to the seminar that set all this in motion was simply deductive reasoning didn't convince her at all. And she thought that Russ was simply anxious now to close up the whole "case" because the supposed accomplice, whether Mr. X or somebody else, either was not that person, or if he was – ought to be left alone. She also figured Russ was afraid of giving Carl dangerous ideas. Maybe that was unfair. But she had undertaken to find out everything she could about what had happened to Robbie Stanson for Carl Peters. And even if she hadn't already accepted his money, by this time she was determined to find out what had happened twenty years ago on the Bashford campus. She owed it to Carl- if only to prevent him from doing something dangerous. At least that was how she explained her behavior to herself now.

§

Back in his room, Russ saw the blinker on his phone. The hotel operator told him someone had left a number. He dialed the number and actually hoped no one would answer. He was sorry this whole thing had taken this turn. He didn't want to be here. But there it was.

It rang twice – then. "Hello."

"Hello, yes, this is Russ Lewis. Someone called me and left a number in my hotel room."

"Yes. I know that. It's Carl Peters. We're all searching for someone, or two people, Russ. My feeling is you're closer than you think. I'm coming out there to join you: Don't give up."

"I don't know what else is here for us," Miriam conceded at breakfast in a way she hoped was convincing, to herself mostly. Russ had thought all night about whether he would tell the other two about the phone call. No one had told him to keep it secret; no one had told him to keep any communication secret. So he decided to tell them.

"There was a call from Carl last night." The other two raised their eyebrows almost in unison. "He's coming out here to join in the search. I don't know if that is good or bad."

His companions remained silent. Finally, Miriam spoke up. "We came out to find some answers; so far we have found zilch. I appreciate you told us," she said. "I'm sure Stuart does, too." She looked at Stuart who nodded back.

Russ was not altogether happy about the situation, to say the least. Like it or not, they had been thrown together. With Miriam, he had begun to feel Stuart had still not confided in them all he knew, or how he knew. But let the cards fall where they may. He had the feeling something was going to happen – soon. It almost seemed to him that they were all held together by a belief that they owed Wendy. He did he knew, as well as Carl, most certainly, but maybe Miriam since she had gotten involved. Less so Stuart, of course, but he had pulled back from thinking about Robbie's rehabilitation as he grew convinced there had been an accomplice. But how far did that extend? A good question, certainly, because it could become a curse. Of them all, he was the only one who had seen her body as Robbie had left it that night.

§

After breakfast they broke up with no plan in mind, waiting for Carl to tell them why he thought their search was not a failure. Russ believed as did they all that Julie's "disappearance" had some significance. Miriam had tried to find out from old connections. He would wait to hear what she might discover. As he entered the elevator, another front desk employee he had seen stepped in quickly. They were alone. He turned to Russ. "Seedloe gave you a brush-off, didn't he?"

Russ took a deep breath. "Not sure what you mean. Mr. -?"

"Prentis, Tom. You know what I mean - about Julie." He waited. Russ said nothing. "You want to know what happened to her - why she left."

Russ waited a bit more looking at his new acquaintance, who was grinning at him. "Look," Russ finally said, "let's take this a step at a time. First, I think I have to tell my companions something about what you think you know."

"Not think about it – I do know. The only question is whether I am going to tell you anything. Look, we can go on with this crazy debate or we can start talking business. Up to you. I think it's worth some C'notes."

"If I say yes, how do I know anything you pass on to me is that valuable?"

"Oh, it is, my friend – it is. For starters let's say someone who looks something like that picture your female buddy showed Julie was in the lodge a couple of times."

"When was this?"

"Quite a while ago, at least a few months back obviously. But I don't say it was him for sure."

"I don't know that we have a 'deal' yet. How can I get back to you?"

"You tell your buddies whatever you want – makes no difference to me – and I'll have someone contact you. Not good for you to be snooping around the way you people are doing. Jesus, like amateurs!"

Russ raised his eyebrows, but he had to admit they had been acting a little bit like Krazy Kops. But this smart-ass Prentis talked about C'notes like a movie-torn guy. Hah. Yet with Carl coming out, he kept his reply civil as he stepped out of the elevator. "What time?"

Prentis pushed the down button and gave a little wave. "I'll decide that. But don't worry - it'll be when you're available."

§

Russ called Miriam and Stuart. "Someone just now told me he has information about Julie. We need a conference to decide on the next steps." He proposed lunch, but not at the hotel. They drove out to a diner at the edge of the park in Russ's rented Ford.

They sat down at an empty booth near the back. The place was nearly full of chattering people who paid them no attention. "O.K.," said Russ, "here's the deal. This guy showed up in the elevator, claims someone who looks - something like the picture Miriam was carrying when she came out here - wants - as he put it, a few C'notes to tell us anything more. The other two stirred their feet at that and stared at him. "Yeah, that's what I thought. For this he apparently proposes to tell us something about Robbie Stanson's time here – and a possible connection with Julie."

Miriam pushed herself back against the booth with both hands on the table. "I suppose you're wondering if Carl will spring for that money."

"Well, I guess he'll have to, unless," he turned to Stuart with a slight smile, " one of you've got that kind of money to spend. Look, I got dragged into this by Carl, and I'm not at all sure about going ahead. In fact, I have big doubts about that. Something about sleeping dogs."

Stuart smiled back. "But they're not sleeping are they?"

Russ acknowledged Stuart's comment with a shrug.

Miriam nodded, but raised the most obvious point. "Why would Carl Peters put out money to a guy who thinks he knows something? I can't ask Carl to put up that kind of reward for information that at most will be little more than rumors that maybe floated around here when the Robbie look-alike disappeared."

"I'm hearing you. It's the way I would normally feel, too. So, you don't even want to ask your 'employer' what he thinks?"

"Look, Russ, I think I agree with you – probably Stuart does, too – so why not give us the name..."

"Won't work that way, he said he'd contact me. I don't have a number. So, do you want to get an early read on how Peters feels about this, or not?"

Stuart had stayed silent.

Finally, Miriam said, "I'll call Carl."

§

"Carl, I'm out here at Yosemite. Russ appears, and I say that carefully, to be in touch with someone who may shed some light on what happened to Robbie and who might have seen him in contact with Julie before he disappeared."

"Yeah?"

"Yeah, but he wants a reward for something that may turn out to be nothing at all."

"Like how much?"

"Like maybe a few hundred - although he may be trying to play us and that would only be a down payment."

"Is there any of bargaining with him?"

"Don't know. I haven't talked to the guy. Russ apparently spoke to someone. It may be worth it, may not, but I'm not at all sure the opportunity will last that long

- if it's legit. I sure wouldn't want to be the one who has to decide. I have no idea what I would say if it was up to me. Whether I'd bargain – try to, that is – or not. Something else."

"Yeah?"

"Then there's Stuart. He's gotten awful quiet – and, also, I don't think Russ is telling me everything about his conversation with this mysterious guy."

"What do you mean about Russ?"

"He said the guy would tell him about people who were seen with someone who looks something like Robbie, but he didn't give me any names or anything, and it was somewhat unclear whether he meant before he supposedly disappeared or after. I think Russ would like to get out of this whole thing, but the guy is talking to him, isn't he? And Russ keeps bringing up how you got him involved. So, he's wondering if the whole thing was a mistake on his part for tracking down Stuart to find out what was going on. Now he's very uneasy, Russ, that is, and Stuart's always been uneasy, dangling between the excitement his paper has brought him, and now out of fear of the ultimate consequences."

"Yes, I can see that."

CHAPTER TWENTY-SEVEN

DECISIONS

Russ picked up a day-old *L.A. Times* in the news shop and settled down in the lobby. He watched a few of the staff wander in from someplace, talk to the clerks, occasionally disappear to some room behind the registration desk, and could not help wondering if Prentis (his real name?) had actually seen Stanson with Julie or was just a clown looking for vacation money. Most likely it was someone who saw the bartender make some big tips and wanted in on the game. But it was up to Miriam to get the word from Carl about what they could "offer" the man. He went back to reading the paper's sports section.

§

Stuart had gone back to his room to make a phone call to Carl.

"I don't think I want to go on with this."

"Why say that, we may be getting close."

"Yeah, well too close. I think I may just pack up and go home – forget about trying to find out about an accomplice – just move on, you know. Not write the article." It seemed his ambition had already shrunk from a book to an article.

"Move on? To where? You're labeled." Carl tried not to show it in his voice, but he was furious.

Stuart couldn't back out now. It was Carl's play now and he wasn't going to let it die. Russ and Miriam had taken the initiative, yes, but now it was his call. *He* was paying the bills and had no intention of losing this chance to find out where Robbie had gone. Damn Stuart. He guessed he needed to show some teeth. "Well, it's a bit too late isn't it? Whoever is threatening you can't ever be sure that you won't decide the other way sometime next month, or next year, or even years later. No, you're in far too deep my friend. You stay there. It was brilliant of Russ and Miriam to think about this rendezvous at Yosemite. This guy who contacted Russ shows how close we are. Bet on it."

Stuart said nothing, and Carl went on: "It's what we all want - a final end to this." With that Carl hung up.

Stuart realized with Carl's voice banging in his ears that he had gotten himself way too involved with a man determined on revenge, at any cost. But what could he do now? He sat on his bed and considered his alternatives. He should never have told Carl about his suspicions. Why'd he do that? He could not make himself understand what had led him to say anything to Carl about an accomplice. Boasting about his research? Yeah, that was the big part of it. To make Carl think he was serious about finding out the truth. But it was really the fame he sought as the person who uncovered the dark secrets of the "Red Slippers" case.

§

He was still thinking about how we all rationalize our desires and decisions when someone knocked on the door. He got up and walked over to answer, completely lost in trying to figure out how to disengage from the search for information about an accomplice without making things much worse for himself. He looked down and saw that a large envelope had been shoved under the door. It probably contained a copy of the hotel bill. They had not indicated they were leaving today, but maybe they kept you up to date, or it was a mistake.

He took it back to the desk beside his bed, went to the mini bar, extracted a beer, and opened it with the church key that hung beside the small fridge. He sat down with the envelope. It was not sealed. He turned the flap back and pulled out an eight-by-ten photo of himself knocking on a door of one of the cabins.

Stuart stared at the photo, breathing hard. He felt light-headed and the room seemed to revolve around him until he shook himself. His first thought was: someone has been watching me, waiting to see if I would turn up again out here. Then he thought more about what that meant. Is this person the one who talked with Russ? He knows. That's why he is trying to set up a meeting, sure. But why contact *me* now? To cement his desire to get Carl to put up money. Hell, he didn't want *anybody* to know he had been out here earlier. It was foolish to believe no one knew.

He had not seen Robbie when he made that trip - but who was going to believe him?

§

Miriam had gone to her room for a nap. Before she could doze off she heard a knock on the door. Going to the door she found a letter size brown envelope shoved halfway under the door into the room. She pulled it through and opened it. Inside was a photo of Stuart looking displeased standing on the porch of a cabin she presumed was one of those for rent here in the park. At about the same time Russ had come upstairs from the lobby to find a similar envelope under his door. The same picture was inside, but there was a typed note as well: "I will wait until 9 to learn if you are interested. Call the bar and ask for me. T.P."

Russ called Miriam's room. He did not mention the photograph – at least to begin with. "I got a message from our 'friend.'"

"Yes?"

"He says he will wait until 9 pm to hear if we are interested. Do you have anything from Carl."

"Nope. But I will try to find out." She did not mention the photograph either, or that she had received the same message.

"OK, keep me advised."

"Right."

Miriam pressed down on the phone twice and got a new dial tone. She dialed Carl's number.

"Yes, I figured you would call soon."

"Well, there's been a big development."

"Oh?"

"Yeah, a person claiming he has real information about Robbie says he'll wait until tonight to hear from us. He wants a big payoff. $500."

"Yes."

"Nine."

"I see."

Miriam had figured the conversation would go something like this way. She could hear Carl's heavy breathing and decided: "There is something else."

"Really, shame on you Miriam for holding out on me."

"Let's have it."

"This person has sent a picture of Stuart Freed standing on the porch of one of the cabins here."

"Jesus!"

"No date, no message, just the picture."

She waited.

Carl grunted. "Stuart wants to pull out, he told me a little while ago on the phone." He paused. "He's scared. And he's been holding out on me. This visit had to be before I heard about his researches and he contacted me. Stuart was looking to do some kind of deal with Robbie if he told him his 'story.' I'm sure of it. He wanted to use me, too. Now he's scared, because someone was keeping tabs. Well, maybe more than just one person. But surely someone who spotted Robbie, knew who he was, and kept a watch, thinking about a payday. Bingo, Stuart shows up. Nothing for a while. But now he's seen Stuart again with you two. Perfect for that guy. That long-ago visit didn't pan out then but it set things up for what's now happened, Miriam, I'm sure of it, not your recent contact with Julie. I believe Stuart's secret visit did it. When you came out maybe Robbie *and* Julie had already made plans. And now she's gone – with guess who."

"Yeah, I suppose that's a possibility - but maybe we're going too fast here," Miriam replied. "We don't *know* that Robbie and Julie are connected, and we sure don't know for sure what Stuart's visit set off. Remember, she had gone by the time the three of us got here."

She waited and then Carl answered. "I'll get back to you in an hour with what I'm going to do. Keep your eyes on Stuart. He may do something. And keep in mind the Julie angle."

"O.K."

He hung up and Miriam sat there for a long time holding the dead phone. No one wanted to tell the truth about this unholy mess. Carl was unbalanced, desperate to find out what had happened to Robbie and the supposed accomplice.

§

She felt very alone for one of the few times in her life. And the cause was whether to go along with whatever Carl was planning, if he even knew where he was headed now from hour to hour. From what was going on it was pretty clear that there was a lot she didn't know about Carl Peters and what he would do to make up for his sense of guilt. Like Russ she was beginning to think she wanted to get clear of this tangle. Too many things happening. She had the distinct feeling she had not been hired just to find someone but was being used to set up some other 'plan.'

With that she picked up the phone to call Russ, and relate to him her conversation with Carl, while taking care not to reveal all her growing reservations. "Carl's not ready to buy into this until he knows more."

"Yeah, that's reasonable, but I gotta tell my caller something when and if he contacts me. Let's the three of us get together for dinner and try to do some planning. Miriam, meantime, there's something else..."

"I know, at least I think I do. Does it have to do with a visual?"

"Yep. I got it, too."

Russ was playing with his ballpoint, wrapping and unwrapping the telephone wire around it. "So, Stuart's been holding out on us – big time. How're we going to handle this?"

"We confront him and ask him what's the story – simple as that," said Miriam, "at least as a starter. I'm not sure he will tell us anything. We let him ramble, maybe and see what spills out – and go from there."

"Let's meet in his room before dinner."

"Do you think Stuart got the picture, too?"

"Doesn't matter because if he doesn't come clean, we just confront him. But let's give him a chance first to tell us before we come down on his holding out on us from the start." After a pause, he went on. "I imagine as well that if he got a copy, he's pretty uptight right now, trying to figure out his best play with us and Carl. Yes, let's see if he's got some explanation."

"Are you going to call him – issue the summons as it were?"

"Sure, I'll do that. And it may turn out that Carl's reluctance to put up the cash will bring this thing to an end right here. It may be that Stuart will convince us that this Prentis guy doesn't have anything."

"Things could end in a worse way, a lot worse. But I don't think that's likely."

"I don't think so either. Still too many cards yet to be played."

§

Stuart had hardly moved since receiving the picture in the envelope. He had no idea what he would tell the other two – or Carl if it turns out that Miriam told him about it

When Russ called, he was more than ready to leave his room that now felt like a trap. No, he was told they would all meet there before dinner. Just after six there was a knock on his door. He opened the door and stood back waving them in with a flourish – as if it was just a casual visit from old friends.

"Welcome to my humble abode. Can I get you a beer – I haven't had a chance to look in that little fridge yet." He continued smiling.

"Whatever's there," said Russ. "Thanks."

"I'd just as soon have a coke," Miriam replied. Neither said anything else as the drinks were passed out.

Stuart took some bottled water. "Well," he said twisting off the cap of his bottle, "what's the latest?" He sat down and waited.

Neither answered. They made much of drinking and just smiling. Stuart smiled back. "Well, he finally said, ... I ... why are we having this meeting, anyway? Whose idea was it?"

"We thought maybe you might have heard something, Stuart," said Russ.

"Me?"

"Yeah, have you?"

Stuart looked from one to the other. "I might have."

They nodded. "And what might that be," asked Russ?

Stuart looked at his bottled water, barely glancing up. "Is Carl going to pony up, then?"

"Why would you think that Stuart," Russ said. "Why would Carl think this new guy has anything to offer? You must have an idea." He tilted his head to one side, a gesture he had perfected way back in Germany to unnerve a suspected smuggler. "We don't even know who actually wants the money, do we?"

"You guys know, because you received that picture of me. So, let's stop playing games. I will admit that I haven't been completely forthcoming."

"Honest might be a better word, don't cha think?" said Russ.

Stuart took a deep breath. "Yeah, I came out here looking for Robbie just before he supposedly went missing. I can't say what happened to Robbie - I didn't see him then. I stayed only a couple of days at a motel. That's it, end of story."

"But he hadn't used his name," said Miriam. "So how did you know to come out looking for him?"

"Well..."

"Yes, Stuart, you've been holding out all this stuff," said Russ.

"O.K., his parents told me." He waited but the others said nothing. "At that time, I hadn't really thought very much about an accomplice."

"So," prompted Miriam, "So, what did you think you were doing then?"

"I don't know, anymore. I guess I thought in terms of forgiveness – well maybe not forgiveness, exactly, more like redemption. One thing I've learned is that we all live 'dangerous' lives in the sense of that old saying 'There but for the grace of God goes...' well, any one of us, really."

"You really think that is the case, Stuart?" Russ said as Miriam shook her head. "I don't believe you for a minute – not a minute."

"O.K., you guys are trained to see the 'bad' in everyone beyond mistakes or momentary lapses."

"Momentary lapses! You were playing Robbie just as you have been playing us. And you went after the accomplice idea – and that changes everything about the crime," said Miriam. "And you got Carl involved, because he hired me to pursue that angle as well. But you opened the floodgates."

"Well, yeah, that's sorta what happened."

"Jesus, Stuart," Russ interrupted before anyone could say more. "Sorta, sorta? That doesn't begin to describe your actions." He waited, but there was no comeback from Stuart. "Not only were you trying to deceive everyone, you were playing out of your league. Suppose Robbie, suppose Robbie's still alive – he wouldn't want that known, and suppose he's dead, suppose the accomplice killed him…"

"I know, I know, the accomplice wouldn't want to be exposed. I get it."

"And you teamed up with Carl – you …."

"I did, ok, I did, once I became convinced that there was a chance that was what really happened. I had come out here to offer help, but Robbie didn't turn up. I thought we had a meeting date. I went back home a few days later, thought some more about the situation, and maybe was a little pissed. But that didn't make me pursue the idea."

"No, then why? You went ahead with that seminar paper, just as you always were. Helping Robbie? Bull, you wanted to write the book. Then the real Mr. X came on the scene."

"Well, I guess it was a little late to pull back."

"A little late! My God, Stuart," Russ exploded.

"I guess I thought no one connected to the case would be at a small private bunch of would be Sherlocks."

"Maybe it also occurred to you that if you could publish this stuff - however it affected Robbie or the supposed accomplice, you would be famous, and no one would dare attack you."

"No, I hadn't thought that – not at first. I've told you everything now - some of it I'm not proud of - o.k.? I admit that."

"But you were seen out here. You slipped up there right at the beginning. Somebody knew you were playing around – well I take that back – injecting yourself into one of your unsolved murders, or something on that order. We know somebody - maybe more than one person - had recognized Robbie despite his efforts to disappear and was putting a watch on who might be seen with him. That's clear from this guy Prentis who wants to cash in now."

"Yes, I guess that's a good way to put it. But after I failed to meet up with Robbie, I guess I didn't think of it that way."

Miriam continued the bad-cop-good cop routine, "Help me understand, what way did you think of it?"

"I also saw it as an intellectual exercise."

"You have more motives than a cat has lives," said Russ. "Not just an article, then, but a new career as Stuart Freed – crime solver. Good God, I can hardly believe what I'm hearing."

Miriam picked up on the theme. "Well, somebody obviously doesn't want people thinking anywhere along those lines. Or, finally, someone was out to have some fun scaring the bejesus out of you. Now, which is the more likely?"

Stuart merely nodded. "Yeah, I guess so.'

"Well, which dammit?" Russ nearly shouted. "Which, Stuart? No more games. By this time you know which - you are in deep – over your head. Who's going to get you – and now us, out of this mess. And you've even got Carl Peters breathing fire again – what if he hires other people, who have..." Russ did not want to finish the sentence with what he was thinking.

No one said anything for several seconds.

Finally, Russ breathed a long sigh, and said, "Look, we need some decisions here, or we could go on like this all night long. Miriam, you need to get back to Carl to see if he has decided what he wants to do – pronto, because I have to expect someone will follow-up on that demand for money. Maybe these are the last decisions we will have to make. Just close up the whole thing. There's not a real shred of evidence that there ever was an accomplice, whatever we might believe. Either way we should leave it alone. The crime was committed the killer confessed

– it's over for everyone. If so, no one has to worry about being exposed. In that case, also, what difference does it make whether Robbie's dead or just missing? "

§

"I still need more first," said Miriam. "So, let's go back to the beginning, Stuart, when you first started reading about this case. Somehow the questions you were asking about an accomplice reached Carl Peters."

"Yes, that's so."

"Did he know that before? Before you met - several times - with him to talk about it?

"Yes, no – but he suspected – like Russ did. But you know all that."

"No! We don't know 'all that,' Stuart. "We didn't know you had been in touch with Carl all the time. You played it for us as if you were just a serious researcher working independently without any special connections specifically to this crime, so that you were simply one of those people who have all sorts of ideas and theories about crimes that have not been tied up – and some that supposedly have been."

"Well, yes..."

"Of course. And you played a game with Robbie, too, with the usual requests for an interview and information by offering to help him find a place to "start over," as it were."

"Shouldn't have done that! I agree. But I never saw him out here. His parents told me he was coming here – and I showed his picture around – well only to this Tom Prentis. That trip ended in failure. Didn't see Robbie."

"Probably, no certainly," said Russ, "the person who directed you to that cabin was the one who must have snapped the picture. What happened is you came out to find no one registered anywhere as Robbie Stanson. You showed the picture around and Prentis probably did not recognize it. He sent you to that cabin knowing there was no one it and figured taking your picture there might produce something for him later."

Stuart nodded. "Yes, could have been that way.

'Then he kept the picture you had asking for a day or two to show it around. Right?"

Stuart nodded again. "Only what he did was have it copied – and found out the whole story of the crime. No slouch Mr. Prentis, no not at all. Now he had something if you or someone else came looking. You were set up by Prentis. He must have been delighted to see all of us - a whole gang of ignoramuses just wandering around. Easy targets for getting taken."

They left Stuart to meet later in the dining room. As they walked down the hall, Miriam said, "I sure wish we could find Consuela to see if it was Stuart at the gas station that day."

"Yeah, but what are the chances of that?"

CHAPTER TWENTY-EIGHT

NO EASY OUT

Miriam had set out originally to find Robbie – or find out at least what had happened to him. Now everything had been transformed – in large part because of Stuart Freed. Finding Robbie had been stymied. But Carl had then ordered her to go to Philadelphia. His long determination to pursue "justice" had been re-energized. Only later did she learn exactly how Carl had got connected to Stuart. Did Stuart tell him from the first about his plan to re-open the case with his seminar paper? Miriam had at least decided that Russ and Stuart were not a "team." But she had little else to explain where they found themselves now.

So she decided to call Carl yet again. Maybe he would play it straight now.

"Hello Carl, anything you want to say about our new informer?

"I've been thinking about this a lot, as you well might imagine. Stuart's first trip was not really a big deal, is it? He never met Robbie. These photos don't prove anything. But there is the Julie angle to pursue. And I don't think I need to pay for something he has already spilled about going on a goose chase."

"Yeah, well Prentis does seem pretty amateurish at this. So, no dice then?" She hoped that Carl would drop things right there. But that's not what she heard him say next: "Right, unless this guy comes up with something far more enticing. Like a positive link between Robbie and Julie."

"He put a deadline on it. Meanwhile, I'm now working to see what I can learn about Julie." She wasn't really but could not say outright that Carl should drop the whole thing.

"Yeah, but it's not like he's a kidnapper, is it," Carl said. "And he's not able to blackmail anyone, either. He just thinks he can hold us up – me rather – for a payday. I'd have to ask for a lot more first, and maybe not then."

"Ok, that's what I'll tell Russ to tell him, and if there's any change in the situation I'll alert you right away."

"Yes, you do that. And meanwhile tell Stuart I'm not too mad at his weak nerves. He can redeem himself. He's put himself at the center of this whole damned thing."

Yes, thought Miriam, what hath Stuart wrought! She was growing more sympathetic to Russ's desire to call it quits – now – before further complications trapped them all.

§

When Prentis called the bar, then, as he had said he would. Russ told him essentially what Carl had conveyed through Miriam: no money for old news. Unless he had real information to sell about Robbie's disappearance, and its relationship to Julie's sudden departure, there was nothing to talk about.

He heard Prentis say, "You'll be sorry." And the phone slammed down. O.K., thought Russ, I'll tell my interested parties what you said, my friend.

§

Miriam's phone call to Carl had made him all the more determined to pursue every avenue to secure final justice for Wendy. Stuart had originally reached out to Carl to ask whether he believed she was really someone who would be willing to stay alone in that miserable shack for even one night, let alone the two that Robbie demanded? Carl responded he hadn't given those questions a whole lot of thought.

In fact, he told Stuart his main focus was how he blamed himself for not "looking out" for her when she arrived in college.

But he was still furious, Carl had said to him, that the judge had not imposed a longer term before parole could be considered. For that matter, of course, he was appalled by the DA's willingness to ignore all the evidence that Robbie had planned to kill her. Carl was not a lawyer. Yet he had always suspected that some sort of fix was in. How had the parole board let him out - even after the scandal? It was almost like all he suffered was an after-school detention!

Until Stuart had come along, however, no one else seemed interested enough to put everything together the way he eventually did in the "seminar paper." Stuart's argument, Carl sensed immediately, put the crime in a new light as a planned execution – to be disguised as a dreadful moment of blind anger. His best option, he had decided immediately, was to get Russ and Stuart working together, even if it was gamble.

And what, then? Meanwhile, no one knew what had happened to Robbie, and no one seemed to care very much. It was like there was a new fix in to protect Robbie once again. Well, maybe that was too strong a way to put it - but if the "system" was through with Robbie, Carl sure wasn't. Was it possible to confirm absolutely what Stuart Freed was thinking about an accomplice? Or to discredit the theory. He had to know. He honestly did not know what his next step would be, but he had to know.

§

It was time to quit the whole confused tangle Miriam said to Stuart and Russ. "We haven't talked to anybody who really knows, or if they do, gives a damn about what happened to Robbie. Carl can settle up with us for expenses and that's an end to it so far as I am concerned."

Russ nodded. "Carl sent me to Stuart in a strange way to get me hooked. Stuart, you've supposedly got yourself in trouble with the accomplice angle, and that worries me, but there isn't anything I can do about it. I think the best thing you can do is go back home and talk to the police about protection if you want. Unfortunately, I doubt very much if they can do diddly-pooh at this point. So, I guess all I can say, is take care, and good luck."

Underneath their seeming lack of concern, however, both Miriam and Russ felt frustrated that there was nothing they could actually do. Stuart shrugged. "I guess it's time to call it quits. This whole thing started with me, … "

Before he could go on, Russ interrupted, "Oh, no Stuart, you might have made yourself a target for someone – but it started with Wendy's death, let's not forget. The killer was tried, and sentenced, and, despite lots of controversy about the parole, let out of prison. He tried to re-establish a place in society and then disappeared. You're just someone who showed up with a theory."

"It's damned worrying, though," said Miriam.

"But not enough to keep on looking for a phantom accomplice like Carl wants to do," said Russ.

"No not enough," agreed Miriam. They could do nothing to help Stuart if he were actually in danger. That's what they were saying, but both knew they were floating excuses that made them uneasy, because, right or wrong, they felt some responsibility for the bumbling Stuart Freed. It sometimes happened that way.

Both feared that Carl Peters had lost himself in false visions of retribution and had become dangerous to others - and to himself. His actions could have serious consequences for them all.

These thoughts passed between them without a spoken word. Miriam had had the more recent contacts with Carl and was in a sense the closest to him of them all. She had come to fear more than ever that she might have to protect Carl from himself. Robbie was now, in her mind, an afterthought because she believed him dead - or gone far away out of anyone's reach.

§

Around ten o'clock that night there was a knock-on Stuart's door. He thought one of them might have left something earlier. He looked around the room first to see if he saw anything: nope not a thing. He shrugged and went to the door. He opened it and stood in the doorway.

The person standing there he recognized from the seminar. Why was he out here? He stiffened and moved back a step nearly closing the door. His visitor had a worried look, like someone anticipating the worst. He did not seem threatening. But that didn't mean anything really. He was wearing glasses with narrow gold-colored rims.

"Stuart, please don't do that, we really need to talk."

"I don't know you. Please leave or I will call the front desk."

"Oh, I wouldn't do that, Stuart. Not until you hear what I have to say."

Stuart hesitated then opened the door wider and motioned the man to enter his room.

"Who are you? What possible interest do you have in me?"

"Oh, come on. Don't be shy, you have pursued a mission – and succeeded - regardless of what damage you might do to some people who got pulled into the mess Robbie made."

"Mess? My God what a way to describe a cold-blooded murder."

"Well, there's still a question about that …. But even if I agree with you, why should Robbie's crime threaten others after all these years?"

"Look, please leave. If it's any comfort I just learned Carl Peters is not going to pursue the search…"

"For now, maybe…"

"How the hell do you know so much?"

"I don't. But it's pretty obvious you three are here looking for information."

"You've been watching me – and now my two friends. You best leave, because they are professionals."

The man just smiled. "Please Stuart, don't try to scare me."

He waited for Stuart who said nothing. "I just want you to know the facts."

He smiled again and still waited for Stuart to say more.

"My only guess is that you are in fact the Mr.X who wrote me those threatening notes, matched with an offer to pay me if I dropped the search into an accomplice."

"Why do you assume there is only one person worried about your research?"

Stuart shook his head, as if he had no answers.

"Nothing to say, come on *Mister* Freed, if Robbie's alive he might be afraid the case will be re-opened."

"He was tried and convicted, served his time and tried to start over."

"But this search for an accomplice obviously involves him. And complicates a disappearing act. And now you've opened the gates, wide."

"You keep talking in the present tense about Robbie. Do you actually know anything?"

"Let's say Robbie ordered me to come out here. Well, that's a little strong, let's just say he invited me. After he learned about this summit conference. He knew where you were headed a long time ago."

"What???"

"Yes, from Miriam's first trip and he figured Carl was behind it or at least in on it. Who else but Carl cared? And he had never really let me go. Every two or three years I would get a card addressed to 'Little Brother,' no name just the card saying the sender hoped I was well. There were also phone calls from someone who hung up right away."

"There's nothing more for either of us to say. I've decided not to pursue my research. I agree with Russ, and I think, Miriam, now, that there's no real point in going any further."

"Nice try. You might be right, Stuart. There's no point in going any further with this."

Stuart nodded vigorously.

"But there's another path that might get us both out of the woods in a safer way."

"Why do you say us? I don't want to even think about this anymore."

"You're in very deep, Stuart, very deep."

CHAPTER TWENTY-NINE
THE CHASE BEGINS

Kent left Stuart's room and went down the stairs until he reached the lobby floor. He started to enter the lobby, then stopped, he did not want to be seen by anyone else just yet, returned to the stairs and went on down to the basement, figuring there was an exit there into the parking lot. He was right and started to look for his car. There it was, and no one in sight. He walked casually so as not to attract the attention of anyone who might be looking out a window down on the cars. Reaching his rental, he got in and sat still for a minute. He needed to catch his breath. He had just outlined a plan to Stuart with a less than sure outcome, far less. When his heart slowed down, he pulled out the key from his sport coat jacket, inserted it in the ignition, started the car and looked in the rearview mirror. Someone had just pulled into the row behind him. God, they seemed to be taking forever! What the hell was keeping them? What were they talking about, Jesus, move, get out – get out of the way!

The passenger door opened and a woman in a maid's uniform got out. She bent back into the car, still carrying on a conversation. "Leave, for Christ's sake," he wanted to shout. "Go on, you 're late, leave." They continued to talk, she got back into the car and leaned over to kiss the driver. Finally, she got out again, closed the door and waved to him from the rear of their car. She walked briskly towards the door he had exited. But the man sat there. Kent was ready to scream. He had to move, get out of there! Finally, the car behind him pulled out and he ducked down.

He backed out and was soon on his way through the park. He reached an exit and drove on to the motel where he had been told to stay. He had told his wife when he left Philadelphia that he had to see a wealthy client who was vacationing in

Yosemite with potential new clients for the investment firm where he was now a a partner. He had said he would stay in touch with phone calls. Kent's wife Ann had her own career as an expert on early American interiors at a famous antique store. She did not worry about him. They had met their senior year at Duke, where he had transferred at the end of his first semester at Bashford, dated, got married, and enjoyed a good life on the East Coast. Their son and daughter had both graduated high school and were happy in college.

But all these years his whole life since that night had sometimes seemed like a suspense movie. He could not watch detective shows on television. But most of the time he could handle it. Once Robbie had confessed, pleaded guilty, and sentenced to prison, he had relaxed a bit because he had understood that Robbie could not implicate him without facing a much more serious charge. After Duke, he had started his career in Philadelphia as a client advisor for a leading investment bank and lived a "normal" life in the suburbs. Still, he got those cards to "Little Brother," and the phone calls. He dreaded a visit. "Hi, it's Robbie." How the hell had Robbie located him? Well it wasn't really that hard to explain. For a time there was a worse fear: a knock on the door: "I'm Lt. Smith, we'd like you to come down to the station."

The phone call had not come. No knock on the door. He had seen the small item in a Philadelphia newspaper about Robbie's parole – and the minor scandal that had caused the Ohio governor to call for an investigation. He sometimes had nightmares about that awful night. Sometimes, instead they were about that bridge. He and Robbie would be walking down to that bridge across the river where the sheriff had found the suitcase. For some reason they would be standing together with the sun glinting off the water. Sometimes he would be alone watching from the end of the bridge. He would see Robbie motion to the sheriff. He had not slept "that" night. He had expected then that whether Robbie said anything about him or not, the sheriff would investigate and find out that he had been there, that he had helped get Wendy into the car, had ridden along with Robbie, had helped him drag her out into the woods, had left something behind in the car, would hear a knock on his dorm room door…

But it had not happened. Years and years passed...

Then a friend asked him to go with him to a crime seminar. "Come on, there's always cocktail hour first along with some eats – and you really meet some neat folk who make it a specialty to discuss old cases from the 19th Century on. There're forensic specialists, defense lawyers, journalists, prosecutors – some retired, some active. It'll be a lot of fun."

"I don't know, that's not really my thing."

"Oh, come on, you'll like it – and maybe make some useful contacts."

Jesus, useful contacts!

He had panicked after the seminar shock and made that stupid threat. But Robbie had now contacted Kent but not because of the seminar paper, but because of Miriam's trip that followed Stuart's failed effort to find him. Robbie actually did not know much about the paper. But he knew Stuart Freed had been seeking him, and where there was smoke there was fire – Carl Peters – his pursuer. Stuart had come out *before* the seminar paper. Robbie wanted to stop Stuart's interference before he even gave the paper. Kent had no idea of all this, of Stuart's trip to Yosemite, but the seminar posed a real issue for him. But none of the how and why mattered now. Robbie had summoned him to come to Yosemite and check in at a certain motel. He had decided there was no other way to get around it - Robbie had summoned him to come to Yosemite by saying a few words: "We are both in danger, little brother."

§

He drove with all these thoughts racing one another again in his head until he reached his motel turn off from the highway. Robbie had picked a large one, a Best Western, and told him to register there for three days. He picked up his key at the registration desk. He had told everyone at the office that he was consulting with some mining executives about some mergers – all very hush-hush. Since there were lots of mines in the state – gold, silver, iron, other minerals it was perfectly logical that a meeting in Yosemite would be arranged for hospitality and convenience.

He got to his room and -"Hello Kent. We have a problem."

It took him a moment to recognize the person sitting in the chair by the bed. He was very Western-looking with boots, jeans, and a shirt that looked like it might have belonged to one of the Sons of the Pioneers in an old cowboy movie – with, who was it, Roy Rogers or Gene Autry? Somehow that seemed fitting because it took him back two decades and more to the time when he knew the person sitting there with one leg crossed over his knee.

The hair was different. He wore a goatee that had grey hair in it. He had on aviator sunglasses. But the recognized the smile. "Hello, little bro."

"Robbie?" The only real surprise was how he got into the room. Kent had followed "orders," as it were, in coming out here. But now he had to hope that Robbie had not somehow learned all he told Stuart. Couldn't imagine that he did, but then...

§

"Oh, I'm not Robbie anymore, Kent. And, of course, I want it to stay that way. But you're getting too much attention, and we have to think what to do about that."

"Well, it's that damned Stuart Freed who's causing us both so much difficulty.

"Of course. You wanted to be free of me, and I wanted even more to be free of someone getting to you."

Kent felt panic rising in his stomach. How much did Robbie know? "I just went to see Freed to try to convince him to stop what he's doing. Isn't that why you got me out here?"

"How the hell did you even get through college, Kent? I'm serious. Why have you been such a success in finance." He shook his head, sadly. "The point was to keep the case buried."

"Yes."

"Well, why the hell did Stuart Freed get started on this Sherlock venture? Julie told me about him when he came out here the first time."

"Julie?"

"Yes, Julie, my wife. It may be, I realize now, too late, that maybe we played it too cool. We shoulda just gone away - far away - figured out some plan to establish my new identity. But Carl Peters probably pushed Stuart Freed from the get-go. He's like a dog with ragdoll in his mouth, he's not gonna let go. And he sent that woman investigator out here - for sure."

"I was there that night in Philadelphia, Robbie. I heard the damned paper. He said the evidence of a 'simple' crime of passion wasn't convincing. But he didn't mention Peters."

"So? That doesn't mean a damned thing. Peters, for sure, is behind it. And that's a danger to both of us. He was all over that investigation, mad as hell about the way it turned out."

Then he suddenly stopped talking, took a breath, and leveled his eyes on Kent in the same way he had that night half-pleading, half threatening. "Little brother, we are both in this - for damned sure."

Kent was nodding again. But he had devised another way of dealing with the situation since he had received Robbie's orders, one that he had half outlined to Stuart Freed while he was still unclear about exactly how it would all end...

"Damn it, stop doing that," he heard Robbie saying in a demanding voice. But Kent kept thinking out what he had told Stuart to do. Some of this he had sketched out in his mind on the plane, but the details had begun to crystallize as he decided to meet with Stuart.

He heard Robbie go on - "I don't want your approving nods you nitwit. We have to stop Peters, and that will end it. Freed would get the point and close up shop."

Kent didn't believe that for a second. But he couldn't keep himself from nodding - as if he really was still obligated to his Big Brother.

"You know," Robbie said, shaking his head, "you're almost as - hell, maybe worse - than those guys." He laughed, slapped his leg and got up from the chair.

"C'mon, let's get you to a safer place."

"No, Robbie, I've got a better idea."

Stanson stopped where he was. "Yes?"

"I don't trust you, Robbie. Sorry. I took some precautions. I left a note in my desk drawer at the office that fills in all the details in Stuart's guess work paper. No, I didn't say in it you were alive because, obviously, it's best for us if you stay vanished. Yes, I panicked when I heard that paper - and have done some pretty foolish things." He paused to let that sink in and watched with a small smile as Robbie's face tightened into a frown.

"Now - you don't know if I'm lying, do you?" It was his turn to smirk as Robbie had a few minutes earlier. "Maybe I am, and I just now thought all this crap up to save my ass. Maybe. But just as likely I am telling you the truth - and telling whoever finds that note that I have gone to Yosemite to look into your strange disappearance because some new evidence has turned up. Obviously, I don't ever want this note to be read because that will mean very likely that I am dead. But it *will* be read if I go missing - oh, and I forgot, I mentioned the Philadelphia Seminar. So people (let's say some police investigators, perhaps) would ask around about that - and -heck - don't you suppose that would set off a real flurry of interest in the Red Slippers case, only now it would be the *new* Red Slippers-Mysteries. Yeah, it would be - with you as a special person of interest again. Alive, after all."

"How, about that, Kent! Damned if you aren't a bit smarter than I thought. I guess we both need to be a bit more careful."

Kent just looked at him. Robbie seemed unimpressed with Kent's warning. "Don't you want to hear my plan? Here's what you're going to do." Then when he finished, he put on his hat and left.

§

Kent sat down in the chair where Robbie had been. It was as if he could still feel his presence and it caused him to pull his hands off the chair arms as if they were red hot. He rubbed them together in a washing motion. He thought Robbie was going to kill him right then and there and had only improvised another plan on the spur of the moment - leaving behind a 38 caliber pistol. You'll need that to...

§

Kent had left no note in his desk! That was why he was shaking now after Robbie had gone. He was cursing himself for *not* leaving behind such a message from the grave. He liked to think that was because he was afraid that someone might see it while he was gone – some busybody secretary maybe. How well did he know that new one who had started just a few weeks ago? Not at all. Had he even talked to her? She put his mail down on his desk in the mornings, reminded him of his appointments. But that was it. He could go on down this path all afternoon and longer, but, hell, the ruse had worked, hadn't it. Hadn't it?

He should be congratulating himself on that at least. Showed he wasn't the dumbass who had helped Robbie that night and given him his best chance. But right now, his biggest task was to get Stuart to contact Carl Peters and get him out here without letting those two investigators who were working as a team in on "the plan," or "plans." Sort of at least.

Meanwhile, he had had to let Stuart know that Robbie was alive - and close by, threatening them both. He felt sure that Robbie wanted him to confront Carl, to admit his role and tell Carl that he was sorry. What a screwy idea. And he knew better. Robbie had something else in mind. He was sure of it. There seemed no other way. Step by step, he thought, step by step.

§

It turned out not to be a problem for Stuart to call Carl and tell him he would have a chance to meet the "accomplice." Stuart had actually leapt at the idea, not giving Kent's name on the phone, merely saying there was yet another informant who had real information, and more than that, who could arrange a meeting between them if Carl wanted to hear the truth. Once again Stuart's quest for a "starring role," as it were, brushed aside all other concerns. Kent had warned him not to tell Russ and Miriam - and he had nodded vigorously.

Once that was done, Kent would let Robbie know if Carl was coming here and that he planned to tell the truth. Then, well, things would fall out. In no case would he allow Robbie to control the "situation." It was a huge gamble that Carl would hear the apology and let go of his death grip on vengeance.

§

Robbie had not gone far after leaving Kent's motel room. He had not decided how exactly to handle things. Kent wasn't really a major threat in the sense that he could be retried for First Degree murder. But what about unwelcome public attention? He had worked to establish a new identity after his "disappearance" - and now he had nearly succeeded. How well that would hold up if Stuart Freed's "researches" continued he did not know. He had sensed there was something wrong when Freed kept trying to "help" him starting all those years ago when he had tried to set up a meeting. Kent did not pose – himself – a physical danger, but Freed's researches could start - had started - a whole new search by Carl Peters. And ever since that moment in the courtroom after sentence was pronounced, he knew that Wendy's brother was determined to keep on searching – and he was a physical danger. The difficulty was in seeing a way to eliminate that danger. Now the pursuers were all together

He had to think of some way to deal with the problem. Behind it all was Carl Peters, always Carl Peters. He turned on the engine of his car and headed out of the parking lot. He could tell Kent had been rattled discovering him in his room – it lent credence to Robbie's belief that he still had the ability to manage his "Little Brother."

CHAPTER THIRTY

WHO TO TRUST?

Carl Peters felt sure Robbie was not dead. But finding a person presumed dead was now only part of what Carl sought. Then Stuart's call came like a door opening on a dark room - the light poured in. Freed had "proved" there had been an accomplice. Now in excited tones he told Carl there was a chance he could be presented to him in person. Could it be true? He heard Wendy's voice telling him it was so. Finding the coward would give her a measure of justice, even if he was wrong and Robbie was actually dead.

It had to be one of those students in Stanson's fraternity, in the pledge class, there could be no other answer. There had been a conspiracy of silence with no one willing to say who Robbie's "Little Brother" had been, obviously to protect that individual. He allowed that they did not imagine that whoever it was had been an actual participant in the murder of his sister. That might have made them "talk." No one had thought such a thing possible. Hell, he hadn't either at first, at first when he had not yet gotten over the shock - but then the rush to trial, the changed prosecution stance, the letters - all of it. And now Stuart Freed had flushed him out. Oh, my God, yes, he had. He wanted to draw him out in the open, this cowardly son-of-a bitch.

He would go to Yosemite to meet the accomplice. The other two could not get in the way – must not. Things were combining to allow him to think after all these years that maybe he could offer some measure of justice for Wendy. Maybe Robbie had made his escape, but now the accomplice had shown himself. He did not question why. What did that matter? He picked up the phone to call for airline reservations.

§

Then he called Miriam without telling her Stuart's news. Miriam told the others that Carl had decided to join them to "coordinate efforts." "That was all he told me on the phone, except that he especially wants to talk with Stuart. That's natural enough."

Stuart said nothing to Miriam's news, effecting to be surprised while pretending all he wanted was to go home. He was no longer sure, he said, if he wanted to write anything else about the 'Red Slippers' case. But he would wait to see Carl along with the others. They all had loads of doubts about what they were doing, he went on talking this way, almost too much.

"Look," Miriam picked up on Stuart's line, "when Carl gets here we can figure out the next steps. I'm sure not going to do anything more without hearing from him. At first, when he talked to me, he just wanted to see if Robbie was still alive, and I agreed to look into it. That wasn't too smart of me, in hindsight, of course, because I wasn't thinking about what he might do. Now it appears that whether Robbie is dead or not – largely thanks to Stuart's 'paper' – we are in totally new territory. And we have to worry about is what Carl has in mind. We have, my friends, seemingly put our feet in some pretty sticky stuff. Getting out is not going to be easy."

§

Hours before Carl arrived the three, Russ, Stuart and herself, had sat down to think about what to say to Carl – and specially to figure out what to ask him if they were to figure out an exit strategy.

Stuart had begun that conversation. "I went out to Carl's place in Upper Arlington, a Columbus suburb, to talk about Wendy. I was barely beginning to think seriously about writing anything on the Red Slippers Case."

Russ intervened. "What did you think Carl could tell you?"

"I really didn't know. Of course, I knew that he and Wendy's parents had been unhappy about the sentence and Robbie's parole. Things along that line."

Staring at Stuart with her old suspicions, Miriam said: "Did he know that you had once tried to contact Robbie with some kind of offer to help him start over?"

"No."

"And you did not tell him, then, did you?"

"No."

"But he might have guessed, might'ened he?"

"I suppose so, but…"

Russ intervened. "Lay off Miriam, let him go on."

She put down a pen she had been holding, nodded, and sat back. "Go ahead Stuart, tell us what happened when you first met Carl. I'll hold off, but I think Carl probably knew more about you than you thought he did at the time. We'll all be interested to know how this got started." She smiled and tilted her head slightly in a sardonic gesture. "Did you talk about your theory?"

"Well, yeah, but I just mentioned that might be a line of inquiry." Stuart hoped his nervousness about what might come next did not show.

No one said anything. Then Russ smiled a rueful smile: "We are all a bit unnerved."

He paused. "I'm not sure of anything, Stuart. Especially not anything you say."

§

By the time Miriam left to pick up Carl Peters, temperatures in the conversation had returned to near normal. He had not brought more than one small suitcase, so that was encouraging.

"Hello Miriam, it seems we have some interesting work to do.

The other two had waited at a corner table in the bar for her to return with Carl, thinking that would be the best place to greet their "employer."

When Miriam and Carl entered the bar, Russ stood up to greet the man he had not seen since that day Robbie was sentenced. "Good afternoon, sheriff," Carl said with a half-smile, extending his hand, "you look like the years haven't done you too much harm. No longer sheriff, of course. Maybe that's the reason."

Russ shook Carl's hand and they completed the greeting in short fashion. Stuart was now standing back of Russ as Carl broke away from Lewis and took Stuart's hand. "Good to see you, Stuart. You've really started something."

Russ spoke up. "I'm not really sure about that Carl, I think we need to talk about that first thing."

"Oh, absolutely, now can we go somewhere private so that you can bring me up to date. We may be on the edge of getting some real answers – that – excuse me Russ – might have been, *really were*, there at the time my sister was killed. Don't you think so, Stuart? Miriam?"

"I don't know, Carl," said Miriam, looking evenly at Carl. "I don't know about that at all, given the situation."

"Sorry, Miriam, if there had been a proper investigation at the time, I think a search for an accomplice would have found Robbie's collaborator. It was..."

"Wait a minute," Russ intervened, but before he could go on to say anything else, Carl took Stuart's arm, turned him away from the group and started walking to the elevators. "Why don't we go back to your room, Stuart, and you can tell me all the details of your future research plans."

Russ and Miriam looked at each other. What were they missing here? Miriam broke the spell. Yes, good idea, Carl. Why don't we *all* go to Stuart's room. We need to think very carefully here before anything else happens."

Carl shrugged, as if it didn't make any difference. But he was grimly holding on to his self-control. The situation did not bode well for an agreeable conversation.

§

"Let me begin, Carl," said Russ. "You got me involved. You now appear to be playing at a lot of different tables – still are."

"I make no apologies for wanting justice for my sister," Carl said in a raised voice. "I don't want anything to happen to Stuart, obviously, but I didn't start this search for the accomplice – now that we all agree there was one."

Miriam looked around the room, to see the reactions. "We're far from sure there was an accomplice. The thing now is to figure out how to end it."

"It only ends for me with justice done," Carl repeated.

"Well," said Russ, "I'm all for that.

"Look," said Stuart, "we don't know how much this supposed accomplice was involved in anything. Maybe I'm alone now in believing there was one. If there was, we can take it as a given that he wants the search to come to an end. But why? The most obvious reason is because he does not wish to be identified. There's another side as well. Suppose that Robbie is not dead. Another question mark. That means that Robbie might want him to be silenced as much as the other wants to feel free of me."

"I'm not sure about that at all," said Russ. "Why should Robbie give a damn at this point? If he is alive, he can't be retried for anything."

"True," said Miriam, "but does this alive Robbie feel secure? He might fear the whole thing getting back in the press, etc. After all, he's killed once - yes, a long time ago, but he never made what you would call a 'full recovery' did he? And if – I still say if - there is an accomplice long in hiding, would we be goading him into some rash act."

Carl exploded, "What the hell is that supposed to mean?"

§

They sat there for a few seconds in silence. Then Carl said, in a different tone than before: "I don't know how you all feel about continuing the search. Maybe we could think about the next steps we want to take – together or individually. Russ, you were never actually employed by me, but I feel obliged to offer you some compensation for all these efforts. And besides, I have never thanked you for your treatment of my parents at a really tough time. I don't want to put Stuart in any more danger, and if he wishes to go to the police or hire a personal guard, I will support him."

He got up suddenly shook hands with everyone, embraced Stuart, and left the three of them standing awkwardly in his room.

Miriam watched him go and wondered. She was the first to speak. "That's not the end of it. He's got some idea of a plan." Then she nodded to Russ and Stuart. "Mark my word," she said with the door open, and left the room.

§

Carl walked back to his room alone. When he got there he saw his phone blinking with a message. Someone back in Columbus likely. But it was Stuart. He dialed his room, "Yes, Stuart?"

"Carl, you should know that the accomplice is here. There is the man who offered information, remember, Thomas Prentis. He wants to meet with you. What shall I tell him?"

Carl sat down hard on the bed. "What are you telling me, Stuart?"

"I'm telling you this guy Prentis knows the accomplice is here and he wants to talk to you. What shall I tell him?"

"My God, my God! Set up a time for Prentis to come to my room. I'll say I have a headache to the others, but you come to the room with him then go back to tell Russ and Miriam I'm not feeling well - which, as a matter of fact - is so."

"O.k., I'll try to arrange it for tomorrow."

Stuart hung up.

Carl was thinking about why Robbie's accomplice had decided to show himself. *Why? He must be afraid that Stuart was very close to identifying him by name. He had lived with his crime – his shame – all these years and now it had been brought to the surface and he imagined that his entire reputation, the fate of his family (presuming, a likely thought, that there was a family to protect), and his reputation. Well, hadn't he lived all these years with guilt about not protecting Wendy! No reason to feel sorry for him – none. He should have come forward at the time.*

Carl wondered why the man had come here? Is he chasing Robbie, too? Maybe that's it. But why is this Prentis involved? Money, of course. He wants money from me to tell how to find the accomplice and confront him. That's it. Sure. It still didn't all make a lot of sense, but he felt close to getting some answers, maybe just the name of the accomplice. But that would be enough to begin the end after all these years.

Maybe, even, if he was keeping watch somewhere close-by, he would know that Carl had checked in - so he might come after him. He would welcome that. Let him come, he was ready. And maybe Robbie, too. Let them both come.

§

Miriam and Russ walked back to the bar for a nightcap – and a recap of all that had happened.

"You know," she said, stirring the glass of crème de menthe and ice cubes, and taking a sip, "there's something else that keeps gnawing at me."

"Oh, just one thing?"

"Julie. When I came out here to try to find out if there had been any visitors to Robbie before he disappeared, she did a pretty neat job of finding a witness to tell me that there had been this man who visited with the Robbie persona apparently, and then drove off a day or so later. Consuela, her informant, seems to be the only person who saw this man – at a gas station before he drove away."

"So, that proved to be a dead end. You reported that to Carl, you said."

"Yes, but suppose it was real and this mysterious person never drove away."

"Yeah, so, where is this heading?" asked Russ.

"Would that mean Consuela and Julie were lying, why?"

"Yes, go on."

"And now Julie and her 'husband' seem to have headed for the hills somewhere." said Miriam. "But maybe not so far, for some reason."

"I get that. Might be the case that... so, if so, what do we tell Carl? That we should take another look, perhaps the accomplice was here."

"I don't think so, at least not yet. We don't know if Carl has other resources besides us, do we? That last conversation today bothered me. I don't know exactly why." Miriam sought the answer in Russ's look.

"No, I wondered about that from the beginning."

"And we don't have any idea what Carl's real intentions are going forward. Let's not say anything to Stuart, either, ok?"

"Yes, good idea to keep it between us at least for now."

§

Stuart sat alone in his room, thinking about all that had happened. waiting nervously for Kent to call. Hurry up. He would surely be happy, Stuart thought, at how well he had handled matters. Stuart was very excited - more so than at any time since he had started his research.

CHAPTER THIRTY-ONE
CHOOSING OPTIONS

Carl's phone rang. He supposed it might be Stuart, but it was an outside number. "Mr. Peters, my name is Tom Prentis. I think I have some information for you."

"Yes?" Carl felt faint for a second but regained his composure. Something he had not told the others: he had brought with him a small tape recorder, thinking he would use it to record their conversations. But he had forgotten to ask their permission in their first conversation. He turned it on now and set it close to the phone.

Then he decided to play it tough. "I damned well don't want to play games. So say your piece or whatever, now, or I will hang up and at once inform the house detective here that someone is playing a very dangerous game!"

A few more seconds passed. "No, don't do that Carl. I think we should talk – just the two of us. Say at the Base Camp Eatery at 10 a.m. Won't be too busy then."

"Why should I do that?"

"I think you know. It has to do with what should have been done twenty years ago."

Carl drew in a long breath. Could it really be happening?

"Alright, I'll be there but I will have left word at the front desk where I will be, and that I am meeting someone. And there will be a note in my room detailing all that has happened in the last few weeks."

He paused for a moment thinking that perhaps he should inform the others. But why? He had not been convinced that they were telling him everything they knew. Their first talk had not been encouraging. He was in no way sure that they were all on the same page. No, he would go it alone for a while.

§

The next morning Miriam decided that her best step would be to contact the bartender she had met on her first trip. He seemed to have more information about Julie and Consuela, more than he let on. The only question was how much to tell Russ. They seemed to be working together now, more so than in the past. She decided there was no point going it alone now, especially since their objectives might not accord entirely with Carl's plans. Actually, "plans" was probably the wrong word. She was pretty sure no one had a plan, so to speak, only some questions, but in one case also an obsession that might or might not lead somewhere. As for Stuart, well he was a central figure who now needed protecting. He clearly had intended his research to bring him some rewards. Was there really a Mr. X who had sent those warning letters to Stuart, or was that part of his sales job to Carl?

She was probably going to have to talk to Russ alone to settle what they planned to do, even though she did not trust him completely. That settled in her mind, she picked up the phone and called his room.

"Let's meet alone for coffee. I have an idea about some way to proceed."

§

Carl arrived at the Base Camp Eatery a few minutes before ten. He realized for the first time that he had not been told how the mysterious caller would contact him. So he tried an obvious thing and asked the cashier if anyone had left any messages for Carl Peters? The answer was no, and he was about to turn around when the phone rang and she picked it up. She looked up at him, "Mr. Peters?"

He took it from her. "Now don't say anything. Just listen to what I tell you to do and be there in fifteen minutes."

"I'm sorry, what kind of deal is this?" The cashier pretended to be busy going over some checks. Then Carl waited.

"I told you not to say anything. If you do, I will not meet you now or next year, or ever."

Carl waited.

"Alright, now listen, because I will say this only once. Go back to your car, get in and drive to the Motel three miles outside the Park on I-580. Meet me in the lobby. We will decide where to go from there. Good-bye."

Carl put down the phone, looked sheepishly at the cashier, and handed it back to her. She smiled back in what he thought was a "knowing" way. He bought a coffee to go and returned to his car.

§

At the motel he parked as close as he could to the main door as he could. He saw that there was a lot of traffic going in and out as it was obviously near checkout time. That seemed wise to him, and it lessened his fears. He walked into the lobby and stood near a couch that sat in the center. Almost at once he saw someone in an elevator door as it opened wave to him with a newspaper. He was a sleight man a couple of inches under six feet with glasses. He wore an open sport coat and no tie. He looked to be in his late forties, and balding with a fringe of light brown hair - a businessman with a perpetually worried expression.

He exited the elevator and walked directly over to him. "I arranged a private conference room. The front desk knows exactly where you and I will be so there is no reason to worry about anything happening here."

Peters frowned at that comment, but then nodded. "Lead the way."

The conference rooms were on the second floor along with a banquet suite and some private offices. His caller led the way into 213, where there was a small table with three seats and place settings. "I ordered coffee to make it seem like this was a 'normal' conference. The third setting won't be used, but it seemed better all around to make it appear this was a 'business' appointment." He gave Carl a rueful look halfway between a smile and a grimace.

"But, then, we do have some business to discuss."

§

As Carl met with his host, Miriam planned out the day with Russ as it would happen in the lodge bar. "The bartender comes on duty at 4 p.m. I plan to be there just after 4. I don't think you should be with me, but if it really bothers you and you think I might not tell you everything, I will accept that decision and we can both meet him."

"That's fine. You met the guy and he will not want me around if he's ready to open up anymore."

§

At shortly after four she walked into the bar and sat down on a stool at the end. Very soon the bartender noticed her, threw his towel over his shoulder and walked down to greet her with a smile suggesting they were old confidants. "Well, well, fancy you being back. Actually, I sorta expected you would be, along with your inquisitive buddy. What can I get you, the same?"

"Yes, that'll do fine."

The drink arrived and Miriam took a sip and smiled at the bartender."

"I guess I didn't get your name last time?"

"That's right, Ms. Stronge, you didn't ask."

"But you know my name, I guess."

"I do - you people are becoming something of an item here. People are curious."

Miriam smiled – a big grin. "Suppose so. But we haven't raised any hackles, yet, I hope. And I really apologize for not asking your name that other time."

"No problem there. It's 'Spokes' Pierson. From the time I was a kid."

"So, you always said your piece?"

"No," he chuckled, "has to do with spokes in a wheel. "

"Oh," Miriam seemed confused, so she let it go. "Ok, Spokes. I wonder if you could tell me a little more about Julie."

"Not much to say. She blew in here several years ago, as you know. She wasn't a native Californian."

"Really? Do you know where from?"

"Not really. But somewhere east. Maybe Ohio, Indiana, some place like that. I don't know much about that part of the country. Been here all my life. I just heard something, but I can't seem to recall anything special in that regard."

Miriam fished around in her purse took out a wallet and fingered some bills. "I hope you might think a little harder about what you might have heard about her background." She pushed some of the bills across the bar.

"Pretty sure now that I think of it," Spokes said picking them up and looking around to see if anyone had observed the transaction. There was no one else in the bar, but Spokes seemed nervous.

"Pretty sure about what state? Anything else about Julie you might recall now?"

"She spent time in Ohio, Columbus. Maybe grew up there." He paused, then went on. "About her life here, you asked. Well, far as I knew she stayed pretty much alone for a long while, til she met and married a man recently. Odd thing was her leaving." Miriam passed two more bills across the bar.

"Was this man a regular?"

"No, never saw him until fairly recently. And then only once or twice."

"So was he what led her to abandon a pretty good job here?"

"Well, some said she was a little peeved that she hadn't gotten a raise, or something. But I always figured she'd find some guy and leave. She looked younger than she was - according to the waitresses. I wouldn't know."

"Did you or anyone else have ideas about him?"

"We're gettin pretty deep here, you know."

Spokes was looking uneasy. Miriam put the last two bills on the bar.

"You're right. I think we're about done here."

"Jesus, you sound like a cop!"

"Really, well I'm not. Thanks. And I gather you never actually met her husband, only saw him around once or twice?"

Spokes shook his head, indicating that was right, picked up the bills and walked to the other end of the bar. He seemed unhappy with the whole business., regretted "telling tales" even taking the money. Didn't want a reputation. Bartenders are supposed to be good listeners, not tattlers. Miriam knew that was it. She slid off the stool, nodded and walked out of the bar.

§

Earlier that day a fateful conversation had happened in the motel between Carl and Kent Crider. "Well, Carl, we've never met. You didn't even know that I existed. Not until Stuart started going back over the case. I know you were unhappy about how Robbie got off with such a light sentence – and even more so when he got out on parole."

"You're not this Tom Prentis, are you?"

"No, I'm not. My name is Kent Crider. I used Stuart to set up this meeting. Oh, we're not in cahoots. I had never met the man who would love to play Columbo." He paused and shrugged in acceptance. "Should've expected someone. Now, I'm leveling with you for several reasons. One, the easiest is, I don't want Stuart to get in any more trouble with anyone. I'm sorry I tried to scare him." He stopped talking and looked straight into Carl's eyes, waiting for a reaction. He could see the red patches rising in his cheeks.

Carl stiffened, and drew back, the veins in his neck stood out. "Go on, he said."

"As I said, my name is Kent Crider. I was a freshman at Bashford College in 1953." He paused and breathed out a deep sigh. "Robbie Stanson was my 'Big Brother.'"

He waited but Carl said nothing. The room seemed to shrink around them. Kent moved to another chair, sat down and began again. "I should've come forward back then, yes. You can believe what you want. But I didn't have anything to do with Wendy's death. I was stunned when I got back to my room that night. There sat Robbie staring at Wendy on the bed. He told me they had had an argument and he had lost it. Then he started crying and telling me how sorry he was, how he loved Wendy, how they were going to run away together. They'd just had a little argument he said, and somehow it got out of hand. She wasn't supposed to leave my room. And so on. Then he stopped crying and turned to me with a terrified look. If she's found here, he had said, *I* would be in real trouble, too. There was only one thing to do, he said. We have to get her out of here – clear out of town, somewhere where she won't be found. I sat there frozen in panic. What was going to happen to me? That's all I could think, *what is going to happen to me?* I had done nothing wrong, and suddenly my whole future was gone – maybe my life, I didn't know about the laws. Who was to say I hadn't killed her if Robbie up and fled. I didn't know shit about the law."

Carl pressed his hands down hard on the table. "Jesus Christ, what do you want me to say? Sorry – what is your name again – Kent? Sorry for all the pain you've had over the years. That son of a bitch killed my sister." He looked at the ceiling. "Then that wasn't enough, he dragged her to a car with you helping, I guess, and drove forty miles. And he *defaced her, destroyed her face*." He looked down at Kent. *And you helped him. What kind of person does that? Tell me, what kind of person does that? And you protected him, you protected the bastard!"*

"I didn't touch her after we got her in the car. All that stuff was Robbie. I couldn't bring her back to life. And it was the prosecutor's decision not to go for First Degree."

"You bastard – you rotten bastard."

"Well, ok, I kept my mouth shut. But once I'd done that, no matter what I said after Robbie confessed would not have made any difference..."

"You'd like to think that, wouldn't you, that's how you've lived with yourself all these years. You're a coward."

"You're right. But I couldn't bring her back to life, could I?"

"Play that helpless bystander role all you want. You had a duty to come forward, didn't you? And instead you let it play out as a panic killing. No, it sure as hell wasn't! Robbie had this all planned out. Why do you think he told her to bring all her stuff and come to West River?"

"I didn't know that did I? And Carl, I'm still not so sure he had always intended to kill Wendy."

Carl shouted out, "Don't you use her name, I don't want to hear it ever from you - or Robbie if I find that evil excuse for a man."

Kent shook his head sadly," I think two or three things might have been going on in his head at this time. I think that he defaced her in the hope that she would not be recognized – but more damn likely, he wanted it to look like he'd lost it completely."

Carl sighed. "At least we agree there – to the extent that there were two or three things going on in his sick - no, evil - head. And now there's one thing for you to think about. We know he's alive, I'm sure of it. And probably you two have schemed out a plan. But tell me, Mr. Crider, don't you think he wants to keep you quiet? And if he is not to be caught out at last for all the terrible things he planned, you have to be eliminated. Count on it, you are not safe after all Freed has set in motion. And if I go public with what you just told me you're ruined. Why shouldn't I – tell me – why shouldn't I?"

Carl just looked at him and smiled a terrible smile, a vengeful smile. "Stuart Freed's the least of your worries." Another smile. "You're such a dumb ass and coward, I almost pity you."

Kent nodded. "But maybe you over-estimate Robbie. You make Robbie seem cunning as hell. We were still pretty young when it happened. Couldn't it just be that it happened the way Robbie said it did. And this was the way it panned out?"

"Well, tell me how he could have gotten rid of the body without your help?"

"He might have managed."

"But why was she in your room? I'll tell you why, because that story he told in his self-serving confession was bullshit. He never planned to take her to that shack – and she would never have agreed to go to that shack. For her that would have been a final straw. But to somebody's room? Sure, she trusted the bastard, despite everything he had done to her, and after those damned letters. And for him to take her across an open field, even at night. And then leave her there in daytime? Somebody might have seen her – so the idea that somebody had seen her became a perfect excuse for him to say that he lost it and choked the life out of her by mistake. Too bad we can't ask him, now, tonight and see what he answers."

Carl said this last with an ugly look, daring Kent to respond. Kent looked up at a spot in the corner of the room. "I agree with all that stuff you just said. But I didn't know it at the time. But suppose we could."

"We could what?"

"Ask Robbie."

"What the hell does that mean?"

"It means..."

§

And later that day Miriam called Russ as soon as she got back to her room. "Russ" she said, "I think we're onto something."

"What's that – I can tell from your voice that you found out something from the bartender."

"Yep, did indeed. Do you remember the episode at the time of Robbie's parole bid that got the newspapers all in an uproar? And the governor calling up the prison warden wanting to know what the hell was going on?"

"I do. What did the bartender tell you?"

"He told me that Julie was not from around here."

"So?"

"He told me he thought she was from someplace in the Midwest – Indiana or Ohio – one of those places."

"So?"

"C'mon Russ! You know what that means."

"Not sure that I do – exactly."

"It means that she was very likely the girl that Robbie was seeing when he was out with the state prison van. I haven't heard back from the Columbus police, but I'm sure of it."

"I know where you're headed with this, but just because a bartender picked up on something and 'thought' she was from one of those places he had never been, doesn't mean a thing. There are a lot of people from those places."

"Yes, sure."

"And we don't have any knowledge about connections after he got out of prison – right – no girlfriend. And if they had gotten together that would have been big news, well not big, maybe, but somebody would have been on it."

"I see that, of course, but what if they kept in contact all those years? Maybe she got married and then divorced and came out here to work. She contacts Robbie, and he comes running. *That answers the question of why he came here, not just because people get lost.* Another reason for him to disappear, and for them to hope that this time they could figure out a way to get together and start over as it were."

"That's a big stretch."

"Then imagine they're putting together some sort of plan – one that might even allow them to stay here. Robbie was only here a few days, remember, and he could have changed his appearance. Dye his hair, grow a mustache, get glasses."

"Yes – and?"

"Yes, and re-emerge as Julie's boyfriend, and then husband. She was not wired in here."

"Well . . ."

"And then I come out and they have to feed me this story about Consuela seeing some stranger at a gas station with an out-of state license with the implication that he did away with Robbie and might even have him in the trunk of a rented car. Or that they got away together – no Julie involved. They had to figure out some story that would cause people to back off. I'm pretty sure that for many years after he got out he was aware that Carl Peters was always there trying to mess up everything for him."

"So, Miriam how do you imagine we are going to find this out? They've done nothing wrong."

"No, but somebody is very upset by what Stuart has set in motion. It all comes back to Robbie, who may now face revelations on two fronts. He must have an even keener sense of things closing in around him and preventing him from his new life."

"So," said Russ, "what's he to do?"

"He would like to be rid of Stuart, and maybe Carl. He might even think that if he got Stuart, Carl would give it up?"

"We're overthinking this," Miriam said. "We have to get together with Carl and Stuart again and see what's on their minds. Carl was got out here in part by that Tom Prentis ploy. Maybe we need to follow that up, too."

CHAPTER THIRTY-TWO
DEVELOPING A PLAN

Russ and Miriam rang Stuart's and Carl's rooms arranging a meeting at Russ's room at five o'clock. As soon as they were seated, Carl began to tell the others what had happened. They looked at one another saying nothing as he went on to describe his meeting earlier that day.

"It was incredible - a search for forgiveness. But why did he come here? I'll tell you. Sure, he wanted to apologize and tell me how sorry he was for all that Wendy's parents and I have suffered, though he absolutely disclaimed any responsibility for her death. I don't know whether to believe him or not. But even if I buy the argument that he had nothing to do with her death, he bears a great deal of blame for the outcome of the trial and the sentence. And that's putting it mildly. But why did he come? Because Stuart told him to? I don't think so - Robbie, that's who. And he's close at hand. The only answer that makes sense. What the hell are they thinking?"

He had not told them everything about his meeting with Kent. Carl waited to see how it was all going down. He looked at each of them with a look of a man unjustly injured and hoping for a chance 'to get even.' No one said anything. Carl took a deep breath and continued. "His name is Kent Crider. He probably knew that if he told me all this stuff I could describe him well enough so that he would be identified anyway. He wants to 'trade.'"

"What the hell does that mean," said Russ.

"That's the question, isn't it?"

Miriam picked up the thread. "What does he know, anyway, about Robbie's fate? Why is he here? Who told him about us? It's all trouble for him. I could go on and on. Jesus, Carl, what dangerous games are going on. He's the only one who got away without a scar. So far. Well, except for his conscience. Look, it makes more sense to me - despite what you say - that he got here through Stuart. That's who contacted you, right?" She stared hard at Stuart. "Right?" she repeated.

"Good question, Miriam," said Carl. "Whoever got him out here, he confirms that Robbie is alive, that he is near, and even that he has spoken to him in the last few days!"

§

"And you believe him?" Miriam asked, looking around the room. "And why would he want to tell you all this stuff? I don't get it."

"I don't know what to believe. It could be that he is simply playing some weird sort of game. It could also be that he is genuinely afraid of Robbie. He assures me Robbie is alive."

"Why in Hell did he come out here, then," said Russ. "To kill Stuart? This makes no sense."

"I don't think he knows for sure why Robbie summoned him," said Carl. "He just wants to put an end, somehow, to all this threat of exposure. He wants me to forgive him, and he wants Robbie stopped before something else happens."

Russ shook his head slowly, a sad smile forming at the corner of his lips. "He sure is going about it in strange fashion. And Robbie stopped from what?"

Stuart answered Russ. "Can you imagine the burden he's been carrying around inside him all these years? But what I'm interested in at the moment is how he knows

Robbie is alive - and near?" That Kent had been in touch with Stuart was no surprise, really, after all that had gone on from the time of the Philadelphia seminar.

Miriam was thinking, of course, that it ran straight through her original visit and the relationship between Julie and - she now supposed - Robbie. He had been trying to start over since getting out of prison, and Carl's effort to run him down.

Russ thought to himself once more about the guilt he had felt since the days of the crime and his sense that he had failed to press Tom Jackson, whose career had taken off after Robbie went to prison. No matter that there was nothing he could have done then to change the prosecutor's mind. And, hell, he had probably been right in taking Robbie's plea. What if Robbie had gotten off some way? It did him no good all these years to think about it. Damn Stuart Freed, anyway, for bringing this all back to life - to his life! He shook his head and tried to pick up on what was being said.

§

Finally, Carl cleared up the mystery about Kent's knowledge of Robbie's presence. "He didn't say exactly, but I gathered they had met in the last few days, Kent and Robbie."

"That's it, then, Carl?" said Miriam in a raised voice, looking at each of them for comments. "He told you all this stuff this meeting!"

Crider had almost literally been begging him for mercy, said Carl. He had no idea how he would eventually play it with Mr. Crider. But he would welcome a meeting with Robbie if Kent could arrange it.

"But," Miriam frowned at him. "How does that solve Kent's problem with you, Carl? And why would you want to see Robbie? What in hell for?"

"I know," said Carl. "I know but he thinks that I will forgive him after what he told me about how all this came down when he went back to his room that night. And I have to say what he said about his shock and despair over Robbie's crime seemed genuine. And remember, he hadn't seen Robbie's damning letters to Wendy then. Only later when the Cleveland newspapers published them."

"So you're ready to forgive and forget?" said Miriam. "But what about Robbie? All Kent's maneuvering doesn't address that."

"No, of course it doesn't. But I'm not afraid of Robbie. I'm willing to play this out to see where it leads, even if only to a chance to..." He stopped there.

"It's wacky, Carl," Russ was standing near the door with one hand on the handle. "Kent's behaving like a man afire. And I guess that is what he is. Why don't you just leave it now, Carl? You've had your confrontation and seen a man who has - admittedly only by his own lights - lived in fear all these years for doing the wrong thing once in his life. But being..."

Carl raised his voice. "*Well short of justice for Wendy?* An apology, that's all it is and what's more that prosecutor was bought off! Dammit, you know that Russ, you know that. Kent Crider owes me big."

"First, I don't know anything like that about Tom Jackson. He told me he was afraid of a temporary insanity plea. And he may have been right. You can't get inside his head now, just as you couldn't then."

"Yes, well, you damn well know that Bashford College sprang for David Wells' fee, don't you?"

"I know they paid for him to represent Robbie, but..."

"Damn right, and why do you think they did that - don't you have the tiniest idea? C'mon man. You don't work there anymore. Oh, excuse me, I meant to say, you're not a sheriff anymore. Tell the truth."

Russ just shook his head and looked at the floor, trying to decide if he was going to walk out or throw a fist at Carl.

"And don't tell me you and Miriam didn't discuss how you were going to play me for a good search fee."

Miriam stood up. "Yes, I admit I expected to be paid well for trying to find out what had happened to Robbie. So? We're not altruists - but I hope people you can trust to give good advice. But all this other business with Crider complicated the search mission. I never expected to get in so deep to complicated moral questions about fit punishments. That's not my field. If we go on with this..."

Carl raised his voice again. "What the hell did you think you were getting into. Russ, you could have backed off right away. No one made you hang around to see what would happen. Miriam, you could have done the same. Like Stuart you both wanted to find out - and if anyone's responsible for the situation it's yourselves. You signed on and now apparently that things are coming to some meaningful point, you want out. It's that simple isn't it?"

He looked at each of them. "You could at least admit I'm right, couldn't you, that you were all too happy to take advantage of my desire to find out what happened to Robbie."

Russ had moved back from the door. "No, you were hounding him all that time. And you wanted still more. He was convicted, served time, and apparently wanted to start a career. What gives you the right to go on with this quest for justice – in order to make amends for your imagined guilt."

§

Carl shrugged, a final dismissal. "Say what you will. I don't give a rat's ass what you think about my behavior. Sure, Stuart's detective work has given me a new lead - one that's only deepened my desire to have the whole story out. It's so much more sordid than I had imagined. Robbie used Kent to get away with First Degree murder. That should be enough to satisfy all of you."

Stuart shook his head. "Look what's happened I never..."

"All those other 'dead' cases you played around with didn't have live characters did they?" said Carl. "Enough is enough. I'm going to meet again with Crider. He's going to set up a meeting with Robbie – the three of us."

Astonished into silence for a second,Miriam shook her head at the notion Robbie would show up. "What is this meeting supposed to accomplish Carl? Are you crazy? Why should Robbie agree?"

"Robbie will show up, Kent's sure of it. Kent's arranging it because he wants to tell me in front of Robbie he was an unwitting accomplice. That it all happened as he said, the result of an unplanned moment of blind fear and anger. And if Robbie had planned to pressure Kent into a rash act, that's out because Crider has left behind a document that will explain all."

"Yes, Carl," said Russ. "That's as you and Kent supposedly see it all working out. And then what? What more do you expect to do? Kill Robbie?"

"Well, what else can Robbie do – maybe he had previously persuaded Kent to kill me for fear his behavior back then will be revealed? But the situation's changed."

"Even so, whatever precaution Kent's taken to protect himself - and you - , or said he's taken why should Robbie not take the risk?" said Miriam. "And why wouldn't you continue the pursuit?"

"You imagine things. I have accepted Kent's account of how it happened; he has suffered some of the same guilt feelings all these years. And Robbie has no alternative but to accept the situation."

Russ and Miriam looked at one another. Then she felt like her stomach would fall out: "This is unbelievable Carl."

She paused to get control of her fears before going on. "Carl, there is absolutely no chance that Robbie will show up for such a meeting -- unless he means violence. Don't you understand? How do you expect him to respond to this final threat you pose? Do you seriously believe he will confess he planned all along to kill your sister?"

"No, but he's a coward. Kent wants to think that now that *he* has 'confessed,' *and* left a note behind telling about his role he is safe from both Robbie and me. He also thinks Stuart will back off."

Russ put his hand to his forehead. "Why should you think any of this could be so? You have no idea, Carl, no idea about how this will turn out. You're delusional if you think Robbie -- if he does turn up as Kent says he will -- won't act to stop you from shadowing him the rest of your lives."

"I don't think he has any choice in the matter."

Russ and Miriam looked at one another. Then Miriam sighed. "I'm leaving this mad house. There's no end to it -- at least not one I want to be around."

Russ nodded. "Goodbye Carl."

CHAPTER THIRTY-THREE

THE LADY OR THE TIGER?

Stuart sat in his room with his luggage packed. He was more than ready to return home. He had no idea what he was going to do about pursuing his publication. He had been eager to "solve" the Red Slippers Mystery. Indeed, he had even imagined taking credit for calling the crime a mystery - something yet unsolved because authorities had overlooked the idea of an accomplice in the hurry to convict Robbie Stanson. It was a miscarriage of justice, well, sort of, to be satisfied with that outcome - well, more like incomplete justice. When he had first tried to contact Robbie he had had on his mind the idea that he wished to help him with his post-prison rehabilitation. When had that changed? Well, of course, he could now admit to himself, almost as soon as he thought about what an accomplice actually meant. What he had not figured on enough was how he was threatening that accomplice more. Whether the guy was an active participant or a dupe - that question - had not really occurred to him? But now he had Kent's story, all that had changed. So what was happening was in a sense a kind of moral lesson. He was prone to argue this way with himself ever since he had started his counseling service. Did his behavior in the "case" demonstrate moral failings in other instances?

He had not told the others that he was definitely leaving, because now he was not so sure even though his bags were packed. He could not stay on forever, obviously, and he was almost sorry he had ever read about the crime. He had no idea what the rest planned.

§

Russ sat in the bar, nursing a Heineken. The bartender was a new man he had not seen before, but that did not seem to matter because he had nothing to ask about Julie or Robbie. Miriam had done all that and Carl had taken over the "search," if that was what to call the events of the last few weeks since he had first walked into Stuart's office. It was the most peculiar "investigation" he had ever been involved in, and he was more than ready to say good-bye to all of it. Kent had now "confessed" his role in the immediate aftermath of Wendy Peters' death to Carl. It was just short of crazy to think that Kent hoped he could dissuade Stuart from pursuing his theory of how things went down. But how did he know they were all coming out here? The more he thought about it, only one answer had emerged that seemed reasonable: Robbie had summoned him! They were in contact. It was still not clear what game was being played now? Carl thought Robbie expected Kent to kill him. That was crazy – surely it was. But if Kent had "confessed" to Carl, did he place himself in a terrible dilemma?

Carl had not told them if Kent had said anything more about his role, whether he had stood watching as Robbie defaced Wendy. What would he have done in Kent's place? Go to the police to confess his role, or keep silent as he had done, rationalizing that he had had no role in the girl's death, so why should he suffer a terrible blow to his prospects - a lifelong one?

Was there any good ending for this? He remembered reading the story, "The Lady or the Tiger" in High School. A young man stood between two doors in the story, forced by the king to choose one. Behind one door was a beautiful woman behind the other was a tiger who would kill him. Had Kent ever read that story?

Russ picked up the phone to call Miriam. They should talk to the police about all this-but it was just talk, that's all it was, no actual threats had been made, and no one had seen Robbie. What would Miriam say? They had headed away from the meeting with Carl as if in a snipe hunt to scare a tenderfoot scout on his first night in camp.

§

Miriam sat in her room alone, and gladly so, because she had no idea how to make sense out of what was happening. She could not count on any of the others for a way out. She had agreed to join in the search for Robbie because it had presented an interesting problem. Carl had paid her well, but he was "using" all of them to do what? Perhaps she should not have ignored the little warning signs that his desire for atonement was leading him down a dangerous path. Now, perhaps her new mission was to restrain him from committing an act of violence, even possibly murder. But how? She had thought about that possibility ever since her report on her first trip to Yosemite. Was he capable of doing something terrible after all these years? Something kept telling her that he was perhaps more capable now of such an act than he had ever been. Was that possible? Yes.

However she rationalized her willingness to join in the search for Robbie, it was clear to her now that she could not run away. She had seen it in his eyes when he first came to her office, a look that combined pleading with anger. Anger at himself almost as much as Robbie for "allowing" what happened to Wendy to happen. He even said at their first meeting, "I was not there for her." She had not known what to say. She hesitated, looking steadily at Carl. Finally, she had replied, half-nodding, "We need to think now about finding out whether he is dead or just missing."

"Yes, that's the first thing." She had not grasped at the time the full intimation of "Yes, that's the first thing." Then he had stood up, pushed the chair back, and moved to the door in a series of purposeful movements. "Keep me informed."

"I will."

After Carl left her office that day she did not see him again until that meeting in the deli on a rainy morning. His disappointment that day had ended their conversation, but she felt responsible. Why, she had asked herself? He had paid her well, and admit it, she had not really extended herself to the limit in the search. She had felt a little guilty, and as things developed and she met Russ she was energized to follow the lead Stuart had produced with his idea. What exit was there? She had imagined it would be a routine job, that a little searching would produce evidence of Robbie's death. Instead, the Mr.X "problem," a.k.a. now as "The accomplice" became the central feature of the search. She had never trusted Stuart, never fully believed in his "paper." Hundreds of false scenarios grow up sometimes like weeds around rational explanations until you can hardly see the obvious answer was always the correct one. But not every time, no, not every time. And so now it appears this was one of those times: that Stuart was right. There had been an accomplice - to what depth he was involved in the murder remained unclear. One thing was clear. Carl was determined to play out the implications in "The Paper" (she now called it) that he had delivered at the seminar.

And then what to do? Carl had been planning for a long time, it was clear to her for a moment of truth. That had never seemed likely to happen - until now. So, what should she do? Bail out, go home, tell Carl she could not be involved in any plan that would lead to violence. She did not know if he were planning to use Kent Crider to lure Robbie to some remote place and kill him or if he was satisfied that Kent had owned up. But what then? She could not read Carl's intensions – nor indeed what Kent might do. Either way she convinced herself that she needed to stay and if necessary, go to the police. Perhaps she could prevent Carl from ruining the rest of his life if she stayed, even if he would not thank her for it. That was it: she would stay. Hoping to know when to intervene if she had to.

But then the next question: What should she say to the others? She had just concluded she must stay when Russ called. "Miriam we can't leave."

§

Russ and Miriam's conversation led to a call to Stuart for an "emergency" meeting in his room. The only one who had actually seen Kent Crider besides himself was supposedly Carl Peters.

Russ shifted in his chair. "Let's not get ourselves totally screwed up here. I think our best way to proceed is to get Carl in here and talk this out. We need answers from him about who it was he met with, and how this 'plan' took shape."

"And we need you to contact Kent Crider – and don't pretend you're not the middleman here, that is the only way this thing is shaping up. You've always had separate conversations with Carl, and it's through you they got together," said Miriam. "Out with it Stuart – now."

"Well, yes, that's pretty much so."

"Pretty much," said Miriam, "that's it – period. Do you realize what you're playing at?"

§

Robbie Stanson sat outside the hotel in his car waiting for Kent Crider. Kent had told him of his conversation with Carl admitting that he had been there "that" night and that he had helped Stanson get Wendy into the car. He did not tell Robbie all about that conversation with Carl and what else was said. Instead, he indicated that Carl had invited him to his room, so that he could complete his "confession" – along with giving him information about Robbie's location.

Robbie was delighted with the idea because here was the way to rid himself once and for all of his pursuer. What Carl – nor Kent - would know was that he would accompany Kent to the room.

§

Carl answered a call from Stuart and came to his room where the others awaited.

"What's going on Carl?" said Russ.

"You know as well as I do. He apologized to me for not coming forward. Now he is looking only to reconcile with me. I just want him to help me smoke out Robbie Stanson."

"Why in hell would he want to do that, Carl?" said Russ. "I just think we all got put off good sense by continuing this search."

Carl shrugged. "He wanted to get twenty years off his bad conscience." He paused. "We've both been living with bad consciences for a long time. Too long."

Miriam nodded. "I guess I understand that, but I confess we have all treated this like we were in some movie. We aren't. And we have no idea what you plan to do. Robbie Stanson killed your sister, confessed and went to prison. We all agree that he got off lightly, but that doesn't give you the right to try to hunt him down, which you've been doing ever since you kept tabs on his effort to start a new life."

Carl stirred and started to speak. "No, Carl, just don't say anything for a while – I'm not finished. I agreed to help you find out if he had died or just disappeared to get away from you. You've made his life a misery."

Carl glared at Miriam. "Don't judge me. And you're not responsible for what I might do?"

"Jesus, Carl," said Russ in a loud voice. "Listen to yourself. You can't be judge and jury. No question we all screwed up by getting involved. But now no more."

Stuart started to speak, but Russ held up a hand, and went on. Now you're going to back off. By God you are. My only problem with not staying another hour in this swarming mess is that I am determined to stop you from making things worse – not just for Mr. Crider or whoever, but for yourself. I don't think you'll ever thank me for this, and I don't give a damn what you think – only what you'll try to do. I hope that is clear."

"Perfectly, Russ, you chickened out from pursuing the investigation. And now you're doing it again. No way can you tell me what I can do."

"No, but I can go to the police."

"Really? What are you going to tell them, please."

"Well, for one thing, Miriam and Stuart are going to back me up in getting a restraining order."

"Restraining order? Carl snorted. "Restrain me from doing what? None of us knows if Kent Crider even stayed around after he came up with what I now see was a delaying tactic. That confession of sorts!"

Miriam picked up where Russ had left off. "Maybe so. Maybe we agree that it is the case here, but you have no standing to carry out an arrest because Stanson served his time, and there's no proof there was an accomplice, and even if there was again the statute of limitations…"

"Statute of limitations be damned, you all keep blathering about that …"

"Shut up, Carl," Russ shouted. "You're not going to do anything. You've done enough to punish Robbie for all these years."

"Hell, man, he hypnotized Wendy! Don't you see that? He had some power over her. She was not a weak personality, my sister. She had been popular in high school, good grades, lots of activities, all of it."

Miriam picked up the argument. "Listen to yourself, Carl. You're raving. You can't make amends by destroying the Robbie Stanson of twenty years ago."

"No, you listen to yourself. I will admit that I have been using you – all of you. But Kent Crider was Mr. X. Stuart's 'paper' was a turning point. Stanson had apparently thought at one time that Stuart was trying to help him. But he quickly found out that was not the case, *Mr.* Freed, and that *you* now posed a danger. As much of one as I did. And so he disappeared. But I've had a bit of a health scare recently that has me all the more determined to find justice for Wendy."

§

No one said anything as Carl moved towards the door. "Don't bother to see me out. I'll manage fine, thank-you all."

And no one spoke after he left until Russ said, "Stuart we have to find Kent. If you've been holding out on us again, you have to tell us. This craziness can't continue until there's another tragedy."

§

Carl left the lodge as the last light of the afternoon sun reflected off car windows in the parking lot. As he turned into the row where he had left his rented Ford Galaxy, he heard laughter back near the entrance. As he did a car without its headlights on came down the row behind him. But because of the laughter he had turned enough to see it coming at him, and he was able to duck in between the parked cars in time. He did not see the driver, nor could he make out any details of the car that had tried to run him down - if that was what had just happened?

Kent Crider had left an envelope on the windshield. He opened it and read: "Tonight." Carl retrieved a package and returned to the entrance and walked up to the desk. "If anyone asks for me," he said to the night clerk aloud. "I'll be in my room, 939."

"Yes, sir, and you are?"

"Peters, Carl Peters, from Columbus, Ohio." He stood there, looking at the clerk. "My sister was murdered twenty years ago. Her killer is here."

The clerk paled, "Sir, I don't -"

"You don't need to say anything, o.k.?"

The clerk's face had gone red, then white.

"Just remember what I told you. That's all. He's here."

Then Carl smiled sadly at the clerk, turned away and headed to the elevators. When he got to his room, he paused for a second, reminding himself what Kent Crider had told him about Stanson confronting him in his room. Would he really take a chance and come here to rid himself? Now he surely must be aware of his mistake. He thought Kent was still his "Little Brother."

He's gotten desperate, so maybe he will? Maybe he will."

§

Downstairs, the desk clerk called the night manager and told him what had happened.

"This Peters didn't say he was going to do anything, did he?"

"No, he just looked sad and tired, as if he had begun to wish it was all over."

"What was over, you're not making sense?"

"I don't know, he just sent a kind of chill through me."

"Look, there's all sorts out there. Maybe he had something to drink, or he took some weird medicine that's making him hallucinate. But if you feel as uneasy as you sound right now, go ahead and buzz Griffin and tell him to make a couple of passes by - what did you say his name was -room. Got that?"

"Yes, sir, I will do that."

"And then take a couple of aspirin, or something. Got it?"

"Yes sir."

§

"He'll be there, Robbie. I promised him I would tell him the truth."

Robbie smiled into the phone. "I'll see you there. Don't worry he'll be so scared, and so stunned this will end it – for both of us."

"How can you be so sure?"

"I am. Once he sees we are together, what choice will he have? And besides, you bring what I gave you."

§

Outside Room 939, Kent and Robbie stood for a second. Robbie nodded and Kent knocked softly. "Carl, it's me. I think I know where Stanson is right now. He's close."

Peters opened the door, and the two pushed in. "Hello, Carl," said Robbie. "I don't want to be here. Why couldn't you just leave it alone? I never meant to kill Wendy."

"Liar - damn you, damn you to hell."

"No, no Carl, it was an accident."

Carl went quickly to the table next to the bed, opened a drawer.

Robbie turned to Kent. "Well, nothing for it then, we'll leave in a minute."

With that he turned to Crider, "Go ahead."

A gun had appeared in his hand, the one Robbie had given him when they met a second time. He had said it was to scare Carl. There was nothing in it but blanks. He'll scare off and get out.

But Kent was shaking.

Carl was searching for something in the drawer.

Robbie smiled and reached to take it in a gloved hand. "Give it to me. No problem, I'll finish. Just like you always were Kent, just like you always were. "

Kent fired.

"Little brother what did you do?" Then nothing more was said in the room for a minute.

"Go," Carl said. "Get out."

§

As the three returned to the bar to have dinner still unsettled about any next steps there was a commotion in the lobby. Russ stood up and went to look. There was a crowd standing near one elevator. He could see EMT workers pushing a stretcher toward one of the elevators. He could also see tan police uniforms keeping people back.

"What's happening," he asked a hotel worker?

"Don't know. Somebody said there was a shooting in one of the rooms, I guess, on the ninth floor. But I only know that a bunch of police came rushing in a little while ago - then these white-suited guys."

By now Miriam had joined them. "There was a stretcher," she told them. "I saw it being pushed into an elevator." They waited with the rest of a gathering crowd - an unusually silent crowd.

One elevator door opened and all they could see was a stretcher with a sheet. A few minutes later another elevator door opened and a thin man with a stethoscope around his neck carrying a medical bag emerged talking to what was likely a plainclothes policeman. Behind them was a second stretcher. On this one they could see the face. It was Carl Peters.

§

"Good God," exhaled Stuart, "what do you suppose happened up there?"

"Well, at a guess," said Russ, "Carl shot and killed somebody. I don't know who but more 'n likely Kent. Robbie's probably miles away."

"Jesus, why didn't he just leave it, instead pursuing forgiveness."

Miriam frowned. "Well, we didn't try hard enough did we? I don't think you, or any of us should make reservations yet - we're not clear of it. We may get hauled in any minute by the authorities."

"Why? We don't know anything." Stuart looked panicked. He knew a whole lot more than the others - a whole lot. He hoped it didn't show too much.

"I take it you're not serious. Of course we do, we know a whole lot. And we don't know if Carl is still alive, or what papers he has here or back in Ohio that connect everything up going back to the trial. I wouldn't be at all surprised if we are called in tomorrow or the next day."

§

At breakfast the three met with copies of the local newspapers scooped up from the newsstand that were filled with stories about a double shooting at the hotel. The dining room was nosier than usual as the hotel guests who had not talked with one another before suddenly found a binding topic: "Did you see that blood on the one man? Yes, he must have died. And the other one..." From what police had told reporters so far one man had been killed, and the other seriously wounded. The survivor had given a brief statement about an intruder who had gotten into his room sometime when he was out, but doctors were concerned about his ultimate recovery and kept him in an intensive care suite. A bullet was taken from his shoulder, but there were complications about other medical issues. So far as was known there were only two shots. Both fired from the same gun as Mr. Peters the hotel guest and the intruder supposedly struggled over the weapon. The details as to how that took place were unclear, and police had not had the chance to quiz Mr. Peters who remained in intensive care.

There were many questions left unanswered the articles said - including the possibility there had been a third person involved, someone who managed to get out in the time between the shots and the first people who came out of their rooms. The shooting had occurred in early evening when many people had not returned to their room, so it was unclear how many people were close by and heard the shots or how soon they came out to see what had happened.

Miriam was the first to comment on this suggestion there had been a third person present. " Could it be that Kent or someone else we don't know about was there? Seems unlikely that Carl could have gotten the gun away from the supposed intruder after he had been wounded."

"Yeah, that's true. If Kent Crider, was there he sure had reason to get rid of all these possible threats to his pursuit of a normal life."

"But we don't know do we?"

"No and maybe we never will."

§

Carl Peters spent weeks in the hospital, recovering from his wound, which was not serious. But doctors had also diagnosed a serious heart issue. During those days in the hospital, he had given out no explanation of how it all happened beyond saying that he had returned to his room and taken off his shoes, when suddenly a man emerged from the bathroom, waving a pistol wildly and going on and on about how Peters had been following him for years. The man came close and fired. But he had somehow stumbled over the shoes as he did and the shot missed a vital organ. Somehow, Peters told police, in the struggle that ensued, he managed to get his hands on the gun and as they wrestled, and it went off. There had been no one else there, Peters told police - just the two of them. It was a hardly believable story, but no witnesses were found.

But a week later the supposed intruder was identified as Robbie Stanson, who had been convicted of killing Peters' sister, Wendy, and had disappeared from Yosemite earlier in the year, assumed another name, then married Julie Converse, an employee of the hotel. They had presumably left the area some time before the shooting took place. She insisted she had no idea why her husband went to that room. He had never mentioned knowing Carl Peters to her. Again, there was no one to contradict her story.

As a result of the discovery of the dead man's identity, police wanted to question Peters again after he had returned to Ohio, where he lived and worked as a chemical scientist in a Columbus research facility. There were unanswered questions. But he was already in critical condition back in a hospital. He readily talked about the murder of his sister. All he would say about the shooting was: "Stanson had come to a room to kill. This time he failed."

There was still no evidence disproving Peters' story that there had been no one else - an accomplice in a planned murder. He died shortly thereafter. He had been divorced years earlier. His former wife and son had moved to Pittsburgh, where she had remarried. She had said during the divorce proceedings that her husband had become obsessed with his supposed blame for his sister's death. Since his parents had died years earlier there were no close relatives at the funeral. He was buried next to Wendy in New York. Years earlier he had left instructions with a stone carver that the legend on his tombstone should read, "I failed you once."

§

Russ, Miriam, and Stuart all left Yosemite and returned to their homes in Ohio and New Jersey. They had been questioned by police, but no one remembered seeing them with Carl Peters late that afternoon or early evening. A few people remembered seeing Carl in the lobby. He checked in but was not conspicuous. Then the history of the "Red Slippers" murder emerged from inquiries into Peters' personal life, and pursuit of Stanson. The story made the newspapers, and reporters did seek out all three.

Russ told the story of how Peters' letter had sent him to Stuart Freed. He also told them that he had had no intention of re-hashing the original murder case. For information on that they should go to court records for Stanson's guilty plea - and for background to officials at Bashford College.

Miriam explained that she had been hired by Peters to look into Stanson's disappearance and to follow up on a clue that there had been an accomplice, an idea that had been advanced by Stuart Freed at a private seminar in Philadelphia that met once a month to study old cases. She said she had had no luck, despite meeting with Freed and traveling with him and Russ Lewis to pool their information. And, yes, she would say that Mr. Peters had paid all three to come out to Yosemite in hopes of finding out what had happened to Robbie Stanson.

Stuart Freed explained that he was not supposed to talk about what had been in his paper for the seminar without the consent of the chair. All he would say was that Carl Peters was interested in his research about things left unknown when Stanson pled guilty, was sentenced, and served his time in the Ohio penitentiary.

When Dan Brockman read an article in the *Columbus Citizen* about the shooting in Yosemite he was stunned thinking of the aftermath and all that had transpired since that morning when he discovered the body of Wendy Peters in the woods. And then his mind drifted back to the argument in the bar about the death of Pretty Boy Floyd. History seemed to be a story of unsettled accounts.

In a few days' time interest in the details of the double shooting fell bck to a few short notices in local newspapers looking for filling material. And then nothing.

§

Kent Crider returned to his Philadelphia office. He did not need to destroy the message he had left in his desk telling everyone who had killed him because there had been no message. Several weeks later Stuart Freed was found dead in his office on a Saturday afternoon by the cleaning lady. The *Trenton Times* ran the story: "Prominent Psychological Counselor Found Dead of Bullet Wound.". Freed's files were found scattered about the office which looked ransacked. "Police had no real leads," the newspaper said, "except the sighting of a former client outside his building and they were seeking other witnesses." But his wife was convinced, she told them, it was not a current patient. "Look for the accomplice," she said, but could offer no name."